# THE ULTIMATE MAN'S SURVIVAL GUIDE

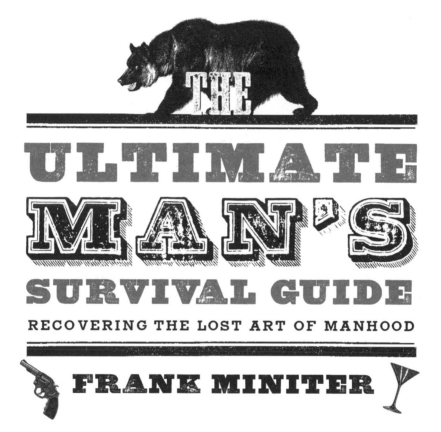

# THE ULTIMATE MAN'S SURVIVAL GUIDE

## RECOVERING THE LOST ART OF MANHOOD

## FRANK MINITER

Since 1947
REGNERY
PUBLISHING, INC.
*An Eagle Publishing Company • Washington, DC*

First paperback edition © 2013
ISBN 978-1-59698-804-0

Cataloging-in-Publication data for the hardcover edition on file with the Library of Congress
ISBN 978-1-59698-570-4

Published in the United States by
Regnery Publishing, Inc.
One Massachusetts Avenue NW
Washington, DC 20001
www.Regnery.com

Manufactured in the United States of America

10 9 8 7 6 5 4 3 2 1

Books are available in quantity for promotional or premium use. Write to Director of Special Sales, Regnery Publishing, Inc., One Massachusetts Avenue NW, Washington, DC 20001, for information on discounts and terms or call (202) 216-0600.

Distributed to the trade by
Perseus Distribution
250 West 57th Street
New York, NY 10107

Interior illustrations by
Lucinda Levine

To Keith Korman, the man who pushed me; Floyd Patterson, the man who taught me to handle myself; Drill Sergeant Richard Pelletier, the man who humbled me; Shingo Matsubara, the man who taught me to flow with a stream; Juan Macho, the man who showed me how to run with the bulls; and to Todd Smith, Scott Olmsted, Max Pizarro, Professor Jonathan Walters, my brother Richard, and so many more who showed me by example what a man can be.

# CONTENTS

# IF

If you can talk with crowds and keep your virtue,

Or walk with Kings—nor lose the common touch,

If neither foes nor loving friends can hurt you,

If all men count with you, but none too much;

If you can fill the unforgiving minute

With sixty seconds' worth of distance run,

Yours is the Earth and everything that's in it,

And—which is more—you'll be a Man, my son!

RUDYARD KIPLING

# INTRODUCTION

## A RITE OF PASSAGE

*"MAN. n. An animal so lost in rapturous contemplation of what he thinks he is as to overlook what he indubitably ought to be."*
—AMBROSE BIERCE[1]

The loudspeakers announced death was due in four minutes. An American grabbed my left arm in the packed plaza in front of Pamplona's town hall and implored, "How do I get out of here?"

Twenty minutes before he was boastful. Ten minutes before he was nervous. Now he looked likely to wet his pants. I shook my head. Like all of the runners in the *encierro*, what the Spanish call Pamplona's "Running of the Bulls," he was trapped.

We'd been waiting nearly a half hour for the bulls. If you wish to run with the bulls of Pamplona you must pass through the barriers before the police close them at 7:30 a.m. You must then stand in the street feeling the anxiety ferment in your gut until the bulls are released at 8:00 a.m. Thirty minutes is a long time to ponder disembowelment.

At 7:57 the men, and a few women, in white shirts and pants and red sashes and bandanas, all looked up and jeered as a couple climbed a drainpipe. As they clambered onto an oddly empty balcony, the woman's dress caught on the rail and everyone in the street got a long look at her bright blue panties. Then she tumbled into the balcony and everyone laughed like it was the funniest thing they'd ever seen.

The light moment flitted away. Stomach acid seeped into my mouth. I wondered how the bulls would get through a packed street that resembled a mosh pit at a heavy metal concert. I looked up at the blue sky and saw onlookers overcrowding tiny steel balconies for six stories above, all hoping to see blood. Below them people perched, legs dangling atop barriers all along the jostling street; they'd been there so long their urine wet the pavement below them.

I stood where the festival had begun two days before with the *chupinazo,* a street party that explodes when the mayor shoots a rocket at noon. When the rocket goes off, people pour water and wine from the balconies on a dancing, singing horde all dressed in white and red. Since the opening ceremony the wine had mixed with urine, vomit, and other things. I shuffled my feet and hoped I wouldn't slip on the slick stone and fall sprawling under the bulls.

Then 7:58 came and men began diving from the balconies onto the street. A group of Brits sang and locked arms as they bounced on the balls of their feet, finding courage in each other. Somewhere drums were pounding, echoing like a far-off avalanche rumbling to the bottom of a Rocky Mountain canyon. Meanwhile, a recurring announcement broadcast in a dozen languages sounded like a conscience: "If you're knocked down, stay down until the bulls pass."

I glanced to my left and saw that the American who'd grabbed my arm didn't understand. He didn't know that in 1995 another American, Mathew Peter Tassio of Glen Ellyn, Illinois, who incidentally had stood right where we were, had been killed because he ignored that advice. Tassio made two fatal mistakes: When the bulls pounded close, he sprinted across the street, not with the crowd and the bulls, as you should; as a result, another runner knocked him down. Then he broke the cardinal rule of running with the bulls—he got up in front of a bull. A Spanish fighting bull is a wild animal. It will destroy whatever moves in front of it. Its horns are sharp and curved forward. The lead bull drove a horn into Tassio's aorta and flung him across the street without even losing its place at the front of the herd. Tassio got to his feet once more before falling dead.

I knew this and other things because Juan Macho, my guide to the *encierro,* a man who had run over eighty times, had taught me how to run, and survive. With the knowledge came understanding and a deeper appreciation for running with the bulls. Knowing how to run controlled my fear. The American beside me didn't know what he was supposed to do, and he found himself trapped in madness.

Suddenly 7:59 was on us and medical workers hurried into spots alongside policemen positioned between a fence and a barrier. The American next to me saw the medical teams and caved into himself. This was real. It was happening. There was no escape.

The crowd began to shudder in waves. One such tremor broke the American. He shouted some awful thing and tried to crawl under the heavy wooden fence and away. A Spanish cop kicked him in the head and shoved him back out alongside me. Blood dribbled from a small cut on his forehead.

Meanwhile, runners were losing their nerve, and some were running early. The Spanish call those who run before the bulls arrive *valientes*, which ironically translates to "brave ones." With their departure there was suddenly elbow room. I anxiously stretched, looked back to where the bulls would come, and breathed deep as I worked to restrain my fear.

On my left the American's expression looked like something in a Goya painting. His eyes were too big; his mouth roved around his suddenly fluid face. He was mad. He had to get out. He dropped onto the ground and rolled under the fence. The cop waiting on the other side clubbed him with his baton and kicked him back into the street. Then the officer bellowed something I shall never forget: "You wanted to be a man and run with the bulls; now you must be a man and run with the bulls."

The Spanish officer's face looked carved in granite. He stood so straight, his spine bent backward. He had the proud bearing of a drill sergeant. He wasn't to be trifled with. But the American didn't want to die. Half the runners had already fled toward the arena. Those left were waiting, set like sprinters, but all with the expressions of people watching a race car lose control and come for them.

8:00. *Boom!* The cannon announced that the bulls were out of the corral, prompting more runners to become *valientes*. We had seconds.

A moving roar echoed closer as the spectators in the balconies sighted the bulls. Six black Spanish fighting bulls and as many steers running to guide them to the bullfighting arena were nearly upon us.

*Nooo!*

The American went under the fence again. The cop swung his club with calculated viciousness, but the American was too panicked to notice. The officer picked up the American who wouldn't be a man and tossed him into a brick wall behind the fence. The American fell limp, wetting himself as he slid to the stone street.

The bulls came. I ran.

Later, I told people about the hapless American. The veteran runners who gather at the Bar Txoko after the run shook their heads. Less experienced men laughed, then grew outraged that the cop had beaten him. I pointed out that if the cops allowed people to clamber over the eight-foot-high wooden fence, then people would get hurt in the panic as they pushed and fell over the barrier. Worse, their desperate escape might cause a jam the bulls would have to horn through in the tight streets of Pamplona. People would be trampled. Such an event occurred right before my eyes at the *callejón*, the gates of the Plaza de Toros (the bullfighting arena) where the street narrows from perhaps twenty-five feet wide to less than fifteen. Dozens were trampled. Several were gruesomely gored. This is where Hemingway decided to have someone killed in *The Sun Also Rises*, and where many others have met their end.

But all that was beside the point. The American decided to prove his manhood, and the Spanish cop was there to make sure he did so with honor. Proving your manhood was once a real coming of age. For a boy to become a man in the Maasai society, he must endure a painful circumcision ceremony in silence, as acknowledging pain brings dishonor. The Cherokee required a boy to sit silently in the forest blindfolded the whole night through, listening to every sound and not knowing if man or beast was about. The bravest Cheyenne warriors would rouse a sleeping grizzly and then attempt to outrun *Ursus arctos horribilis*. Many nations had mandatory military service—some European nations still do. A few cultures, such as the Spartans, had tests of endurance and skill. Others used brandings, body piercing, and other acts of mutilation, during which a juvenile had to remain stoic in order to enter manhood.

Today the transition from boy to man is a subtle shift, marked more by ages than feats. At eighteen we can vote, smoke, and die for our country. At twenty-one we can drink. These are earned merely by living, not doing. Just a few generations ago only the wealthy stayed in school and out of the trades into their teens, but now we pamper youth and grumble that they're growing up too fast, when what we really mean is they're exposed to sin too soon, not to manhood—strip clubs, alcohol, and tobacco are considered manly things, but surely don't make men of boys.

So how do we become men when there's no test to pass? After all, despite the lack of a rite of passage, being a man is something we try to achieve, at least the best of us. And there's more to being a man than climbing the Matterhorn, shooting 100 on the sporting clays range, or dropping a bully with a right hook. There's being a father, a husband, a good brother, and citizen. Being a man is being a *mensch*. Being a man means doing the right thing regardless of who's looking; it means biting the bullet and taking the hit (in life) even when you're not going to profit—especially when you're not going to profit. Being a man means suffering in silence, knowing how to keep your mouth shut, but still not being afraid to speak up. It means being the white knight, Robin Hood, George Washington, and Roland all rolled into one. It means speaking softly, yet carrying a big stick. It means knowing how to say you're sorry, and mean it. It means keeping your own counsel and knowing when to seek advice—very tricky life stuff. It means understanding the words "Duty. Honor. Country." It means having the know-how to solve a crisis. It means not panicking in an emergency. It means being a hero when no one is looking. It means knowing how to survive, lead, and show others the way.

Being a man means standing your ground when you must, but not seeking glory by harming or dominating others—a man is never a bully. The underlying reason Ahab in *Moby Dick* is a monster, not a man, is because he holds his wrath higher than the lives of his crew.

Being a man means finding the correct path even if you don't have a guide. Hamlet doesn't become a man until he dies, because, left fatherless, he is forced to take the steps to manhood alone and so attempts immature machinations before standing up boldly for justice and then dying as a man of courage and honor. Characters such as Holden Caulfield in J. D. Salinger's *The Catcher in the Rye* are tragic because they're rudderless in adolescence and so, like Hamlet, tread a dark path to manhood. Others, such as Harvey in Rudyard Kipling's *Captains Courageous,* become men because a man takes the time to show them the way.

Being a man means having the moxie to choose your own destiny. Gus in Larry McMurtry's *Lonesome Dove* is a man because he controls his emotions and makes the decision to go up against a group of outlaws alone in order to free the damsel-in-distress. Then he affirms his manhood by not wallowing in his heroism or making the event about himself. In fact, Westerns have retained their popularity because cowboys are our white knights, men who stoically follow a masculine code of honor. Many of John Wayne's characters were men who lived by a tough, manly code, a set of rules often not taught to youth these days. Today, the American male has no code. We have laws, but legalism is a poor substitute for a code of honor, because legality doesn't always parallel morality.

The ultimate man, as reconstructed in this book, is that "one thing" Curly referred to as the meaning of life in *City Slickers.* He is virtue and action forged into something we can comprehend without advanced degrees in a dozen fields. He is an evolving concept characterizing right and wrong in a heroic, comprehensible figure; he is someone to look to and question as we encounter worldly problems.

He is fundamental because, despite the absence of clear rites of passage, every male must learn how to be a man as best he can; after all, such knowledge isn't written in our genetic codes. Training shapes a soldier, a poet, and a boxer, not just courage, intellect, and brawn. Indeed, the American who wouldn't be a man and run with the bulls failed himself because of his ignorance. Knowledge instills confidence. Through understanding comes self-reliance. That American's fate in Pamplona could have been mine, but because I understood what was happening, I steadied myself with the knowledge of what had to be done to survive. That's what this book is about. There isn't one way to be a man. Running with the bulls isn't necessary for everyone, but having self-confidence is. And that assuredness comes from edification. Here is as much of that knowledge as can be packed between the covers of a book.

# PART 1

# SURVIVOR

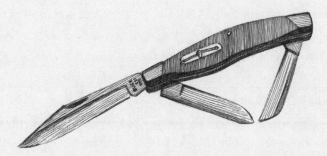

*"Do what thy manhood bids thee do, from none but self expect applause."*
—SIR RICHARD FRANCIS BURTON[1]

"Just call me 'Big Jim,'" booms the Brooklyn contractor whenever he meets anyone. His hands are beaten rough from swinging hammers and laying brick most of his fifty-eight years. His handshake hurts. His massive shoulders sway atop spent knees, giving him a swagger. He hunts deer in Saskatchewan's big woods every autumn because he likes to go where wolves add background noise, because the primal experience is a concrete connection to a time when men were men. Then, a few seasons ago, his throwback self-image was tested.

The thermometer read thirty below Fahrenheit as the sun set on the northern poplar forest. His guide was late and his feet cold, so Big Jim climbed out of his deer blind. He began to walk in order to get his blood pumping. He decided to meet his guide along the trail. A snow squall started but he didn't think anything of it. Snow had come and gone all day. He trudged on. As he grew warmer he considered the turns he had to take in the web of trails that wove for miles before finally leading back to pavement. The snow fell more heavily. He saw that the wind was blowing over his tracks. He clicked on his flashlight, but couldn't see more than ten feet as the falling snow reflected back the light. He began to worry he'd taken the wrong path. There were many. He started to walk faster. Then he began to jog. Soon he was running.

His guide found him sprinting, stripped to his bare chest. He had to run Big Jim down with a snowmobile; had to jump on him to restrain him. Big Jim's heart was going too fast. He was screaming and flailing. He was already suffering from hypothermia. He'd tossed his rifle, then his coat. He had become sweaty as he sprinted and tossed more clothes. He lost his mind. The guide had taken one trail and then another in a mad attempt to find him. Blowing snow had washed out Big Jim's tracks. The outfitter, a retired logger renowned for hefting logs three men couldn't, had trouble wrestling Big Jim down.

When I saw Big Jim, he was sitting humbly in a corner at the lodge. He never thought he'd lose his head, his manhood, so easily. He'd thought of himself as manly. He didn't know that word had lost its meaning.

The American Heritage Dictionary defines "manly" as "having qualities generally attributed to a man: mainly courage." This vague, overly simplistic definition supports today's popular contention that manliness has something to do with looks, taste, bearing, bravado, and sexual preference, but is largely an indefinable word. The feckless notion that manliness can't be defined is a symptom of what has left many of today's men bereft of the skills once thought compulsory. Peoples from the Babylonians to the Greeks to the Romans and all the way up to recent history could not only precisely define what "manly" meant in their cultures, they also taught their boys how to survive, to fight, to hunt, to navigate by the stars, to build a shelter in a storm...in essence, how to be men.

Since man learned to write, he gave his evolving definition of manliness roles in mythology, epics, and novels where he had names like Solomon, Hercules, Odysseus, Aeneas, Sir Gawain, and, more recently, Natty Bumppo (*Deerslayer*) in James Fenimore Cooper's *Leatherstocking Tales*, and Horatio Hornblower in C. S. Forester's seafaring novels. Beyond works of fiction, the ultimate man was the ideal represented by Michelangelo's *David* and the warrior-philosopher as described in Plato's *Republic*. He was an evolving archetype for individuals to measure themselves against. But today's scientific age has dismissed the essence of what a man should be as indefinable because philosophy, not science, is needed to define "manliness." As a result, we have been left without our age-old guide.

In fact, not only have we recently dashed man's definition, but we also ignorantly assume something called "instinct" will kick in and men will intuitively know how to survive. As if we're Hollywood action heroes, we assume real men simply overcome dilemmas with sheer force of will and bravado. But the truth is more premeditated according to today's ultimate survivors, U.S. Navy SEALs. To shape individuals into SEALs, an initial twenty-five-week curriculum at the Naval Special Warfare Center's Basic Underwater Demolition School is divided into three phases: The first eight-week phase tests and builds candidates with long runs, swims, and difficult-to-master water and survival skills; the second seven-week phase teaches and forces individuals to survive in horribly stressful conditions; finally, a ten-week-long third phase concentrates on land warfare, survival, and navigation.

After those intense twenty-five weeks, SEALs move to specialized schools for advanced weaponry, demolition, and more. In the end SEALs receive more training than most college graduates. So today's ultimate survivors don't just tough out a crisis, they've been taught to survive. Certainly you needn't undergo a SEAL's training regiment to learn to survive. But you do need the skills in this chapter. After all, if you go camping, hiking, or even driving in the mountains, this know-how can save your life, calm you, and make you the man of the moment, the one who kept his head. You need to know these things because knowing how to survive trounces the trepidation that comes from skiing a virgin route, climbing a mountain, or kayaking a remote stretch of river. You need to know how to survive because with this knowledge you'll know what to say when your son or daughter asks how to sharpen a knife or to light a campfire. And you'll know what to do if your child's canoe flips. And, as Big Jim learned, you need to know what to do if you get lost.

## Lost

> **Adapt or perish, now as ever, is Nature's inexorable imperative.**
>
> H.G. WELLS[2]

No one knows exactly how many people get lost in the forests, mountains, deserts, and swamps of the more than one million square miles of public land in the United States every year; the federal land agencies don't keep national records. More people are hiking than ever before—the number of people going into the wild has increased nearly 50 percent to almost 70 million since 1994, according to the National Survey on Recreation and the Environment.[3] And those who search for lost hikers say the number of people who get lost is increasing. For example, the Oregon-based Mountain Rescue Association (MRA), which has member teams in about twenty states, has seen a surge in the number of lost hikers, says MRA president Fran Sharp. The group's ninety search-and-rescue teams now complete more than 3,000 missions each year. As a result, survival know-how is increasingly relevant in today's age of outdoor recreation.

# Emergency Gear

## YOUR PACK/CAMP

Here's what Air Force F-16 pilots carry in their seats and life vests. It's a good list of the survival gear you should tote in addition to the supplies you'll need for your particular excursion; however, the raft, beacon, and sea dye are optional and you can probably skip the face paint, unless you're so tough you're going hiking behind enemy lines.

1. Survival radio (if your cell phone has coverage, all the better)
2. Global positioning system (GPS)/compass
3. Distress signals
4. Mirror
5. First aid kit
6. Face paint for camouflage
7. Tourniquet
8. Signal kit with personal distress flares
9. Whistle
10. Strobe light
11. Knife
12. Container with matches (a survival lighter is better)
13. Raft
14. Water
15. Blanket
16. Packet of sea dye
17. Survival pamphlet

18. Drinking storage bag
19. Firearm
20. Personal locator beacons (PLBs)—these are now available to the public; hit a button and rescue personnel will come and save your butt anywhere on the planet.
21. Survival food

## YOUR TRUNK

A tough veteran logger in Vermont's Northeast Kingdom once told me he won't leave home without a chainsaw in case a tree falls across the road. "Laugh," he said, "but it has saved my butt a few times." I carry a handy, fold-up saw instead. It's less bulky, and it still gets the job done. Here's what else you need to be the man of the moment.

1. **A Working Jack:** Don't trust the one that came with your vehicle, as they often have small platforms that sink into mud or snow, and can only be used on table-flat asphalt. If your jack is small, carry a small piece of plywood to set your jack on so it won't sink on less stable surfaces.

2. **Spare Tire:** Here's a secret: tires rot. The life of a tire (even one not being used) is three to five years.

3. **Saw:** A tree that falls in the forest may not be heard, but it can block a road or trail.

4. **Flares:** These warn drivers to go around you as you fix a flat and can make you the prepared man when you come across an accident.

5. **Rope/Chain:** These will pull you (or a damsel-in-distress) out of a ditch.

6. **Duct Tape:** Trust me, you just never know what you'll need this miracle tape for.

7. **Extras:** Tote extra clothes, blankets, a flashlight with extra batteries, a GPS, a first aid kit, food, and water when driving into the backcountry.

   **TIP:** Your grandfather's tire chains are still relevant on dirt roads, especially in spring mud.

## WHAT LEWIS AND CLARK PACKED

In May 1804 Meriwether Lewis and William Clark set off on their Corps of Discovery—one of the manliest missions of all time. Here's what the men on the exploratory trip to the Pacific Ocean were probably issued (per man): 1 tall felt hat; 1 regimental coat; 2 shirts made of either strong linen or flannel; 1 woolen waistcoat; 1 pair of white woolen overalls for winter; 1 pair of white linen trousers; 1 pair of white linen overalls; 1 pair of black leather low quarter shoes; 2 pairs of socks; 1 frock or shirt; 1 rifle or musket (Harpers Ferry Model 1803 rifle, Charleville-like "Model 1795" U.S. 69 caliber musket made at Springfield or Harpers Ferry Armory, or a Kentucky Rifle); 1 pipe tomahawk; 1 powderhorn/ammo pouch or cartridge box; 1 scalping knife and belt; flints; 1 gun sling; 1 ball screw; 1 brush and wire; 1 haversack, oil cloth; 1 bullet mold; 1-pint tin cup without handles; 1 steel for starting fire; 1 iron spoon; soap; 1 knapsack; 1 wool blanket; tent; 1 brass camp kettle (shared by four men in mess unit). Could you survive for two years on this list?

## THE PERFECT POCKETKNIFE

Chuck Buck of Buck Knives—a historic American knife-making company—carries a Gent, a small single-bladed knife, everywhere he goes. He says it's the ultimate knife because it's always on him. I carry a three-bladed Cabela's penknife with a box cutter, a bottle-opener, and a three-inch blade. I once used it in a Manhattan boardroom to open a package a few stuffed suits couldn't open—not quite a Crocodile Dundee moment, but the Japanese president of Kabuto was impressed because he knew he wasn't just talking to an editor of

*Outdoor Life*, but to the real deal. He became an advertiser. The perfect pocketknife is not an all-purpose Swiss Army-style knife—you'll never carry that bulky thing. Try Buck's Stockman, Spyderco's Co-Pilot, or W.R. Case's Working pocketknife.

## SURVIVAL KNIVES

Many think of the huge Rambo-style knives when survival knives come up; however such knives, though as manly as axes, have serious drawbacks. Their scary-looking serrations were originally intended to allow air crewmen to cut through the metal skin of crashed aircraft. They don't function as saws. Also, Rambo knives have hollow handles (for storage) that weaken the knives structurally. Avoid those gimmicky knives and look for quality. For example, the U.S. Army redesigned the bayonet to include survival knife features because historically bayonets have functioned poorly as field knives. Here are three stout survival knives to consider:

1. Cold Steel SRK, approved by the U.S. Coast Guard and U.S. Navy
2. KA-BAR® 1218/5018 USMC fighting/utility knife
3. SOG's SEAL 2000, approved for use by the U.S. Navy SEALs as an assault knife

## SURVIVAL GUNS

Guns are only manly when they're treated with respect; for example, I only saw my grandfather's handgun twice—when he killed a poisonous snake with it, and when I saw him take his shoulder holster off after a long hike. When I

### MAN FACT
Switchblades and butterfly knives are for juvenile delinquents, but today's "assisted opening" knives snap open and will make you the prepared (and hip) man. Check out Heckler and Koch's Nitrous Blitz.

was finally taught to shoot, I followed his example and took the lesson reverently. Brandishing a gun is not manly.

There are three reasons to carry a survival gun when leaving civilization: 1) to provide sustenance; 2) to signal help; and 3) for self-defense. I once interviewed a backpacker who was anti-gun until he ran into a British Columbian black bear that wanted to find out if he was edible. It took a lot of screaming and pot clanging for the hiker to convince the bear a vegetarian hiker was probably too tough and stringy to bother with anyway. He now carries a survival gun. A gun is an important tool, as long as it is treated with respect.

A survival gun needs to be light, easy to pack, and able to do the job. No firearm is perfect for every scenario, but some are made for emergencies. Traditional survival guns disassemble and stow in small carrying cases that can be broken out for use should you find yourself stuck in the backcountry. Here are six smart options:

1. **The Henry U.S. Survival:** This takedown .22 weighs just over two pounds. It breaks down and all parts fit in its hollow stock.

2. **Springfield Armory M-6 Scout:** This fold-down gun is compact and offers both .22 and .410 barrels.

3. **Kel-Tec SU-16 Rifle:** This semi-automatic rifle is chambered in .223 Rem. It features a fold-down stock that holds spare magazines.

4. **Marlin 70PSS Papoose:** This stainless, seven-shot, semi-auto .22 offers a takedown barrel and synthetic stock.

5. **Thompson/Center G2 Contender:** This single-shot is known for accuracy and comes in a number of different calibers.

6. **Smith & Wesson AirLite SC Revolver:** Smith offers a whole family of AirLite revolvers in a number of calibers

A SURVIVAL GUN NEEDS TO BE LIGHT, EASY TO PACK, AND ABLE TO DO THE JOB.

**9**

and configurations that are excellent choices for survival use.

## SURVIVAL KITS

Many survival kits are either too big to carry or too little to be of any use; however, one good kit I've used was put together by Ultimate Survival. Its Ultimate Survival Deluxe Tool Kit's hand chainsaw cuts through blow downs. Its "Blast Match Fire Starter," the kit's "Wet-Fire Tinder," will start a fire in a downpour. A whistle and signal mirror are also included. All of these items come in a watertight plastic case that's small enough to carry in a cargo pocket.

## SIGNALING DEVICES

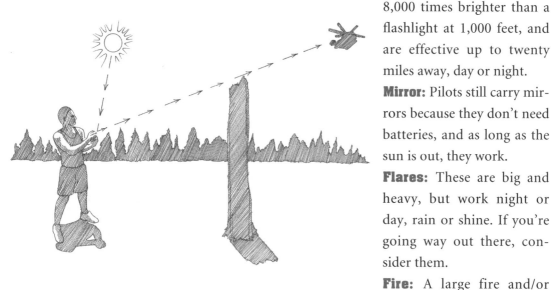

**Rescue Laser:** One smart tool is Greatland Laser's Rescue Laser Flares, which are small enough to fit in a cartridge belt, 8,000 times brighter than a flashlight at 1,000 feet, and are effective up to twenty miles away, day or night.

**Mirror:** Pilots still carry mirrors because they don't need batteries, and as long as the sun is out, they work.

**Flares:** These are big and heavy, but work night or day, rain or shine. If you're going way out there, consider them.

**Fire:** A large fire and/or smoke is a great way to signal for help. Use damp wood or green pine branches on a hot fire to create a lot of smoke.

## PERSONAL LOCATOR BEACONS

Personal locator beacons (PLBs), which have been saving the lives of mariners and pilots for decades, were approved by the FCC for use by civilians on land in 2003. Now a lost person in the continental U.S. can use one without paying a federal fine. In a worst-case scenario, at least your remains will be found.

Before I went to the Montana Rockies, I registered my PLB with the authorities and carried this 17-ounce guardian angel on an elk hunt. Once activated, it transmits a 406 MHz signal encoded with a unique number identifying its owner. Orbiting satellites pick up the signal and relay it to search-and-rescue teams. Thankfully, I never needed to turn it on. A field test was tempting, but because some backcountry hikers have been fined for calling for help in non-emergency situations (so they could get an easy ride out), I thought it best not to summon a rescue team.

**MAN FACT**
Being lost in the wilderness works to your strengths, as there is no one to ask directions, so your inherent self-reliance will be the right reaction.

# Navigate the Wild

## MAP AND COMPASS

Though GPS units have become mandatory, they don't work everywhere—mountains and dense tree cover can block satellite signals, and batteries die. Here's how to roam the backcountry the old-fashioned way, with a compass and a topographic map.

1. Orient the map by aligning its magnetic north (MN) indicator with your compass's reading of MN.
2. Pencil the MN line across the map, then anchor the map in this north-facing position; instead of turning the map as you head toward your destination, pivot around it as if switching seats at a table.
3. Draw a line between where you are and where you want to go. To further orient yourself, look for landmarks such as mountains or rivers.

4. Fold the map parallel to your line of travel, leaving a two-inch margin on the side that you hold. Place the map between your thumb and index finger and begin "thumbing the map" to check off terrain features as you travel so you can look away from the map without losing your bearings.

**TIP:** Estimate how long it will take to get to your destination—on level terrain a healthy man walks about three

# Make a Compass

The ultimate man should be able to make his own compass. Here's all you'll need: a sewing needle (or other small, straight piece of metal), a magnet (silk will work in the place of a magnet, though not as well), a piece of cork (or a plastic bottle top), and a cup of water.

1. Your compass will work better if you first run a magnet over the needle a few times, always in the same direction. This action "magnetizes" it to some extent. Drive the needle through a piece of cork (or a similar material). Cork from wine bottles works well. Cut off a small circle from one end of the cork, and drive the needle through it, from one end of the circle to the other.

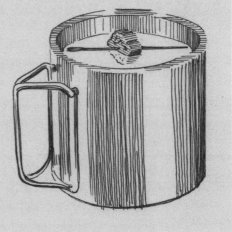

2. Float the cork and needle in a cup of water so the floating needle lies roughly parallel to the surface of the water.

3. Place your "compass" on a still surface and watch what happens. The needle should point toward the nearest magnetic pole—north or south as the case may be.

miles per hour. Then, as you pass landmarks, see if your estimate is holding up.

## MAP READING 101

"To the right and up" is an old U.S. Army catchphrase. In other words, to find, for example, grid 23-04 you start at the left hand side at the bottom of the map and then move right until you find the vertical gridline with the number 23. Then you place your finger on that 23 vertical grid line at the bottom of the map and run it up (north) until you come to the gridline numbered 04 along the right or left vertical (east or west) edge of the map. Where those two lines cross is the lower left hand corner of the grid square designated by the coordinate YD 23-04. Somewhere in that grid square is the site you're looking for. You can narrow the area by using the additional numbers each grid contains—better maps have more grid coordinates.

## DETERMINE NORTH WITHOUT A COMPASS

Don't fret about which side of the tree the moss is growing on—that doesn't work anyway. If you're stuck for a long period of time, use the sun. It rises in the east and sets in the west. Find a straight, slender stick that is about two feet in length. Securely place the stick in the ground so it's pointing directly at the sun. (There shouldn't be a shadow.) Wait 10–15 minutes, or until there

> "You have a choice. Live or die. Every breath is a choice. Every minute is a choice."
> CHUCK PALAHNIUK[4]

**NORTHERN HEMISPHERE**

**SOUTHERN HEMISPHERE**

is a shadow about four inches long. The shadow will be pointing east. Stand with the stick on your left, with the shadow extending to your right. You are now facing toward the north.

## FIND NORTH WITH THE STARS

**Northern Hemisphere:** Polaris, the North Star, is the last star in the handle of the Little Dipper constellation. The Big Dipper's two rightmost stars point to the North Star. If you're having trouble, remember that the constellation Cassiopeia is always on the opposite side of the North Star from the Big Dipper. Draw an imaginary line straight down from the North Star to the ground. This direction is true north; if you can find a landmark in the distance at this point, you can use it to guide yourself.

**Southern Hemisphere:** In the southern hemisphere, the North Star is not visible, and no single star always indicates north or south, but you can use the Southern Cross as your guide. This constellation has five stars, and the four brightest stars in it form a cross that is angled to one side. Identify the two stars that make up the long axis of the cross. These stars form a line that points to an imaginary point in the sky above the South Pole. Draw an imaginary line from this point to the ground, and try to identify a corresponding landmark to steer by.

# Exposed

*"People get caught up in the chase. We get calls from all over the United States, someone saying their loved one is lost in the Beartooth Mountains, and they want us to find them. Well, that's hundreds of miles of backcountry. Some of them we just never find."*

–SHERIFF CLIFF BROPHY OF
STILLWATER COUNTY, MONTANA

# AIR FORCE CAPTAIN SCOTT O'GRADY

On June 2, 1995, Captain Scott O'Grady was enforcing a NATO no-fly zone over Bosnia. Serb forces were firing at American planes daily, but he didn't see the Soviet-made anti-aircraft missile coming. As his F-16 exploded, O'Grady ejected over enemy terrain. Tense seconds ticked by before he made a safe landing. As he jumped into action he didn't know that his wingman never saw his parachute.

He hid his parachute and plunged into the forest. Serb forces saw him land. Within minutes he heard gunfire and saw Serb forces around him. He lay face down in the brush, cupping his camouflaged flight gloves over his head and ears. "Thank God there were no dogs there," he later told military de-briefers. He evaded the enemy by sleeping during the day, covering himself with camouflage net-ting, and moving only between midnight and 4:00 a.m. Armed Serbs were never far away. Equipped with a 121-page survival pamphlet, a radio, a first aid kit, distress flares, and a compass, he used the lessons he'd learned during seventeen days of Survival, Evasion, Resistance and Escape training. He used a sponge to soak up rainwater and fill a con-tainer. He ate grass and bugs. The survival pamphlet included instructions on cooking insects as big as grasshoppers and explained that you should eat them only after removing their hard legs. He didn't know exactly where he was. He was lost behind enemy lines.

The 29-year-old pilot hid for five days before he made radio contact. He had been taught that downed pilots are often captured after calling for help too soon, giving away their position. An American voice responded, and the rescue operation was put in motion. The 24th Marine Expeditionary Unit used a CH-53, a big cargo helicopter, to carry a total of forty-three marines—riflemen, assault climbers, medics, a communications team, and an interpreter—along with two AH-1W Cobra gunships and two AV-8 Harriers. The rescue team flew head-on into the sunrise. When they were close O'Grady "popped a smoke," a smoke canister that marked his location. A CH-53 landed and marines scrambled down its back ramp to secure the perimeter. Seconds later O'Grady ran out of the pines, pistol in hand. Enemy fire whizzed around them as they flew towards friendly skies, but they made it out with no injuries. Training and self-control pulled O'Grady through.

It's ironic in this technological age of advanced wicking fabrics and instant-heat devices that fewer people than ever understand how to survive the smallest calamity in the wild. But fear not, here's the know-how that'll keep your manhood intact whether you are caught in a white-out or stranded without water. Here's how to dress for any temperature/weather, how to build a survival shelter, how to start a fire without matches, and much more.

## ULTIMATE CLOTHING SYSTEM

You don't have to resemble the Pillsbury Doughboy to stay warm. You just have to know how to dress in order to harness your body's heat while keeping moisture (sweat) off your skin.

1.  **Wicking Layer:** Survivalists use the phrase "cotton kills" because cotton absorbs and holds moisture. When you sweat as you hike, cotton keeps the moisture next to your skin. This moisture later freezes when you stop. To avoid this use a breathable, wicking layer next to your skin.

2.  **Insulating Layer:** This layer mostly consists of polyesters treated in a way that makes the fibers stand up and trap air between them—fleece is a good example. This trapped air becomes the protective layer of still air forming the main insulation. Wear this over your wicking layer.

3.  **Shell Layer:** This outer protective layer is waterproof and breathable.

## FIRE STARTERS

Store-bought fire starters such as WetFire are effective and easy to pack. WetFire comes in small, individually packaged dry pellets of compressed fire starter that can be shaved into a tinder bundle or broken up and spread among kindling. They burn very hot (over 1,300 degrees), even when wet. Fire Paste is another effective commercial fire starter. Smear it into a tinder bundle or wipe it on some kindling, then pile more kindling on top and light it. Fire Sticks are a little bulkier but also work well. They are made of compressed sawdust and infused with an accelerant to help the solid material catch and hold a flame.

## NATURAL FIRE STARTERS

- **Pitchwood:** When sap floods into a tree wound, the wood becomes heavy and brittle as pitchwood is formed. A few slivers of pitchwood stuck into a tinder bundle or in among the kindling almost guarantee success in starting a fire.
- **Bird's Nest:** If you can find one, these are ready-made tinder bundles.
- **Dry Grasses:** You can make your own bird's nest by twisting dry grass stalks together into a tight bundle.
- **Shredded Tree Bark:** Some trees, such as juniper and cedar, have an inner bark layer that can be shredded and also twisted into a tight tinder bundle.

## BUILD AN EMERGENCY FIRE

Remember that scene in *Jeremiah Johnson* when Robert Redford starts a fire under a snow-laden pine and it dumps melted snow on his fire? Don't do that. Build the fire on the downwind side of a rock or bank to block the wind. Clear the ground, then gather fuel. To find dry wood, look for standing deadwood and broken branches stuck in tree limbs. Place the material against your cheek; if it feels cool, it's too wet to burn efficiently. Form a teepee with three six-inch-tall sticks and place smaller sticks on the floor as a platform for the tinder. Lean the smallest sticks on the tepee, leaving a doorway to face the wind. Place the next size of sticks on top.

> **MAN FACT**
> Carry a candle. It will hold a flame after a match has died and will make all but the worst situations more romantic for your damsel-in-distress.

> **MAN FACT**
> You can make a fire starter from dryer lint or cotton balls by saturating them with melted candle wax or Vaseline and compressing them into marble-sized pellets. Store them in a plastic bag or plastic 35mm film canisters.

Pack the teepee with the tinder and light it. Slowly add the larger sticks in a star pattern.

## SHELTER

Remember you're building a shelter not just to keep the rain off your head, but also to keep the wind out of your face. Wind is one of the biggest factors in heat loss, so always consider the wind's direction when choosing a shelter's location and orientation. In most of North America the predominant wind direction is from the west. Look for simple, natural protection like boulders and upturned trees. Moisture is your next consideration. This may simply require a roof over your head, but may also require a floor and walls that separate you from melting snow. A small tarp is ideal, but don't overlook overhanging rock ledges, boulders, overturned trees, and so on. Lacking everything else, cut enough boughs and branches to fashion some sort of primitive lean-to. Cold is your third consideration. In low-snow situations, consider grasses, evergreen boughs, leaves, or moss as insulators. In snowy conditions, use snow. It is the paradox of snow that this water crystal, a product of the cold, can effectively insulate us from the cold.

- **Snow Tree Pit:** Snow shelters do not have to be elaborate to be effective. Often you can combine a natural feature with snow to help build your structure. A prime example of this is an evergreen tree. In deep snow conditions, skiers and snowshoers are well aware that they

# Make a Fire without Matches

This is an art, but it really can be done. It took me two weeks and two very blistered thumbs to prove it in my backyard. To start a fire without matches you'll need a knife, kindling, wood, bow (a curved stick about two feet long), string (a shoelace, parachute cord, or leather thong—primitive cordage can be made from yucca, milkweed, or another tough, stringy plant), a socket (a horn, bone, piece of hard wood, rock), lube (ear wax, skin oil, a ball of green grass, lip balm), a spindle (a dry, straight, 3/4 to 1-inch-diameter stick approximately 12 to 18 inches long, that's round on one end and pointed on the other), a fire board (select and shape a second piece of wood into a board approximately 3/4 to 1 inch thick, 2 to 3 inches wide, and 10 to 12 inches long and carve a shallow dish in the center of the flat side approximately 1/2 inch from the edge. Cut a V-shaped notch into the edge of this dish), a tray (a piece of bark or leaf inserted under the V-shaped notch to catch the ember), and dry bark, grass, leaves, cattail fuzz, or some other combustible material, formed into a bird's-nest shape.

1. Tie the string tightly to the bow.
2. Kneel with the ball of your foot on the fire board.
3. Loop the string in the center of the bow.
4. Insert the spindle in the loop of the bowstring so that the spindle is on the outside of the bow, pointed end up. The bowstring should now be tight—if not, loop the string around the spindle a few more times.
5. Take the hand socket in your left hand, notch side down. Lubricate the notch.
6. Place the rounded end of the spindle into the dish of the fireboard and the pointed end of the spindle into the hand socket.
7. Pressing down lightly on the socket, draw the bow back and forth, rotating the spindle slowly.
8. Add pressure to the socket and speed to your bowing until you begin to produce smoke and ash. When there is a lot of smoke, you have created a fire ember.
9. Immediately stop your bowing motion and tap the spindle on the fire board to knock the ember into the tray.
10. Remove the tray and transfer the ember into your "nest."
11. Blow steadily onto the ember. Eventually the nest will catch fire.
12. Add kindling. When the kindling catches, add larger pieces of fuel.

need to be cautious of falling into a snow pit around a tree. Use the pit as your shelter.

- **Snow Trench:** You can dig a trench in the snow a little wider than your shoulders and a little longer than your height. Keep in mind that the smaller the space, the less body heat you will lose warming that space. Dig the trench deep enough so that when the sides compact, there will be enough height for you to crawl in and out. Over the top of the trench you can place some supports to pile snow on top, such as skis, snowshoes, boughs, or branches.

- **Snow Cave:** If the snow cover is adequate, snow caves are wonderful and can be built in a reasonably short period of time. The ideal situation is a large drift on the leeward side of a bank or ridge where snow has dropped in the relative quiet of the downwind side of a ridge. You must plan your cave so that there will be at least one foot of snow overhead. Keep the entrance downwind and sheltered. Also, if the drift is big enough, start the entranceway below where you anticipate the floor of the cave to be, since warm air rises.

## WATER

### Find Water Anywhere

On average the body loses four quarts of water per day. In an emergency, examine your map not only for springs and streams, but also for man-made

> **MAN FACT**
> Living trees give off heat; the melted-out space around a tree trunk can be significantly warmer than the surrounding environment.

structures like wells, cattle tanks, and windmills. As you hike, look for bright green vegetation. There may be a seep or spring nearby. Keep an eye out for cottonwoods, sycamores, and seep willows growing in dry streambeds. If you find damp sand, dig down. Search out places in canyons where flash-flood waters have scoured away the sand and gravel, exposing bedrock. Shallow depressions in the bedrock, called "tinajas," may have trapped pools of rain-water. If you're hiking the ridges in hilly terrain, examine the canyon floors below you for the bright flash of sunlight reflecting in a water-filled pothole. Lava and limestone are porous rocks that often contain springs. A cave in a limestone cliff or a place where lava abuts a sandstone cliff may contain a seep or a spring. Look for the dark stains and green moss that mark seeps in sandstone cliffs. In the high desert in the winter months, examine the shady north sides of cliffs where the sun never shines. Lingering snow patches may provide a source of water.

### Get Water from Vegetation

By placing green vegetation under a piece of clear plastic in direct sunlight, you can gather the evaporated water from the plants by catching the moisture in a container positioned below. You can also fill a plastic shopping bag with green vegetation, blow in air, and tie it like a balloon, then leave it in the sun. The sun's heat will draw out the plants' moisture.

### 5 Ways to Purify Water

1. Boil water for five to ten minutes.
2. Add eight drops of liquid chlorine bleach per gallon of water, sixteen drops if the water is cloudy, and let stand for thirty minutes.
3. With a 2 percent tincture of Iodine (from your first aid kit), add twenty drops per gallon of water, forty drops if the water is cloudy, and let stand for thirty minutes.
4. Use water purification tablets.

**MAN FACT**
An old Bedouin trick is to turn over half-buried stones in the desert just before sun up. Their coolness causes dew to form on their surface.

5. Use a commercial water filter that removes bacteria, protozoa, viruses, and chemicals.

## Woodsman Know-How

### HOW TO SHARPEN A KNIFE

A dull knife is useless and, because it takes more muscle to complete a task, more dangerous. Here's how to hone a blade the way your grandfather did—with a combination stone that has a coarse side and a fine side. The trick is to hold the blade at the correct angle and keep it there. Most blades have a 22- to 25-degree blade, though Japanese knives and fillet knives typically have a 12- to 15-degree blade.

1. Lubricate the coarse side of the stone with water.
2. Push the blade across in a sweeping motion, like you're cutting a thin slice off the stone.
3. Flip the knife and work the other side until a slight burr forms along the edge.
4. Switch to the fine side of the stone; lift the blade to a slightly higher angle and hone off the burr to create a razor-sharp micro bevel.

### RESCUE A CAPSIZED BOATER

Move fast and approach a capsized boater by directing the bow into the current and the wind; then swing the bow toward the person in distress. If you're in a motorized boat, when you get close, put the engine in neutral to minimize danger from the propellers. If the swimmer is conscious and can swim, tie a loop in a rope (or use a safety flotation device) and toss it to the victim. If they're unconscious or can't swim, position them at the stern and maneuver them so they face away from the boat, arms in the air, then grab their wrists and pull them into the boat. If you're in a canoe or kayak, don't try to pull the person in, as doing so may flip your boat. Hold them alongside and paddle to land. Stay with them until help arrives.

## Attacked

*"The bear put me down twice. I knew if it put me down again, chances are I wouldn't get up. It wasn't fight or flight. It was live or die."*
–JIM WEST WAS ATTACKED BY A BLACK BEAR
IN BRITISH COLUMBIA ON OCTOBER 7, 2008,
AND KILLED THE BEAR WITH A MAKESHIFT CLUB

# Paddle a Canoe

On still water the J-stroke keeps the canoe tracking in a straight line. Reach forward so the "catch" (the start of the blade's pull through the water) is well in front of your knees. At mid-stroke, the blade should be vertical and fully immersed. The upper arm extends diagonally across your body as though delivering a cross-punch and finishes on the outside of the gunwale (top edge of the canoe). The motion delivers power through a lever action; use the shaft hand initially as a fulcrum, then pull back on the shaft. The second half of the stroke traces the hook of the letter "J." When you draw the blade out of the water, the power face (the side pulling against the water) is parallel to the canoe. This way your paddle performs as a part-time rudder.

Being attacked by a wild animal is perhaps the most primal, hair-raising death imaginable. However, today we think of such events as anomalies, or at least as last vestiges of a wilder time. But the truth is there are more bear, cougar, and alligator attacks on humans today than in any other time in recorded history. (See part 4 to learn how to fight off wild animals.) And most of these attacks are happening in well-used campgrounds and in our backyards, not in the hinterlands.

To prepare you for the worst, this section is designed to deflate long-enduring myths about predators and to show you how to survive. You never know if you'll be tested. For example, on January 8, 2004, at about 4:25 p.m, Anne Hjelle, a 30-year-old Californian, was bicycling on a well-used trail in Whiting Ranch Wilderness Park in southern Orange County when a cougar jumped off a 4-foot rise and knocked her off her bike. Her riding compan-ion, Debi Nicholls, grabbed Hjelle's legs and screamed as the mountain lion dragged both of them thirty feet down the slope. The screams brought two men, Nils Magnuson and Mike Castellano of Long Beach, to the scene. They called 911 and fought off the mountain lion by throwing bowling-ball-sized rocks at it. Authorities later killed the cougar. Hjelle would recover from her injuries. And the two men walked quietly off, as heroes should.

## TREATING ANIMAL BITES

A wild animal bite should be treated as infected. The animal may suffer from rabies, a deadly disease carried in its saliva. Alligators in particular carry many pathogens in their mouths. Scrub the bite with plenty of soap and water to remove the saliva. Cover the wound with a sterile bandage and get the victim to a doctor.

## SAFETY IN BEAR COUNTRY

Bear attacks are more common than cougar attacks. According to Steve Her-rero, an environmental science professor at the University of Calgary, there were at least 131 verified human deaths from bear attacks in North America during the twentieth century, and more are occurring every decade. Here are some tips on how to avoid a bear attack:

**Hang Your Food:** Put your food in Ziploc bags or airtight containers and put it all in a garbage bag. Select two trees that are about twenty feet apart. Throw a weighted end of the rope over a branch about seventeen feet above the ground. Tie the line to the trunk of the first tree. Throw the weighted end of the line over the branch of a second tree. Attach your food bag to the middle of the line and pull it up and adjust so it is centered, at least twelve feet above the ground. Tie the other end of the line to the second tree.

**Cook Downwind:** Place your cooking fire downwind of your camp. If you're camping in mountainous terrain, place your fire fifty yards downhill from your tent. This way evening thermals will blow the scent away.

**Avoid Thick Areas:** Avoid thickets and densely wooded areas and make noise on the trail. If you're hunting, stay with a partner.

**Self-Defense:** Carry bear spray and/or a firearm. It's critical that the bear spray you buy has an EPA registration number so that you know it meets EPA standards. However, many bear sprays say they have high oleoresin capsicum ratings, but the stuff that counts is capsaicin. Spray needs at least 1 percent capsaicin to stop a grizzly.

## COUGARS

While only four cougar attacks were reported in California from 1890 to 1990, that number has been exceeded since 1992. As of January 2008 California had verified a total of seventeen attacks on humans by mountain lions since 1890, and thirteen of those attacks have taken place since 1992. But you can't believe those numbers. Many attacks, even killings, slip through the administrative cracks. States often don't share reports and some are better about keeping records than others, and organizations that maintain databases often have political agendas. The USDA's Wildlife Services keeps records of livestock loss, but not attacks on humans. In fact, according to Doug Updike, California Department of Fish and Game's senior wildlife biologist, "An attack doesn't become official until it meets very strict criteria." Perhaps someone should tell that to 7-year-old Shir Feldman. He was holding his father's hand while hiking up a trail when a cougar jumped on him. The mountain lion grabbed Shir by the jaw, but the boy's family counterattacked. They pelted the animal with sticks and rocks and the cougar quickly dropped the boy and ran away. The 7-year-old received a broken jaw and other injuries. Luckily his family was with him when the cat attacked. This attack, because there wasn't a fatality, wouldn't be recorded "officially."

### Cougar Avoidance

**Fight Back:** Cougars don't attack out of pure aggression; they attack because they want to eat you. (See part 4 to learn how to fight a cougar.)

**Safety in Numbers:** When in cougar country, keep small children close.

**Don't Feed Deer:** Mountain lions have followed deer (their traditional prey) into the suburbs. If you attract deer to your property, you'll also bring cougars.

## ALLIGATORS

As of March 2008 there had been 21 people killed and 449 attacks by alligators in Florida since 1948. More than 150 of those attacks had taken place since 2000. Florida alone has over 1 million alligators—there are more than 3 million in the southern United States. While there are more people and alligators living side-by-side than ever before, perhaps the biggest reason is that some large alligators—they grow to more than 14 feet and over

**MAN FACT**

People live through cougar attacks because the large cats typically don't know how to kill an erect person. All their life they've been trained to kill four-legged animals by biting the back of the neck and separating the spine or by clasping their jaws around the throat and suffocating their prey.

1,000 pounds—are fed by people in the backyard canals and swamps that permeate Florida. When alligators are fed, they lose their fear of people and become especially dangerous.

- Be aware of the possibility of alligator attacks when in or near fresh or brackish waterways. Attacks may occur when people who are working or recreating near water do not pay close enough attention to their surroundings.
- Never allow small children to play unsupervised near water.
- Do not swim outside of posted swimming areas or in waters that might be inhabited by large alligators.
- Alligators are most active between dusk and dawn. Therefore, swim only during daylight hours.
- Never feed or entice alligators—it's dangerous and illegal. When fed, alligators overcome their natural wariness and learn to associate people with food.
- Seek immediate medical attention if bitten by an alligator. Alligator bites often result in serious infections.

## SNAKES

Real men don't scream when they spot a snake. They move to a safe distance and stoically say things like: "Oh look, a Western diamondback rattler, a member of the viper family. Its venom is primarily hemotoxic." Here's the knowledge you'll need to be such a man.

**Rattlesnakes:** Like all but one of the dangerous snakes in North America, rattlers have a heavy, triangular head with elliptical (or cat's-eye) pupils. They also have a rattle and use it. There are more than a dozen different species of rattlesnakes in North America. Gopher, pine, and bull snakes can look like rattlers, but their comparatively slender heads and lack of rattle tell them apart.

**Cottonmouths:** These are hard to identify. They range in color from coppery brown to black to greenish, and can be solid colored, blotched, or banded. There are a number of common water snakes that are very difficult to tell apart from a cottonmouth by color alone. Rely on the distinctive "raccoon mask" feature, a white stripe along the side of their heavy, triangular head, and their cat's-eye pupils. Cottonmouths are often found in or near water, but are quite comfortable on dry land and can adapt very well to living inland and feeding on mice and rats.

**Copperheads:** These are closely related to cottonmouths, and have a similar body type but much brighter colors, ranging from coppery brown to bright orange, silver-pink, and peach. These snakes are often found in wooded or hilly areas. Like rattlesnakes, they are attracted to shady areas that offer cover to hide, and they prey on mice and rats. Look-alikes include the corn or rat snake, which has similar colors but rougher scales, a slender head shaped like an oval instead of a triangle, and round pupils.

**Coral Snakes:** These are distinctively colored in black, yellow, and red, with a solid black band on the nose and a bright yellow head. The old rhyme, "Red touch yellow, kill a fellow. Red touch black, friend to Jack," is one way to tell coral snakes from non-poisonous snakes, such as the scarlet snake.

## Tricks for Identifying Poisonous Snakes

1. Non-venomous snakes usually have a round pupil; venomous snakes in the U.S. (except for the coral snake) have an elliptical pupil like a cat's eye.
2. Non-venomous snakes usually have only one color.
3. Most non-venomous snakes have a spoon-shaped round head and venomous snakes will have a flat head.
4. Look for a rattle—some non-venomous snakes do shake their tails.
5. Most venomous snakes have a small depression between the eye and the nostril. This is called a "pit," which is used to sense heat from their prey.

## Snakebites

1. Have the victim lie down and rest the bitten part lower then the rest of the body.

**MAN FACT**

Size doesn't matter. It's a remarkable fact that young rattlesnakes actually have more potent venom than older ones. And snakes can kill. An Eastern diamondback rattler, for example, typically yields 500 to 600 milligrams of venom when milked, while a dose of just 100 milligrams can be lethal.

2. Put a constricting band two to four inches above the bite to slow the spread of venom.

3. Remove the venom with a Sawyer snakebite kit or by squeezing it out.

4. Treat the victim for shock.

5. Get medical help. If possible, identify the snake.

## SPIDERS

When someone screams "Spider!" and runs out of the tent or cabin, it's a man's time to shine. There are more than forty species of spiders in North America that can bite and harm you. But only three are really dangerous.

**Black Widow:** An adult black widow has a shiny black body with a red or orange hourglass marking on its belly. Its venom contains neurotoxins that can be fatal. Its bite causes redness, pain, and swelling. The victim may sweat and have severe muscle pain.

**Brown Recluse:** This spider is most commonly found in the southeastern and south-central U.S., but it ranges as far north as New York. It has a dark-brown, violin-shaped mark near its head and measures just three-eighths of an inch. Its venom is necrotic, causing swelling and death to the tissue around the bite. Untreated, this wound can grow.

**Tarantula:** These have large, hairy bodies and can be up to three inches long. They are most common in the southwestern U.S.

### Spider-Bite Treatment

Wash the area thoroughly and get to a hospital. If possible, kill and bring the spider so that it can be identified.

## TICKS

Ticks carry many diseases and are currently responsible for more than 15,000 cases of Lyme disease annually in the U.S. Other tick-borne diseases include Rocky Mountain Spotted Fever, ehrlichiosis, and babesiosis. Use a permethrin-based spray on outer clothing and dress so that ticks cannot get on your skin. Showing a date, spouse, or kids how to avoid ticks before hiking is manly. But if a tick still manages latch on, here's how to get rid of it:

1. Use small, pointed tweezers to grasp the tick by its mouth parts. Tug gently until the tick is removed.
2. After removing the tick, wash the area with soap and water and use antiseptic on the bite and the tweezers.
3. Save the tick in a small vial and mark the date and victim's name. In case of infection, this will help in diagnosing health problems due to the tick bite.
4. Watch the bite and the victim's general health and see a doctor if you notice anything out of the ordinary.

## BEES

Bee nests can be in trees or even holes in the ground; as a result, getting stung isn't always avoidable. Relieve the pain of insect bites with ice water or a cold towel. If the stinger is still in the skin, use a bee-sting kit or flick it away with your fingernail. Ask the person if they're allergic. In rare cases bee stings can kill. If they're allergic, ask them if they have prescription medicine and get medical help as soon as possible. If you get stung, you have to suck it up. Complaining isn't manly.

## JELLYFISH

The jellyfish and Portuguese man-of-war have thousands of stinging cells on their tentacles. When touched, the poisons of those cells cause a sharp, burning pain. Wash the affected area with diluted ammonia or rubbing

**MAN FACT**
The Cherokee pounded the large rootstock of goldenseal with bear fat and smeared it on their bodies as an insect repellent. (Note: This will probably keep women away, too.)

**31**

alcohol. And no, pee won't make it all better and urinating on someone is far from manly. Typically urine doesn't have enough acid to neutralize the sting.

# Injured

> *"People head out into the wild full of themselves, stumble, then remember they're mortal. That's when they find out if they're men. The tough and smart live. I find more dead every year."*
> –DON FOOTE, VICE PRESIDENT OF
> THE WYOMING SEARCH-AND-RESCUE ASSOCIATION

Falls resulting in broken bones and sprains are by far the most common outdoor emergencies, and so it is essential that a man knows what to do in these situations. In fact, in October 2007 near Reading, Pennsylvania, Boy Scout Troop 226 from Rockledge in Montgomery County came to the rescue of a hiker who had fallen and hit her head on the Appalachian Trail.[4] They built a stretcher from scratch and carried her three miles to help. They earned their survival merit badges—and found a rite of passage to manhood. Whether saving a damsel-in-distress on a hiking trail or dealing with a serious injury in the backcountry, you need to know these emergency medical procedures. (For further reference, the U.S. Army "Firefighting and Rescue Procedures in Theaters of Operation" is an excellent and free resource. As a bonus, it'll teach you how to survive behind enemy lines, while under fire, and other such macho scenarios.)

## THE PERFECT FIRST AID KIT

### Your Daypack
1. Adhesive bandages of various sizes
2. Triple-antibiotic ointment

# MARK MATHENY

Mark Matheny carried a longbow into the Montana wilderness in September 1992 with his long-time friend Dr. Fred Bahnson. Snow had fallen overnight, lying white under aspen flaring autumn gold. Early that morning Dr. Bahnson downed a four-point mule deer in the crisp air, and both men smiled and felt triumphant. As the sun rose the snow melted, letting them slip silently along hoping to see more game. Matheny was leading as they emerged onto a wooded beach. He looked across a clearing and a saw grizzly sow lurch up, tossing her cubs off her teats in the process. Then the grizzly charged.

She grunted madly as she came. Matheny spun and looked vainly for a tree to climb. Bahnson was twenty yards farther up the trail. Matheny ran toward him, yelling, "A bear, get your spray!" Weeks before the hunt Bahnson had read about the increasing use and success of pepper spray as a bear deterrent, and had bought a small canister of "Karate In A Can," a spray designed for people, not bears. He even fashioned a homemade leather belt holster to keep the spray within reach. As Matheny ran, Bahnson groped for his spray, then leaped off the trail.

Matheny jumped behind a log. When the grizzly followed him he thrust his bow at the bear and yelled, "Get out of here!" The sow hit the bow out of his hands and leapt on him. The grizzly dug its teeth into his face and neck. He screamed, "She's got my head. She's killing me!"

Then he remembered he was supposed to play dead.

Just then Dr. Bahnson came screaming up and the sow charged him. Matheny jumped up and began to run. The bear turned and ran him down again. This time the sow started tearing his arm off. Despite the anguish, he lay still, which is just when Bahnson hit the bear in the mouth and nose with the pepper spray. The bear shook its head, spun and ran away with her cubs.

Bahnson assessed Matheny's wounds. The left side of his face was torn open. His cheek was hanging. Bahnson rigged a pressure bandage, but blood from puncture wounds on Matheny's scalp kept pouring into his eyes. As they neared their Jeep, Matheny decided to stop and take pictures of his wounds. A photo of his face bathed in blood would make him famous.

Matheny spent the next spring in the mountains coming to terms with his fear. He finally walked down from the mountains and became a spokesman for a bear-spray company, travelling around the country teaching bear safety tactics and touting the message that grizzlies shouldn't be irrationally feared, but need to be respected. He has since developed products designed to fend off grizzlies and has accrued piles of testimonials from people who've used his products to stop charging bears.

He dealt with and adjusted to the attack like few men could.

3.   Sunscreen

4.   Lip balm

5.   Insect repellent

6.   Antiseptic hand wipes or soap

7.   Moleskin for blisters

8.   Dimenhydrinate (Dramamine) or meclizine for nausea

9.   Ibuprofen or acetaminophen for pain relief

10.  Diphenhydramine or fexofenadine for allergies

### Your Backcountry Pack Should Also Include

1.   Compression bandage at least 5x9 inches

2.   Several 4x4 inch sterile bandages

3.   Roller gauze bandage two inches wide

4.   Roller gauze bandage four inches wide

5.   Elastic bandage for support or swelling

6.   Thermometer

7.   Tweezers for splinters

8.   Scissors

9.   Topical pain reliever

10.  Chemical cold pack

11.  Zipped closure freezer bags

12.  Iodine and alcohol prep pads

## BLEEDING

**Severe Bleeding:** Cover the wound with a pad and press hard. Hold the pad in place with a bandage. If the pad becomes soaked, do not remove it. Put another pad on top of the first and continue pressure. Get medical help.

**Arterial Bleeding from Leg:** Control it by pressing the artery with the heel of your hand against the pelvic bone.

**Arterial Bleeding from Arm:** Control it by squeezing the artery with the flat of your fingers against the upper arm bone at a pressure point.

## DISLOCATIONS

Dislocations are the separations of bone joints causing the bones to go out of alignment. These misalignments can be extremely painful and can cause an impairment of nerve or circulatory function. You must place these joints back into alignment. Signs and symptoms of dislocations are joint pain, tenderness, swelling, discoloration, limited range of motion, and deformity of the joint. Without an X-ray, you can judge proper alignment by the look and feel of the joint and by comparing it to the joint on the opposite side.

It is possible to treat a shoulder dislocation in the field; however, when possible, taking the injured person to a hospital is the safer option. Just after the injury, the muscles are not yet in spasm, which offers an opportunity for a shoulder dislocation to be fixed with some basic maneuvers.

1. Lay the injured person flat on his or her back and ask them to relax their muscles.

2. With the elbow flexed at 90 degrees, apply steady pressure by pulling the arm away from their body. At the same time rotate the forearm slowly. If the patient complains of pain, stop. Allow the victim to relax and let the shoulder muscles stretch while you continue to maintain traction. Resume rotating when they are calm. Using this method, full external rotation alone will reduce most anterior shoulder dislocations.

# Make a Tourniquet

1. Using a wide length of cloth, fold several times until you have a bandage three to four inches wide and several layers thick.
2. Tie close to the wound, but above the elbow or knee.
3. Put a stick on top of the knot, and tie another knot around the stick.
4. Twist the stick until the bandage is tight enough to stop the bleeding.

**Note:** A limb that's in a tourniquet for several hours may need to be amputated, so it's important to be sure that the tourniquet is necessary and to get to medical help as soon as possible.

3. If you do not feel or see the shoulder joint reduce, maintain traction as you gently move the arm until it is next to the patient's chest. Then slowly rotate the forearm against their chest. Most shoulder dislocations can be reduced this way.
4. You'll know the shoulder joint is back in place because the injured person's pain will decrease dramatically.

## FIVE WARNING SIGNS OF A HEART ATTACK

1. Uncomfortable pressure, squeezing, fullness, or pain in the center of the chest behind the breastbone. The feeling may spread to the shoulder, arms, neck, jaw, and back. It may last two minutes or longer, and may come and go. It need not be severe. Sharp, stabbing twinges of pain usually are not signs of a heart attack.
2. Unusual sweating: for instance, perspiring even though a room is cool.

# Perform CPR

**A**merican Red Cross guidelines for administering CPR (cardiopulmonary resuscitation) on adults no longer include using "rescue breaths," so those scenes in sit-coms where less-than-manly men argue about who should give mouth-to-mouth resuscitation to some unfortunate fellow are no longer relevant.

Here's how you can try to save a life. First, if the person has passed out from choking, you have to clear their airway before they'll be able to breathe (see "Choking"); however, if they're not breathing due to cardiac arrest, drowning, or for an unknown reason, here's how to administer CPR. (The American Heart Association [AHA] and the American Red Cross offer CPR courses; to find one, contact the AHA at 800-AHA-USA1 or contact your local American Red Cross chapter.)

1.  **Check for Signs of Life:** Tap on their shoulder and ask loudly, "Are you okay?" If you don't get a response, call (or better yet have someone else call) 9-1-1. Next, check to see if the person is breathing.

2.  **Begin Chest Compressions:** If the person is unresponsive and isn't breathing, roll them on their back. If possible, they should be on a hard surface. Lace your fingers together with both palms facing downward. Place the heel of your bottom hand on the center of the person's chest (their breastbone). Keep your elbows locked in a straight position and your shoulders directly over your hands. Push hard and fast. You should compress the person's chest at least 100 times per minute. Push down at least 2 inches and then let their chest rise completely before pushing down again.

3.  **Continue Chest Compressions** until help arrives or someone else takes over.

3.  Nausea: stomach distress with an urge to vomit.
4.  Shortness of breath.
5.  A feeling of weakness. (The American Heart Association has the most comprehensive advice for diagnosing and treating heart attacks.)

## CHOKING

To perform the Heimlich Maneuver, step behind a choking person and put your arm around their midsection. Clasp your hands together with the knuckle of one thumb over the person's navel. Drive the hand up under the rib cage. Food should pop loose. Repeat if necessary.

## BURN/SUNBURN

**First Degree:** Treat immediately with cool water. Keep the burn under water until there is little pain. Apply a moist dressing and a bandage.

**Second Degree:** Do not break the blister. This will compound the injury by causing an open wound. If the blister is not open, place the injury in cool water until pain lessens, then apply a moist dressing. Do not apply cream, ointments, or sprays.

**Third Degree:** Do not remove any clothing; it may stick to the flesh. Wrap a clean sheet around the spot. Get medical help as soon as possible.

## SPRAINED ANKLE

If you're far from the trailhead, do not remove your shoe. It will give your ankle support. Tie an ankle bandage around the shoe and your injured leg. Raise your leg and reduce swelling with an ice pack, cold soda, or whatever you have.

## PUNCTURE WOUNDS

Take out any foreign matter and then squeeze gently around the wound. Wash with soap and water. Apply a sterile bandage and get to a doctor. A tetanus antitoxin shot may be needed to prevent lockjaw. If someone has been snagged by a fishhook, cut the line and push the barb out through the skin and snip it off with pliers. Then back the now barbless hook out of the wound.

## SKIN POISONING FROM PLANTS

The poison in poison ivy, poison oak, and poison sumac is contained in oily sap throughout the plant. The sap of poisonous plants takes about twenty minutes to bind in the skin. Rinse immediately with soap (if you have it) and water, or water alone. Calamine lotion may relieve itching. Try not to scratch the area. Remove lingering sap by laundering clothing that has come in contact with poisonous plants.

## HEAT STROKE

Heat stroke is usually caused by exposure to the sun. The victim's body temperature soars, making heat stroke a life-and-death matter. Get medical assistance at once. Get the victim into a cool, shady spot. Place him on his back with his head and shoulder raised. Douse the person with water or do whatever you can to cool them down.

## FROSTBITE

Frostbite typically begins when someone's ears, nose, fingers, or feet feel numb and then begin to hurt. Move the victim inside a warm tent or building and thaw the frozen area. If an ear or part of the face is frozen, have the person remove his gloves and cover the part with his warm hand. Do not rub or massage frozen skin. You can also warm a frozen area by holding it in warm (not hot) running water, or by wrapping it in a warm blanket. When the area has become warm, exercise the injured area. Go to a doctor.

> **MAN FACT**
> Boneset tea was one of the most frequently used home remedies during the nineteenth century. The Menominees used it to reduce fever; the Alabamas, to relieve stomachache; the Creeks, for body pain; the Iroquois, for fever and colds.

## HYPOTHERMIA

When you hear that someone "died of exposure" or "froze to death," the killer was probably hypothermia—from hypo, meaning "low," and "thermia," meaning "heat." Hypothermia occurs when the body is losing more heat than it can generate. A victim of hypothermia begins feeling chilly, tired, and irritable. Next they'll begin to shiver. Their shivering will become violent and they won't be able to think clearly. If they continue to freeze, their shivering will stop and they may die.

Get the victim inside some sort of shelter. Get their wet clothes off and zip them into a dry sleeping bag. If hypothermia is far advanced, the victim will not be able to warm himself. The rescuer must strip down and get into the sleeping bag so that body contact can warm the victim.

## TREATING FRACTURES

A closed fracture is a broken bone that has not caused an open wound. A victim will complain of pain around the injury. Swelling may occur, and the victim may suffer from shock. An open, or compound, fracture has the same symptoms plus the sharp edges of the broken bone have cut through the skin. The great danger in treating a fracture is that incorrect handling may turn a closed fracture into an open one.

**Collarbone or Shoulder Fracture:** No splint is necessary. Place the forearm in a sling with the hand raised about three inches higher than the elbow. Tie the upper arm against the side of the body with a wide cravat bandage.

**Lower Arm or Wrist Fracture:** Use splints long enough to hold the wrist, forearm, and elbow motionless. Place the splinted arm in a sling with the thumb up and the hand slightly higher than the elbow. Use a cravat bandage to tie the upper arm against the side of the body.

**Upper Arm Fracture:** Tie one padded splint to the outside of the upper arm. Place the forearm in a sling. Use a cravat bandage to tie the upper arm against the side of the body.

**Lower Leg Fracture:** Apply two splints, each as long as the distance from the middle of the thigh to just past the heel. Place the splinter on either side of the injured limb and bind them together.

**Thigh Fracture:** Use padded splints, one for outside the leg extending from heel to armpit, and one for inside the leg from heel to crotch. Bind the splint together. (Note: All knots should be square knots.)

## TRANSPORTING A VICTIM

**One-Person Carry:** This is best done piggyback. Kneel in front of the person with your back to their belly. Bring your arms under the patient's knees. Hold onto their arms.

**Four-Hand Seat Carry:** Two people can transport a conscious patient with this carry. Each bearer grasps his own right wrist with his left hand. The two bearers then lock hands and wrists with each other. The patient sits on their hands and places his arms around their shoulders.

**Stretchers:** If a person must be moved for some distance or their injuries are serious, they should be carried on a stretcher. Start with two poles. Use strong saplings, skis, oars, etc. Button up two or three shirts or coats and push the poles through the sleeves. You can also use blankets, a tent fly, or a sleeping bag with the bottom-corner seams opened. Lashing together three metal pack frames is another good option.

## ICE RESCUE

Don't rush onto the ice to save someone—foolhardiness is not manly. Try to reach the person from shore with a pole or by throwing a rope. First tie a loop in the rope for the victim to put his arm through. Use a bowline knot. If you have to go on the ice, distribute your weight as much as possible over the surface. Lie on your belly and snake over the ice until you are close enough to throw a rope. If there is help, form a human chain. Crawl out onto the ice while one person holds your ankles and another hangs onto his. Grasp the victim by the wrist and get back.

# LON
# MCADAM

Late in the afternoon in April 2007, during the third day of a nine-day solo trek in Arizona's Superstition Wilderness, 56-year-old Lon McAdam lost his footing on the bottom of Rough Canyon. His scream echoed between the red rocks as he rolled in pain. His left kneecap was shattered. He was helpless and alone, days from a trailhead, and no one was expecting him back home for six days. He'd been hiking solo for thirty-two years, and nothing like this had ever happened. He couldn't stand, let alone walk. There was no cell service. When the pain subsided he searched his pack for his satellite phone, but the fall had burst his water bag, shorting out his phone.

He lay looking up at the sky and listening to the silence that drew him into the wild. He felt harmony alone with the wind singing through the canyons. Being out there healed his soul. But he never thought his fate would be to die crippled in a wild Arizona canyon. He shook those thoughts from his mind. He knew how to survive. He knew a plan can conquer panic. He'd talked to his wife, Toni, earlier that day, letting her know everything was going well. He looked back at the sky and remembered the bear scat he'd seen all through the area. He pulled out his can of bear spray and kept it close

He mentally cataloged his gear. He knew he had enough food, though he would ration it in case he had to wait longer than six days. He realized he needed to get to a spot where a rescue helicopter could spot him in the canyon. Night came. He slept little. Every noise and shadow became a bear in his mind. Days passed. His knee swelled grotesquely. It took him three days to slide along his butt to an opening 100 feet away. Once there, he laboriously set up a large blue tarp with an "X" on it. Then he waited.

After six days injured and alone, McAdam sighted an Arizona Department of Public Safety helicopter hovering over Rough Canyon. He used his survival mirror to signal it. They zoomed in, and McAdam was soon lifted out with the help of the Pinal County sheriff's Superstition Search and Rescue squad. Within hours he was in a hospital surrounded by his family.

He told the *The Arizona Republic*[5] he plans to go back; though next time, he'll tote a personal locator beacon. How many men would have survived his ordeal? His tale is proof we need to be prepared for any injury or calamity.

# PART 2

PROVIDER

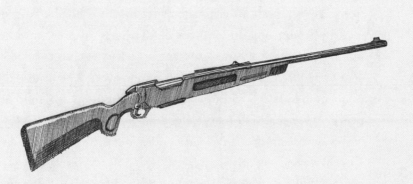

*"One does not hunt in order to kill; on the contrary, one kills in order to have hunted."*
—JOSE ORTEGA Y GASSET[1]

Even in these whitewashed times, somewhere under the crumbling trusses of our once patriarchal, male-chauvinist society, stinking like rotting corpses will, is the fact that from the beginning men have been judged by how reliably they bring home meat—and it's mostly the women who've done the judging. In fact, it's a safe assumption that before recorded time, not coming back to the missus with a wooly mammoth rump roast, or at least a snared rabbit or two, wasn't just tempting death by starvation, but an emasculating night at the cold end of the cave.

Indeed, no matter what today's politically correct spin purports, at the end of the work day, a man is someone who can proudly answer the question, "What do you do?" And it doesn't matter what he does as long as a man brings home enough meat, has pride in his work, and respects where his meat comes from. It's this last condition that many of today's men are uncertain about. This is because the process of literally earning our own meat, and thereby learning how nature truly functions, is a critical segment now largely missing from man's education. Tellingly, man's loss of a tangible role in nature is a recent phenomenon. In 1790, about 90 percent of Americans were farmers, but the percentage of Americans farming fell to 64 percent by 1850, to 38 percent by 1900, to 12 percent by 1950, and to about 2 percent of the American population today.[2] So, just two or three generations ago, more than one out of every ten people in America still dealt with the wildlife that ate their crops, and with insects, droughts, and floods. And even those who didn't farm in 1950 likely had a relative or a friend who did; as a result, they were still close enough to the natural process to understand how food was grown and what farmers had to do to control depredating wildlife and insects. But now, with just two out of every 100 Americans still tilling the land and six out of every 100 Americans hunting,[3] we have in just the last two generations transitioned into a society that is so successful the bulk of the public doesn't know where its food comes from—and doesn't have the slightest notion how to grow or kill their own. This is a staggering thing. The world has never seen this kind of society before. This is why for the first time in history there is real antipathy toward and misunderstanding of hunting, fishing, and shooting.

Theodore Roosevelt, hunter, conservationist, and president, noted our waning connection to nature in 1899, when he wrote, "Over-sentimentality, over-softness, in fact washiness and mushiness are the great dangers of this age and of this people. Unless we keep the barbarian virtues, gaining the civilized ones will be of little avail."[4]

Roosevelt thought that, whatever the women are up to, men not accustomed to getting their fingernails bloody, or at least dirty, can hardly be expected to remain manly. Indeed this, more than any other factor, has softened men's hands and feminized their behavior. Though it's fashionable among conservatives today to blame feminism for creating metrosexuals, the truth is sissified males aren't the result of women donning suits and toting briefcases. Males don't get manicures, have highlights put in their hair, and have their eyebrows plucked because a woman has the corner office. No, the cause is a lack of concrete connection to the earth. Just travel to any third world country where men still have to till the earth with their hands and hunt to fill the pot, and look around and see if you can find a "girlyman" admiring his reflection in a stream like Narcissus and wishing he had a fuller-bodied shampoo. Such men don't exist far off the pavement.

So the domesticated man asks, does shooting a pheasant really give an understanding of nature? Not necessarily. But really studying pheasant hunting, learning where the birds move and feed and hide, is necessary to becoming a good hunter, and it's those things that connect a man to nature and his place within it. The reality is that being environmentally responsible is manly when it's based on reality—a reality in which we are an active participant—and not on emotional idealism. Men, after all, are supposed to be the rational ones.

# On Shooting

hooting well has very little to do with physical strength and everything to do with mastering yourself. To succeed at archery, skeet, sporting clays, or long-range rifle shooting, you must first learn to be stoic, which is why shooting has always been a manly art. To succeed at hunting you must do even more: you must control yourself when a large animal is near so you can make a clean, ethical kill. This not-so-simple lesson has turned boys into men from the beginning.

Firearms, and learning how to use them responsibly, teach discipline and respect. They are tools to provide food for the table and security against thugs. Firearms exist, and government regulations won't change that, so as men we have to understand and respect firearms. Such things only come from education.

# How to Shoot

Shooting well is a mechanical exercise. Shotguns are pointed and rifles aimed. In each case, to shoot well you must subdue your emotions. You have to overcome and ignore the fear of recoil and of the loud boom. You need to concentrate your mind on the target, whether it's a flying clay pigeon or distant bull's-eye, while your body moves the gun or bow and your finger pulls the trigger by smooth instinct without a conscious thought. That's the key to shooting well.

Eugen Herrigel (1884–1955) was a German professor of philosophy who went to Japan to study archery as a way of experiencing Zen. In his classic book *Zen in the Art of Archery* (1948), he writes that a shooter has to transcend technique so that shooting comes from the unconscious. Herrigel practiced archery with a Zen master, who drilled him in the art until his body responded without any conscious interference from his mind. Many shotgun shooters joke that they can hit a moving target that appears suddenly, but they'll miss the same target if they see it coming.

I learned this lesson the hard way. Jim Carmichel, who was the shooting editor for *Outdoor Life* magazine for more than three decades, once taught me to shoot skeet.

"What are you thinking about, young man?" Carmichel is a refined, old-school southern aristocrat, but he knows how to cut to the root of the problem.

"Um?"

"Stop thinking. Start doing," he barked.

"Huh?"

"*Huh* is all you can muster? Your pampered generation doesn't even know the basics of manhood, yet you have the arrogance to assume you do, as if such things are intuitive to men."

As he shook dismay from his head, I dropped the gun from my shoulder, looked him in the eye, and said, "I'm listening."

His mustache fluttered. "You think you are. Trouble is you're really only listening to that crowd behind you."

I tossed my head. There was no one on the range but us.

"You don't see them, do you? Well, I'll point them out for you." He raised a long index finger and began, "Right there is doubt. Over there is ego. And there's angst hiding behind that tree. Stubborn is sitting on your right shoulder and confusion on your left. Your body is crowded with your emotions, and shooting, young man, is a mechanical exercise. You have to master all those emotions by forgetting them. Clear them from your head. They only get in the way. This is what video games don't teach you and why your generation is lost."

Carmichel has earned his biases and he really did have a lot to teach, so I said, "All right," and really tried.

"Now shoulder the shotgun and turn your body as if you're moving with the target. You're right handed, so plant your feet so your left toe is facing where you will shoot the target. When the target comes out, shoulder your gun fluidly as your whole upper body—turning at your waist—moves with the clay. The gun should move as an extension of your arms and body. Because you're right handed, push your left hand a little farther down the forend and point your index finger toward the muzzle—that's the end of the barrel," he mocked. "You point a shotgun; you don't aim it. It's like raising your finger to point out a star in the sky. The gun should just follow wherever you point."

I nodded and realized shooting is fundamentally simple, which is a tough concept to grasp in this increasingly complicated world.

"Forget about the bead on the end of the barrel," instructed Carmichel, "it should be out of focus as your eyes and your body behind it focus on the target. When your index finger passes the clay target, your trigger finger should shoot without being told to by your conscious mind. You calmly, fluidly swing the shotgun behind then past the clay bird as if there is a ribbon tied to its end—never stop to shoot; if you stop you miss. Let the gun go off naturally. It's that simple . . . if you can forget the crowd I still see milling about behind you."

Then I began to shoot. After a few shots the crowd grew quieter. After the second round of skeet I even began to tune out Carmichel's grunts and sighs, which was when I began to hit targets. On my third round I hit twenty-three of twenty-five.

# Gun Safety

Even those who don't plan to own a gun should know the National Rifle Association's ten rules of gun safety:

1. Always keep the gun pointed in a safe direction. A safe direction means that the gun is pointed so that even if it were to go off it would not cause injury or damage.
2. Always keep your finger off the trigger until you are ready to shoot. When holding a gun, rest your finger on the trigger guard or along the side of the gun.
3. Always keep the gun unloaded until ready to use.

4.   Whenever you pick up a gun, immediately check its safety device if possible, and, if the gun has a magazine, remove it before opening the action. If you do not know how to open the action or inspect the chamber(s), get help from someone who does.

5.   Be absolutely sure you have identified your target beyond any doubt and be equally aware of the area beyond your target. Never fire in a direction in which there are people or any other potentials for mishap.

6.   Just like other tools, guns need regular maintenance to remain operable. Regular cleaning and proper storage are a part of the gun's general upkeep. If there is any question concerning a gun's ability to function, a knowledgeable gunsmith should look at it.

7.   Use only the correct ammunition. Most guns have the ammunition type stamped on the barrel. Ammunition can be identified by information printed on the box and sometimes stamped on the cartridge.

8.   Wear eye and ear protection. Guns are loud, and the noise can cause hearing damage. They can also emit debris and hot gas that could cause eye injury.

9.   Never use alcohol, over-the-counter, prescription, or other drugs before or while shooting.

10.  Store guns so they are not accessible to unauthorized persons.

# Shooting Guide

## SHOTGUN

Fit is the first step to shotgun shooting. When someone tries shooting they often borrow or rent a shotgun that has too long or short a length of pull.

**MAN FACT**

Whether you are interested in recreational shooting, competition, hunting, or personal protection, NRA Basic Firearm Training Courses can teach you the safety principles and help you develop the necessary knowledge and skills. NRA Member Programs can be reached at 800-672-3888 or by logging on to www.nrahq.org/education/training/basictraining.asp.

A gun with the wrong length of pull will often bruise a shooter's cheek and frustrate him because the gun won't shoot where it's pointed. So the first time you shoot, go to a professional range and ask to be measured. Most major public ranges will have shotguns of various fits.

First, some terms every man should know about shotguns:

- **Length of Pull:** The distance from the center of the trigger to the center of the rear butt plate or recoil pad.
- **Over/Under:** A double-barrel shotgun with one barrel set vertically over another.
- **Semi-Auto:** A shotgun that cycles shells with each pull of the trigger.
- **Gauge:** The term used in the identification of most shotgun bores—12 is the most common and versatile.
- **Choke:** The constriction at the end of the barrel; a "tight choke" keeps shot pellets together at longer ranges and an "open choke" lets pellets spread apart faster. There are three standard chokes, from the least constrictive to the most constricted: improved-cylinder, modified, and full.

Most skeet and sporting clays ranges have over/under shotguns available for purchase or rent. If you want to be the envy of a skeet or sporting clays course, you'll need an over/under, and not just any over/under, but a Beretta,

Perazzi, Kreighoff, or other fine firearm. Such snooty guns can cost more than those diamond earrings your lady has been eyeing, so if you're not a high-roller, consider Browning's Citori, Ruger's Red Label, Kimber's Marias, or another quality brand/model that can be had for a grand or two. Increasingly affordable yet quality over/unders are coming from Turkey, a country with cheap labor and quality gun-makers. Only a trained eye can tell whether a shotgun came from Turkey or Italy. A good example of a fine Turkish over/under is Smith & Wesson's Elite Silver, which costs around $2,000. At the bottom of the price range are the workingman's guns. They lack the elegant styling of more expensive guns, but a real man doesn't need a pretty gun, right? For a good over/under shotgun in the sub-$1,000 class, consider Remington, Winchester, Mossberg, Marlin, or Savage/Stevens.

Another popular design for the clay sports and for wing shooting is a semi-automatic shotgun, which automatically cycles a new shell into the chamber when you pull the trigger. Because most semi-automatic shotguns use some of the "gas" from the shot to eject a spent shell and to load another, they typically have less recoil than other designs. They can also give a shooter three shots

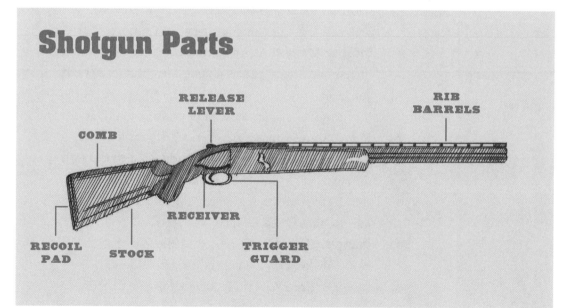

## Shotgun Parts

RELEASE
LEVER

RIB
BARRELS

COMB

RECEIVER

RECOIL
PAD

STOCK

TRIGGER
GUARD

or more, though two is the traditional limit on clays courses. Semi-autos are more commonly used by upland bird and waterfowl hunters. Consider Remington's Model 1100, Winchester's SX3, or Benelli's Legacy Sport.

## RIFLE

A rifle is a precision instrument. It's designed to hit a distant target with predictable accuracy. Rifling—grooves in the barrel that spin the bullet— was invented in the mid-fifteenth century, but didn't become common until the nineteenth century. Smokeless powder came about in the late nineteenth century.

First, some terms every man should know about rifles:

- **Sub-MOA:** If a rifle is "sub-MOA" it's accurate. "MOA" stands for "minute of angle." A minute of angle is 1/60th of a degree; it subtends 1.047 of an inch per 100 yards of range.

- **Rifle Scope:** Most rifles are topped with optics. You'll see these referred to by numbers: 3-12x-40. This means it is a variable 3-12 powered scope with a 40mm objective.

- **Trigger Weight:** A two-pound trigger is light and a three-pound trigger is usually considered about right. If you hear a shooter damning his heavy trigger, he means it takes an inordinate amount of pressure to pull it.

- **Bolt-Action:** A manually operated action that uses a handle-like bolt to load, eject, and lock a round into the chamber.

- **Semi-Automatic:** A firearm that fires, ejects, and reloads once for each pull of its trigger.

- **Pump-Action:** A manual-action firearm that uses a moveable forearm to load and eject cartridges.

- **Lever-Action:** A manual-action firearm that uses a moveable lever to load and eject cartridges.

- **Bullet:** This is not the entire cartridge, but the portion that shoots out the end of the barrel.
- **Load:** The amount and type of powder used to propel the bullet.
- **Caliber:** The type of ammunition. Hunters typically use different types of .30-caliber ammunition, such as .30-06, .300 Win. Mag., and .308 for big game.

Today, rifles are mechanical wonders designed with the capability of putting three shots in a one-inch circle at 100 yards. However, if you pick up a scoped rifle for the first time and hold its crosshair on a distant object you'll see Hollywood, once again, is lying: you can't hold a crosshair steady on a small object at long range without a solid rest and a disciplined shooting style.

The bolt-action rifle has a special reputation for accuracy. This design has dominated hunting and long-range shooting (including sniper rifles) ever since Paul Mauser designed his famous Model 98 over a century ago. Today

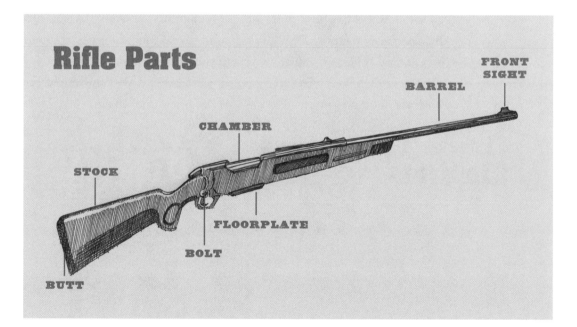

**Rifle Parts**

FRONT SIGHT

BARREL

CHAMBER

STOCK

FLOORPLATE

BOLT

BUTT

**MAN FACT**

"Black Guns" are in; Remington, for one, recently introduced two AR-type rifles that emulate the configurations and accessories of their battlefield cousins.

there are so many bolt-action options that the question isn't so much which is the best rifle, but which rifle is right for you.

At one end of the scale is Savage's Model 12, an affordable, accurate rifle made in America. On the other end are custom-made bolt-actions built on Model 700, Kimber 8400, and other reliable platforms that can be modified until they're proven tack drivers with certain loads and bullets. In between are rifles such as Browning's X-Bolt and Winchester's controlled-round-feed Model 70, which is now back in production. New Model 70s sport the company's MOA trigger, a three-lever system factory-set at 3 pounds, 12 ounces.

As for semi-automatic rifles, the effect of the M1 Garand (developed by John Garand, it was the military's primary rifle from 1936 to 1957) and M16 as infantry rifles led to today's sleeker models. In terms of civilian sales of semi-automatic-only rifles, derivatives of these two rifles dominate the American marketplace. Today, the hottest-selling rifle segment is the black gun, AR-15-type rifles that emulate the configurations and accessories of battle-field rifles. The AR-15 has evolved into a product line that offers a model for practically any type of shooting scenario. Chambered in everything from .22 LR to .50-caliber hog busters, the AR-15 is exhibiting the same adaptability in civilian circles that propelled the M16 family to the longest-serving standard issue infantry rifle in the history of the United States military.

Although many prefer the recoil mitigation of the AR-15's straight-line stock and intermediate chambering, there will continue to be a demand for a

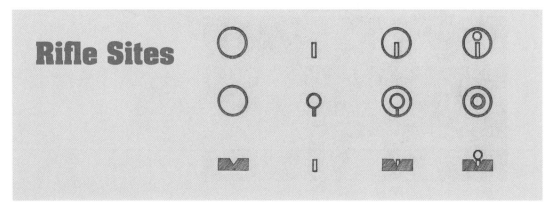

**Rifle Sites**

full-size, full-bore semi-automatic rifle. No rifle fills that void as succinctly as Springfield Armory's M1A line of semi-autos chambered in .308 Win. From National Match versions to the wonderfully versatile SOCOM, the popularity of the M1A echoes the U.S. military's resurgent use of the M14 service rifle. Simply stated, the rifle has capabilities unequaled in the M16 family, a shining testament to the final application of Garand's genius.

Though military-inspired semi-automatic rifles dominate civilian sales, there remains a consistent crop of rifles chambered for deer-stopping rounds and marketed primarily for hunting big game. The Winchester SXR, Browning BAR, Remington Model 750, and Benelli R1 are the contemporary maturations of John Browning's Model 8 and Winchester's popular lines of early self-loaders. With gas systems that more closely resemble modern semi-automatic shotguns, these rifles feature lightly stressed receivers with bolts locking into barrel extensions.

## MARINE CORPS SNIPER TACTICS

The U.S. military's snipers quietly altered the war in Iraq. Flat, open terrain made it possible for Marine snipers and snipers from other branches of the military to target enemy forces at long range and take them out with precision.

Sniper Guns: There are two basic types of sniper rifles now used by the U.S. military: a .30-caliber bolt-action, such as Remington's Model 700, with a range in good conditions of about 1,000 yards, and a .50 caliber, bolt-action rifle, such as the M107, which can effectively reach out to 2,000 yards.

Techniques: Most snipers use a spotter who helps spot a target, and uses a rangefinder to get a precise reading distance to the target. He then

> **MAN FACT**
> Sniper schools run by ex-military marksmen can be a manly vacation.
> For example, the Sportsmen All-Weather, All-Terrain Marksmanship
> course is a sniper school run by former Navy SEALs in Texas and is open
> to the public.

> **MAN FACT**
>
> Sorry, Dirty Harry, the most powerful handgun in the world is no longer a .44 Magnum. Several handgun cartridges are now more powerful than the .44, most notably, the .500 Smith & Wesson Magnum. When the .44 Magnum was called "the most powerful handgun in the world," its standard load produced about 900 foot-pounds of muzzle energy. Today, the .500 S&W Magnum will produce almost 2,600 foot-pounds of energy at the muzzle.

calculates the bullet's drop and wind drift; for example, a .30-06 Springfield using Federal Cartridge's 150-grain Sierra HPBT bullet that's sighted in to be dead-on at 200 yards will drop 13.5 inches at 350 yards; meanwhile, a 10 mph crosswind will blow that bullet 10.1 inches at that same range. Such variables make a spotter who helps quickly calculate bullet placement and who then watches to see where bullets are hitting, critical. Snipers and their spotters lie in a prone position and use terrain and camouflage, such as Ghillie Suits. Often, they will have to move between shots to keep the enemy uncertain about their position. To stay out of sight, modern ballistics and rifles enable snipers to do things like shoot "loopholes," meaning a sniper avoids enemy detection by shooting through a fist-sized hole in a building from dozens of feet away.

# Handguns

### REVOLVER

As any Hollywood producer could tell you, revolvers are retro. But, despite the reliability and accuracy of semi-autos, the revolver is the sidearm of choice when a hunter needs all the power he can handle to deal with large animals. And, for the less-experienced shooter, a revolver is easier to operate since it does not have manually operated safeties to disengage or a reciprocating slide that can tear flesh from the top of a misplaced thumb. Furthermore, revolvers have evolved. It is now possible to pack the excellent stopping power of the .357 Mag into an 11-ounce revolver, as Smith & Wesson proved with its Model 340PD. In the more remote areas of this country, those who need to pack a handgun daily more often than not choose a powerful revolver in .44, .45, or even .50 caliber.

## SEMI-AUTO PISTOL

First of all, when a man shoots a semi-automatic pistol, he holds it straight up and down—not horizontally "ghetto-style." You not only can't aim when you hold a handgun on its side, but when you shoot a semi-auto this way hot brass will bounce around your ankles or fly at your head. A gun maker at the 2008 SHOT Show, an annual guns-and-hunting trade show, designed a semi-auto 9mm with sights on the side of its frame to mock such hipsters. Shooters came by all day and went off smirking, knowing they'll outshoot the thug who holds a gun that way.

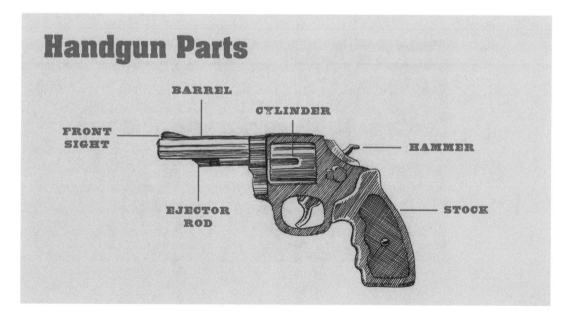

# Handgun Parts

BARREL

CYLINDER

FRONT
SIGHT

HAMMER

EJECTOR
ROD

STOCK

Next, you need to learn how to grip a semi-auto handgun, because if you leave a thumb in the wrong spot, the gun's action will fly back and cut it to the bone. You shoot with two hands, with the top hand pulling the trigger while keeping the thumb along the frame. The bottom hand stays below and serves to tighten and steady your grip. Take a course at a range near you before you shoot.

Now, the cool part: technology has made semi-auto pistols smaller, lighter, and more powerful. This trend started with the Glock 17 and has continued with firearms such as the Springfield XD and the Smith & Wesson Military & Police. These days you can find a 9mm or .45 ACP as small as a PPk. Many compact semi-autos are chambered in .40 S&W, 9mm, and .45 ACP.

### Which Caliber Do You Need?

A 9mm is used by military and police because it's easy to shoot, fits in a small-frame handgun, and has plenty of knock-down power. If you want a home-protection gun, you can choose any caliber you like, but when you're carrying for personal protection, you want something light and portable. Today there are more choices than ever. Some handguns can even be tailored

**MAN FACT**

In 1139 AD, the Second Lateran Council, under Pope Innocent II, banned the use of the crossbow against Christians: "We prohibit under anathema that murderous art of crossbowmen and archers, which is hated by God, to be employed against Christians and Catholics from now on." But today crossbows are hip again. A crossbow fires a short (often about 15-inch) shaft called a "bolt." A crossbow is able to fire a bolt with much more velocity than a bow can fire an arrow, but because a bolt has less weight and therefore less potential kinetic energy than an arrow, a bolt slows down faster and has less killing power at longer ranges.

to you; for example, the Sig Sauer P250 is a modular pistol that allows you to change caliber and grip size. The P250 is available in 9mm, .357SIG, .40S&W, and .45ACP.

## WORLD'S FASTEST QUICK DRAW

Sure, the quick draw in the white hat is a masculine icon, but there is very little historical evidence that cowboys ever squared off in a street to see who was faster. But the myth did create a tough-guy sport. These days a world-class competitor can draw and fire a shot from a revolver in under half a second; the current world record for open-style standing blanks is 0.208 seconds, which includes the time it took to react to the signal. The reaction time of the best fast draw shooters is 0.145 seconds, which means that the gun is cocked, drawn, aimed (from the hip), and fired in just over 0.06 seconds. To make a World Fast Draw Association record, a second shot must be fired in the same competition that is no more than 0.03 seconds slower than the first—this rule is designed to prevent a shooter from setting a record by guessing when the signal is coming. Quick draw artists use two hands: as one hand draws, the other cocks the hammer and lets go, causing the shot to go off. Quick draw shooters don't raise the gun to eye level or even much away from their bodies. They fire as soon as it clears the holster.

# Bow

In *Rambo II*, Sylvester Stallone used his bow to shoot explosive tipped arrows at North Vietnamese communists. But because the bow was too quiet for some Hollywood producer, they added a sound effect that made shooting a bow sound like a fighter jet taking off. Bows are supposed to be quiet—and most are. Today, about four million hunters use compound bows to hunt deer and other game. Hunting with a bow and shooting in 3D tournaments is as manly as it gets.

The first thing you'll need to do is have a bow fitted to you—you can't just pick up and shoot someone else's unless their strength, experience, and arm length are the same as yours. Go to an archery shop and get fitted for a bow. Even if you only shoot recreationally, you'll soon learn why the Japanese and Chinese have used archery to discipline the mind.

Here are some terms every man should know about bows:

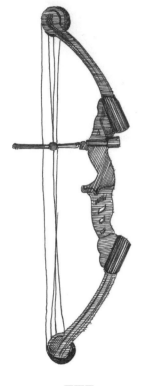

**THE COMPOUND BOW**

- **Compound Bow:** This bow uses wheels or cams to generate torque.
- **Recurve Bow:** This bow has recessed limbs to generate torque.
- **Long Bow:** This is what Robin Hood toted.
- **Release:** A mechanical trigger used to release the bow's string.
- **Peep Sight:** A small ring, usually located on the string, that an archer looks through to be sure his sight is lined up the same way every time.
- **Sight:** Usually pins attached to the riser. You line up a pin with your target and sight different pins for various ranges.
- **Stabilizer:** A weight screwed into the front of a bow's riser that keeps a bow level and easier to hold steady.
- **Broadhead:** This is a razor-tipped arrow point.
- **Draw Weight:** This is the amount of weight you pull back.

Shooting a bow is like firing a rifle: you aim and look through the sight to the target as your shooting hand fires. To shoot well, you need to develop the same instinctive shooting skills that go with firing a gun. If you use a release, you'll even be pulling a trigger. If you use a tab or shooting glove, you'll need to learn to release the string smoothly. There are many good bows on the market from makers such as Mathews, PSE, BowTech, and more. Nothing will help you learn to master yourself more than shooting a bow. Many manufacturers still make longbows and recurve bows as well. They'll build your strength and require you to control your mind and body.

## Why Men Hunt

A man doesn't have to prove his manhood by killing game, though that is what some urban non-hunters think sportsmen do. Hunting actually humbles the egotistical. Try waiting long hours in the cold woods, reading deer sign, and mastering your nerves as a bear comes close, and you'll know hunting increases knowledge and respect for wildlife. Though it's no longer necessary for men to kill game to survive, it is necessary for men to understand that some deer must be killed—that when deer overpopulate they starve in winter, are more susceptible to disease, and over-browse habitat to the detriment of other animals. A man can't sit at a San Francisco café and mock where his food comes from and be manly.

For me, respect for nature comes from being a predator. And, because I know the science behind what I'm doing, and I know men have always had an active role in nature, I recognize my role in the natural world by showing respect to fallen game. The Finns, who still have a strong hunting culture, ceremonially close a slain moose's eyes and place a small piece of food in the animal's mouth as they thank it for giving them sustenance. Afrikaners do the same thing. Native Americans had many rituals for thanking wildlife for their lives and sustenance. American hunters, however, don't practice any form of ritualized respect. I've long thought this an oversight. So when I got the chance to hunt with the Jicarilla Apache, I was looking forward to seeing if they still follow the old ways.

Because the illiterate leave few records, to learn the Apache rituals I was forced to turn to books written by people who knew and even fought the Apache. Colonel John C. Cremony's *Life among the Apaches*, for example, is an insightful and epic book published in 1868 and written by a man

> **To waste, to destroy, our natural resources, to skin and exhaust the land instead of using it so as to increase its usefulness, will result in undermining in the days of our children the very prosperity which we ought by right to hand down to them amplified and developed.**
>
> THEODORE ROOSEVELT[5]

**63**

who fought and grew to know and respect renowned Apaches such as Mangas Colorado. But the book that taught me the most was Frank C. Hibben's *Indian Hunts and Indian Hunters of the Old West.* Re-published in 1992 by Safari Press, it's a compilation of hunts Hibben made decades earlier in the Southwest with a dying breed of Apache who were still in touch with the ancient ways. Hibben explained, "To an Apache Indian, good or bad fortune in hunting is attributed to Killer of Enemies or Child of Water, two deities of the past who taught the Indians how to hunt and the ceremonies and rituals that go with hunting." Hibben then described the rituals. I jotted them down in my memory, not so much to follow, as to respect.

But my first sight of the reservation wasn't enlightening about the old ways, it was a symbol of the times: a casino. The Jicarilla Apache's casino looked like a large, white circus tent haphazardly erected in the desert, and had more tumbleweeds than cars in its parking lot. The U.S. Government gave the Jicarilla Apaches this mountainous reservation in the early twentieth century. Little did the U.S. Congress know at the time that they'd granted oil and gas rights to a courageous people who would one day sap Americans with high-stakes poker and dollar slots.

The next morning I met my Apache guide, Shelby. He pulled up in a full-sized pickup and declared, "They're bugling hard. Let's go find a big one!" Shelby had amber skin, deep, dark eyes, and a wispy smile that belied a cutting sense of humor. We drove into the high country and hiked for miles before the sun rose to find us in an open, sweeping canyon listening to elk bugle. We spotted a bull feeding in a lush spot under a cliff two miles away. As we stalked the feeding bull, I tried to slow down Shelby (who I was already calling "Fleet Foot") by teasing that maybe we should follow an old ritual or two, so the hunting gods would smile on us.

First I asked if Shelby had fed crows at his previous kills. "If you don't leave something for the crows to eat then the crows warn the elk you're coming," I said.

Shelby smiled and replied, "Yes, I leave the gutpile."

"Okay then, did you ever leave a deer or elk head facing where the sun rises, and then leave without walking in front of it?"

"No. Hunters always want the head. As do I. My elk watch over my living room."

"Well, that's the modern ritual of respect, maybe they'll let us get away with that one. Did you pray this morning to Elk Chief, to give us a bull to feed us through the winter?"

"No."

"Well, I asked the hunting gods for luck this morning," I chided, "so maybe they'll forgive you, Fleet Foot."

As we walked over red dirt in the afternoon sun, Shelby looked down a long time, then finally asked, "Where did you learn such things?"

"Books."

"Maybe I should read those books."

I was disappointed he didn't know these things, or other, deeper things, but not terribly. Not knowing your own history is a common failing.

Shelby guided me past two cow elk bedded just fifteen yards away in oak brush and padded down a red sandstone ridge to where elk bugles were echoing. We crawled onto a slab of rock that jutted out over the canyon, giving us a perfect view of the herd below. Bugles were ricocheting up the precipices, and there was a bull with antlers better than four feet wide. Cow elk were bedded in conifer islands on a sage flat. A small bull was feeding on the right. We needed to keep very low and very still.

As we waited, the immature bull inched closer to the herd. A dozen cows and calves were between him and the mature herd bull. The young bull meandered within a dozen feet of a cow, and the big bull bugled, shook his head, and began to saunter over to show who was boss.

The small bull slunk off. The herd bull looked majestic in his dominance. This was the moment non-hunters don't understand, can't comprehend. I admired the bull and whispered thanks to the ancient Apache hunting gods as I settled the crosshairs. The bull went down in his tracks before the roar of the .338 Federal's report ricocheted back again. The small bull ran off with the herd.

Shelby boasted we'd celebrate with beers at the cleaning shed, which was anticlimactic as I was hoping for a ritual Indian dance around a campfire. Only one thing remained constant: the hunters gathered to tell tall tales, but also to express their reverence for the elk. The mix of the old and the new spun together, and it was good.

# Hunting How-To

### THE HUNTING LINGO

There are strict vernaculars used in hunting. So if you go on your first duck, pheasant, or deer hunt with experienced hunters, be humble. Remember what a fool Senator John Kerry made of himself when he bragged to the *Milwaukee Journal Sentinel*, "I go out with my trusty 12-gauge double-barrel, crawl around on my stomach. I track and move and decoy and play games and try to outsmart [deer]. You know, you kind of play the wind. That's hunting." Anyone who has ever hunted knows deer hunters don't crawl around on their stomachs. Kerry got his alleged Swift-boat antics confused with his hunting hallucinations, when all he had to do was play it humble.

On your first hunting trip, ask questions on the car ride out, then shut up, listen, and learn in the field. To get you started, here are a few words and terms hunters use.

**THE BLIND TREE STAND**

- **Blind/Tree Stand:** A place where a hunter waits for game.
- **Bugle:** The high-pitched cry of a bull elk. Hunters use a tube call with a reed to mimic this call because bull elk will sometimes come to a bugle.

- **Decoy Spread:** A waterfowl hunter's decoys positioned to mimic feeding or resting ducks or geese.
- **Glassing:** Using a binocular to spot game animals.
- **Grunt:** A sound bucks make when they're chasing a doe in estrus. It sounds like the guttural rumbles often heard emanating from Taco John's bathroom stalls.
- **Gutpile:** The remains left after a hunter cleans his kill.
- **Rattle:** Taking two antlers and banging them together to simulate two bucks fighting. The sound will often lure bucks in.
- **Rub:** A small tree a buck has rubbed its antlers on. "Did ya see the size of that rub?"
- **Rut:** The rut is the breeding period for deer. It typically occurs in early to mid November outside the Deep South. Hunters use the words as both a noun and an adjective, sometimes in the same sentence: "I know the rut's here, because I saw a buck so rutty he was chasing horses."
- **Scrape:** A patch of ground a buck has cleared to deposit its scent in.
- **Spot and Stalk:** A tactic comprised of using a binocular to find game, such as deer or antelope, and then sneaking closer.

## NATIVE AMERICAN STRATEGIES

**The Surround:** A tribe would encircle a certain section of terrain (especially one with natural boundaries like rivers or cliffs) and then tighten the noose. Game would run away into the closing circle. When the circle got small enough, the deer, bears, turkeys, and so on would try to bust out, giving the braves a chance to shoot them.

**The Fire Drive:** Tribes would use controlled burns to push deer and other game to waiting ambushers.[6]

**A Wolf in Sheep's Clothing:** Indians would drape themselves in deerskin and a "deer mask" and walk just downwind of feeding deer. When close enough, they'd shoot one with an arrow.

**The Duck Snag:** Indians would submerge themselves in a pond with their back facing toward the bottom and slowly swim while sucking air through a reed. They'd approach feeding ducks, grab them by their feet and yank them under. If they did it well, the other ducks would think the duck was just diving down to feed on aquatic plants.

**The Buffalo Jump:** "Look at all them bones," guffawed Tom Mankin, a cowboy now at the end of his trail, as we stood on a blind bluff near Casper, Wyoming. "This here's a 'buffalo jump.' The Cheyenne would drive them down this flat and get 'em really movin', too. Just look at the cliff, you can't see it as you approach. So those buff would just run right off." There are many known buffalo jumps all around the West.

## HOW TO READ DEER SIGN

**Tracks:** When reading tracks, first look at their direction, and then their size. A whitetail doe or young buck might make tracks between 1.5 and 3 inches long, while an old buck's can be as big as 4 inches long. To determine when they were made, look at how sharp the track's edges are. It's critical to know what the weather has been doing to age the track, as rain, wind, and even humidity will age a track at various rates.

**Scat:** Deer pellets range in size from .5 to 1.75 inches long. A trained eye can tell what deer are feeding on by looking at scat. Fresh scat (moist in dry weather) tells you deer are currently using the trail.

**Buck Sign:** During the fall rut whitetail bucks rub their antlers on trees (called "rubs") and clear small sections of ground to deposit their scent in (called "scrapes").

**Beds:** These are places where deer have laid down. A deer bed can measure from 25 to 42 inches long. Deer bed in thick cover and on southeastern facing slopes in cold weather.[7]

### The Ultimate Deer Stand

The best deer stand is in a place where the terrain forces deer trails together between where deer are actively feeding and bedding. Look for a stand on the downwind side (the predominant wind is usually from the west) of the trails. And locate a way to get in and out without leaving your scent or spooking deer (deer are skittish and they'll become nocturnal if they know you're in the vicinity).

## SET A SNARE

If you're lost and starving, this is the easiest way to get meat. You can use a shoelace, but a supple copper or brass wire is better as it will hold its shape and won't hold scent. Locate a rabbit trail or any path small animals are using. Look for places that force animals to use a certain spot, such as a space between deadfalls or a stream crossing, and look for tracks. Use a slipknot to tie a loop big enough to let in an animal's head, but not to allow its shoulders and front legs to pass through. The loop should be three to five inches wide for a rabbit-sized animal, and the loose end should be about eighteen inches long. Position the snare in the path being used by the rabbits so it's high enough off the ground that the animal's head will naturally go through it (about four inches for a rabbit) as it follows the path. When the animal's

**MAN FACT**
"Rabbit starvation" is a real condition. You can't live entirely off rabbit because the meat is too lean.

**69**

shoulders and front legs hit the snare, the string/wire will tighten around its neck. Tie the end of the wire/string to a sapling or log so that when the animal gets to the end of the line, the noose will tighten.

## HOW TO CALL GAME

With today's manufactured calls for turkey, geese, elk, or other game, it's easy—most calls come with a CD or DVD that plays the sound you want to reproduce. Try practicing in your car as you drive. If you're lost in the wild, or just want to be the ultimate woodsman, here are three calls hunters used to make.

### Wingbone turkey call:

By using a straw or other small tube, or by fitting together the hollow bones in a turkey's wing, you can make a good turkey call. Just suck air out of the tube and control the pressure at the bottom.

### Single-reed duck call:

Carve a hollow tube from wood or even use your hands to hold a single reed that's attached on one side and loose on the other. A leaf or piece of plastic can be used to make the reed. Experiment with pressure on the reed, the size of the reed, and the airflow through the tube, and before you know it you'll be able to make everything from buck grunts to cow elk mews to duck quacks.

### Slate-and-peg call:

By using a small piece of slate and a wooden peg, you can easily produce turkey hen yelps.

## MAKE AN ETHICAL KILL

When hunting with a bow, you need to shoot an arrow through your prey's lungs. A shot one-third to halfway up the chest and right behind the front leg or shoulder is ideal. Just be sure the angle of the shot will allow the arrow to get both lungs. An arrow that does this will kill a deer in twenty seconds or less and is relatively painless. If you've ever been cut with a really sharp razor, then you know it doesn't hurt, but it bleeds—a hunting arrow is tipped with razor-sharp blades.

When using a firearm, you can also shoot the animal just behind the shoulder. But a chest-shot deer can run up to 100 yards before expiring. If you're hunting dangerous game and don't want the animal to run, shoot for the shoulder and break it down. This is a good shot because if the bullet strays forward it will hit the base of the neck, which is instantaneously lethal; too far back and it takes out the lungs; too high and it hits the spine, which will drop it in its tracks, but may need a follow-up shot; and too low and the bullet will hit the heart.

## FIELD DRESS YOUR DEER

If you're man enough to kill it, you're man enough to clean it. Remember, someone cleaned every piece of meat you've ever eaten. It's a natural part of the process.

1. If you're in an area that uses tags, put the appropriate one on your animal immediately.
2. Carefully cut a circle around its anus so it's free and can be removed from within.
3. If it's a buck, remove and discard its testicles and cut the penis free so it can be removed by the same route as the anus.
4. Start from the pelvis and cut open the stomach cavity up to the ribcage. Only cut through skin and a thin layer of meat. This is what a guthook (a curved portion on the back of some knives) is for.
5. If you want to have the buck mounted, don't cut any farther than the bottom of the chest. If you don't, then continue to cut up to the neck.

6. Sever the windpipe and esophagus at the base of the skull.

7. Open up the animal's stomach and roll out its intestines. Cut through the diaphragm and remove the lungs, heart, and everything else.

8. Cut the muscle holding the hips together and be extremely careful when you remove the bladder. You must reach up into the pelvis and pinch it shut while you cut it free.

9. Clean any debris from the cavity.

10. Drag the animal out or quarter it by cutting it into four sections and putting the quarters into game bags. Get the meat out of the forest and clean it with cold water as soon as possible. If the weather is warm, get the meat to a butcher so it can be hung in a cooler as soon as possible.

> **The gods do not deduct from man's allotted span the hours spent in fishing.**
>
> BABYLONIAN PROVERB

### Make the Best Tasting Jerky in the World

Making deer jerky is easy, and your wife will be left wonderfully perplexed with your sudden interest in the oven. Just cut two pounds of venison steaks into thin strips. Mix them with 2/3 cup of soy sauce, 2/3 cup Worcestershire sauce, 1 teaspoon garlic powder, 1 teaspoon onion powder, and 2 teaspoons of seasoning salt and let them marinate over night. Then drain the excess marinade, use paper towels to get the meat as dry as possible, and place individual pieces of meat on a rack in your oven at 140 to 160 degrees for seven to 12 hours, or until the meat is thoroughly dried.

# THEODORE ROOSEVELT

He was a sickly youth, wheezing asthmatically as he squinted through spectacles. His will to live, to strive for the horizon, grew, and he shrugged off his ailments, eventually becoming a big-game hunter, an outdoorsman, as well as a boxer during his days at Harvard. He went west to the banks of North Dakota's Little Missouri and learned to ride, rope, and hunt. He rebuilt his life and health. To find adventure, he became a deputy sheriff. One day he hunted down three outlaws who'd stolen his riverboat. After capturing them, he took the thieves by himself to jail while guarding them for forty hours, at one point reading Tolstoy to stay awake. After one of his hunting expeditions, "Teddy" bears were named after him. He became governor of New York, led a famous charge as a colonel in the Spanish-American War up Kettle Hill, and became the twenty-sixth president of the United States.

When in the White House, Roosevelt turned his attention to conservation. He declared, "All hunters should be nature lovers," and fostered a humane conservation ethic by recasting hunters as not just predators, but as cultivators of the wild, as game managers. As a hunter, he understood the wild and preached a bold concept, a melding of European game laws—where wealthy landowners possessed the animals in their woods and fields and forbade others the meat—with the American free-for-all that had nearly eliminated buffalo. He wanted the American people to understand that hunting is humane and beneficial, but destroying game populations is not; and he wanted to use sportsmen as caretakers of nature—and he succeeded.

Roosevelt created the first National Bird Preserve (the beginning of the Wildlife Refuge system) on Pelican Island, Florida. He recognized the imminent extinction of the American Bison and co-founded the American Bison Society in 1905. He pushed Congress into establishing the U.S.Forest Service in 1905. He set aside more land for national parks and preserves than all his predecessors combined (194 million acres). Roosevelt expounded, "There is an intimate relation between our streams and the development and conservation of all the other great permanent sources of wealth."

Hunters and fishermen have since paid for and fought for reintroduction of deer, turkey, elk, waterfowl, and other game, and have preserved millions of acres of habitat.

# Why Men Fish

Many think of fishing as a child's sport. And it is a fine one. Casting a bobber and worm to sunfish on a Saturday afternoon is an American pastime, an experience every child should try, at least once. Fishing is more than child's play, though. Fishing can be an adrenaline sport, but mostly fishing seduces you into falling into harmony with the water, and through it, with nature herself.

Fly-fishing on a stream coursing over free stones is madness at first cast, then less so as you learn what's happening in the turbid scene. Finally, when you master the line and insects hatching and the trout flitting in the seams of the current so well you move with waters and play fish like the moving stream itself, fishing becomes a simple romance again. This is why fishing is good for men, and always has been. There's boyish delight, then deep problems to overcome, then a Zen experience as you fall in harmony with the natural world gurgling by your feet.

If you learn just one pond, lake, or stream, really learn its processes, understand how the nymphs hatch into insects and move up and out of the water and fly free and how this makes the fish move as they feed, and what weather fronts and barometric pressure do to fish, and what happens when the water temperature is 58 or 68 degrees, and all the other pieces in the natural puzzle . . . if you learn just one place like that, you'll know all places, a little. And you'll begin to sense the depths of the ecosystem, and with that knowledge will come appreciation and harmony. And all that is something to guide a son or daughter through. Such fluid reality washes away bias and with it idealization and you realize just where we as humans fit into the natural system and know when it is okay to eat a fish and when it isn't, because we should be rational men, not emotional things built on bias.

When you're in the middle of this learning curve and look up to see someone so perfect and knowledgeable they seem not to be as much fly-fishing as a natural part of the ecosystem, you're drawn to that person.

This happened to me some years back on a Wyoming river, miles from the popular pools. I heard his line first. *Wisp . . . wisp . . .* his fly line traversed a seam in the current and then softly fell right on target—tight loops and a low arc; no wasted motion. The fly was up, over, and then back in the water. He was a master, as anyone who makes casting look so effortless must be. I wondered if he would be willing to teach me a little, just a little.

After shadowing him for the better part of an hour, watching, barely fishing, I observed him roll the line in with his left hand and spin it back out with a light, smooth motion with his right. As if in a trance, he didn't even glance at me. Just watching the seams, flitting his line into the next, biting off a fly, replacing it with a quick twist, he moved almost mechanically, but was too fluid to be a machine.

I could have approached him, but fly-fishing etiquette required me not to cross a certain invisible line in the water. He was fishing the head of the pool; I had to wait.

So I decided to be daring. I moved in below him and tried to mimic his motion. We were on the North Platte in early August. The evening turned shades of amber and birds sang from cottonwoods on the banks. I changed my posture . . . leaned in a little . . . stood with my left foot facing the upstream current . . . tried to make my face look content, without a care in the world, like his.

The master cast and so did I, he to the seam at the top, me to the same seam sixty feet below; his fly was inhaled by a fish, mine escaped their attention. At the risk of all humility lost, I pretended to play his fish. Rod at 45 degrees and shaking like a tree in a hurricane, he kept his wrist loose and let the fish run until he got him on the reel. Turning to let the rod tip follow the brown downstream, he looked right at me turning with my rod unbent and empty.

I stepped out of the way as he played the fish down the hole.

The master let the fat brown go like he was teaching it to swim, then sat on a rock with his legs splayed. I seized the opportunity.

"Beautiful day on the river, huh?"

He smiled, said, "You walked right by the fish."

"Huh?"

"To the right of the boulder is a brute. I left him for you, but you walked right by him. Instead you cast everywhere I did. Come on, let's see if you can catch him."

The master opened his fly box. He was a minimalist. He pulled out a better stonefly than I'd tied on. Biting off my fly, he tied a new fly on with one quick improved clinch with knot. He barely had to snip the excess line.

"There, you see him? He's eighteen, maybe twenty inches, a smart old bugger. Your first cast means everything with a fish like that. Drag the fly by him and you're done; he'll sink and wait. You cast too much. False casts kill leaders and spook fish. Make a practice cast below him to get the distance, then drop the fly four feet above him. It needs to sink a foot."

My nerves fired as I felt the rod's action. I cast and the line landed with a little splash.

"Don't force it," said the master.

I picked up the line, let it straighten, then threw it forward, pretending it was a false cast and hit the mark. The fly followed the seam my line stopped. I set the hook. The fish ran first upstream and then across. I followed him with my rod tip, letting him have line just as the master had done. He turned and went down. I forgot the world around existed. I moved down the rocks with the current, keeping just enough pressure on the fish.

He ran into a pool and around. My rod jittered and shook. The trout made another run, this one shorter. I was in waist deep, reeling fast. He was circling. He jumped one more time. Then he was in my net. I carefully let him go and turned around to thank the master, but he was gone. I stood there in the stream thinking, *He's even a master of exits.*

## Fishing Guide

> *"Many go fishing all of their lives without knowing that it is not fish they are after."*
> –HENRY DAVID THOREAU[8]

## BASS FISHING

Every man should know how to cast a spin reel and a baitcaster, as those reels with the big buttons on the bottom are for children. A spin reel is the most common and versatile. They come in various weights and sizes. Choose one right for your choice of fish. A listing of weights will be on the reel's box. One listed between four and twelve is right for most freshwater fish. Match the reel size to the rod. A spinning rod will have a large low guide (the rings the line passes through), because the line spins off the top of the spool. A spinning reel is cast by holding the line with the index finger of your casting hand, flipping the reel's bail (a piece of wire around the top of the reel), and when the lure is tossed letting go of the line when the rod is pointing to where you wish the lure to go.

A baitcaster is something altogether different. This reel has a spool that spins toward the rod tip. The line doesn't spool off, but comes off as the wheel spins. To cast one properly, you'll need to control the spool's speed with your thumb. Put too much pressure on the spool and the line won't cast, too little and the spool will spin too fast and the reel will snarl into a bird's nest of line. Like riding a bike, the only way to learn to cast a baitcaster is to cast one. Baitcasters are popular for bass fishing in the southern U.S. because they are versatile and accurate.

### Fishing Lures

Some men earn a living tossing artificial lures to black bass. And there is great depth in such fishing if you look. But for most of us it's a summer pastime, though an art you should know enough about to show to a boy. Here are the top lures/baits and when and where to use them.

> **Poppers:** These topwater lures are typically made from wood and float. They attract bass by popping and gurgling like a wounded insect on the surface when you jerk them.
>
> **Stickbaits:** These long, minnow-shaped lures will dart back and forth on or just under the surface like a wounded baitfish.

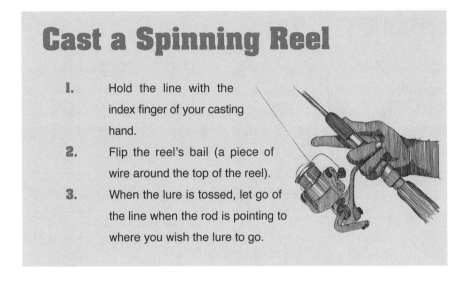

# Cast a Spinning Reel

1. Hold the line with the index finger of your casting hand.

2. Flip the reel's bail (a piece of wire around the top of the reel).

3. When the lure is tossed, let go of the line when the rod is pointing to where you wish the lure to go.

This technique is called "walking the dog." Use this lure in shallow water in the morning and evening.

**Propbaits:** These large plastic or wooden lures stay on the surface and have metal props or spinners. They mimic wounded fish or frogs. Fish them on warm summer evenings in places where bass feed.

**Crankbaits:** These mimic minnows and usually have one or more treble hooks. They are great for aggressive bass in open water. They become snagged easily in brush or vegetation.

**Spinnerbaits:** This lure has a plastic skirt, a large hook, and a blade that swings above the hook. It doesn't look like any natural forage, but only worms catch more bass than spinnerbaits.

**Jigs:** A typical jig is a hook with a weighted head and a soft rubber body, usually with a tail. You can cast and retrieve them or drop straight down off a boat or dock and just bounce them to catch bass and sunfish.

**Plastics (Soft Baits):** Worm-, lizard-, or fish-shaped plastics are great for fishing when bass or panfish aren't actively

# Cast a Fly Rod

1. Pull about twenty feet of line out past the tip of the rod and lay it on grass straight away from you. Hold the rod in your casting hand and pinch the line between your fingers and the rod handle. Hold the rod parallel to the ground with the reel down and your thumb pointing along the spine of the handle.

2. Lift the rod tip until it reaches the 10 o'clock position, then quickly flip the entire line behind you.

3. Stop your hand sharply when your thumb points straight up. The rod should be at a slight angle behind you, with the tip pointing toward one o'clock.

4. Pause for a moment to let the line straighten out behind you. You may look to see the loop uncurl, but, with practice, you'll feel the line pull at the rod tip when it straightens.

5. Begin the forward cast and accelerate the motion of the rod by lowering your elbow.

6. As your thumbnail comes even with your eye, snap your wrist forward to a full, immediate stop.

7. When the loop has unfolded forward and the leader straightens, lower the rod tip to follow the line and fly to the water.

> **MAN FACT**
>
> Women learn to cast a fly-rod more easily than men do because men muscle a rod, and try to force it to literally bend to their will. Casting doesn't go like that; you have to forget yourself and fall into harmony with the three-count rhythm.

feeding. Rig them with weights or "Carolina-style" by running a hook through the tip, pulling the hook through up to the hook's eye, and then pushing the hook's tip into the soft bait so the hook's tip doesn't go all the way through.

**Natural Baits:** If you ever really want to catch a fish, bring some night crawlers. If there are fish in the water (and you get the bait to them via weights or a bobber) you'll catch them at any time of the day or year. They are so effective they are illegal in professional bass tournaments. But they won't let you target big fish, because every fish with a mouth big enough to swallow your bait will bite.

## FLY-FISHING

The best way to gear up for fly-fishing is with a package deal. Orvis, Cabela's, L.L. Bean, and other catalog retailers have economical packages for different types of fishing. Buying one bypasses much of the learning curve necessary to matching line with reel with rod. For example, if freshwater trout is what you'd like to try, you can get a trout rod (4–6 weight), reel, line, backing, leaders, tippet, and an assortment of flies for just a few hundred dollars.

### Understand Insect Hatches

When a fly-fisherman enters a stream, he looks in the air for hatching insects, on the water for rising fish and/or flies on the surface, and he picks up rocks to see what insect larvae are close to hatching. He then matches the hatch and adjusts what he has tied on as the day progresses and the natural cycle develops. To get a sense of what to do, here's the life cycle of a very common aquatic insect, the mayfly, and how fly-fishermen change flies to mimic the cycle: A mayfly begins as an egg. Its gestation period is only a few days, and the hatched nymph is a miniature of the adult except for the wings and tail. The nymph seeks out cover, such as weed beds and gravel. The nymphal stage lasts from a few months up to three years. Fly-fishermen mimic this stage with nymph patterns as they fish subsurface. Then the mayfly hatches. To do so, it swims to the surface, often on still, overcast afternoons, and sheds (or shucks) its skin as it breaks through the surface tension of the water. At this stage fly-fishermen tie on emerger patterns or spinners. The mayfly then rests on the surface tension of the water until its wings dry. This is when fly-fishermen use a dry fly pattern. The mayfly has an adult life of only a few days before returning to the water (often with others) to lay its eggs. During this stage the adult mayfly is again eaten by trout and dry fly patterns work again. The mayflies then die. To mimic this last stage, fly-fishermen use wet fly patterns that they drift just under the surface to feeding trout.

### Speak the Fly-fishing Lingo

A man should be able to correctly use some of the common terms in whatever endeavor he attempts. These shouldn't be used in a know-it-all fashion, as any real angler will see through a bluff, but should be used as an American tourist uses French phrases in Paris, to show a general interest and respect.

> **Tippet:** The section of line that is tied to the fly.
> **Seam:** A place where water of different speeds meets—you can often spot seams by looking for a line of bubbles.
> **Hatch:** Insects that are changing to a flying stage.
> **Dead Drift:** A perfect float achieved when the fly is traveling at the same pace as the current.
> **Drag:** Term used to describe an unnatural motion of the fly caused by the effect of the current on line and leader.

**MAN FACT**

Fly-fishing schools are a great date. You don't have to worry about what to talk about. You'll be doing something together. She'll think of you as an adventurer. Just be humble and laugh when the line twists around your head. Orvis has great fly-fishing schools.

# SHINGO MATSUBARA

If you've ever felt a fish living, tugging at the end of a light line, and played it well and landed it unharmed, wriggling, and alive from its element to yours, then you know why some men fish. However, though fishing well requires knowledge of and harmony with the natural world, the Japanese have a deeper technique. Shingo Matsubara, a master ayu angler, showed me the ancient method of *tomo-zuri*.

Shingo took me to an icy, freestone stream between volcanic mountains in central Japan, slapped me on the back, and said, "Now you will learn to be one with the fish." Sounded like new-age Zen to me. But he insisted, "You're not fishing today. You're going to learn from fish, not me. You won't catch an ayu. I didn't catch any my first season. Just don't force him. You have to guide him. Do that and he'll teach you how to be an ayu. Then maybe someday you'll catch one."

Ayu are sea-run char that migrate into freshwater rivers in summer. They vary in length from eight to twenty inches and are a shimmering, opalescent color that changes with the whims of sunlight. Before we started fishing we bought a half-dozen live ayu and put them in small live wells tied to our belts. We had 30-foot extension rods without reels. The complicated line/leader system is a little shorter than the rod. At the end of the leader is a tippet attached to a "fish harness." We waded into a fast-flowing, freestone stream, and then, as instructed, I took an ayu out of my livewell and snapped a little nose ring through its nostrils (this is attached to the line) and ran the line back to its anal fin where I attached a small hook. The end of the fish harness holds a small barbless treble hook that swings in the current just behind the ayu's tail. Now mind you, I did all this with a slippery little char while holding a 30-foot rod in a swiftly flowing stream.

Shingo showed me how to hold the surprisingly light and nimble rod at the proper angle, and the fish on my line began to swim upstream. I tried to guide the little char to deeper water. My concentration grew so intense hours passed like minutes. The rod tip is so fine you can feel the fish's tail moving. I learned how they swam; what harms them; that I couldn't make the fish go where I wanted; that I had to will him there. I had to switch ayu three times. The sun was beginning to set when I coaxed my ayu into a likely spot. As Shingo had instructed, I raised the ayu's nose a touch to guide him off the bottom and up six inches. This induced the ayu to circle, which is what they do when they're getting aggressive with another ayu. I was picking a fight. When ayu fight they bite each other's tales.

Sudden madness came and my fish, which had been swimming smoothly with the current, began to flail. I picked up the rod. Another ayu had bitten the treble hook dangling near my ayu's tail. The line (remember, there is no reel) swung as both fish lifted out of the water. I grabbed the oval-shaped net stuck in my belt. Shingo said I had to catch the ayu on the first pass. If you don't you'll likely lose the second ayu at the other end of the pendulum—remember, the hook is barbless.

They came in wide. I reached . . . and fell into the water.

Rods up and down the stream went vertical as the Japanese men watching the Westerner attempt the ancient art of Japanese ayu fishing were delighted. Rods shook as anglers laughed and passed my plight up and down the stream. Shingo fretted—the rod cost $4,000. Then, when he saw it was in one piece, he laughed more than I thought it was proper for a conservative Japanese male to do in public.

As he left me again, he advised, "When I said be the fish, I didn't mean swim with them."

It's not manly to play the fool, even if you don't speak the lingo. I got frustrated. Ayu fishing is even harder when you're angry. You have to clear your mind and be the fish. I settled down and guided my ayu to another likely spot. I asked my ayu to circle and he did, and my rod tip bent again. I lifted. Set my feet. I pulled out my net, and scooped my first ayu out of the air.

Shingo splashed down to me. Shocked. I was the only Westerner on the stream. Japanese are polite. They rarely stare. But the sight of a red-haired Yankee catching an ayu was too much for them. They stopped and glared. I was no longer the foolish American. My manhood was intact after all.

**Dry Fly:** Any fly fished upon the surface of the water.

**False Cast:** Standard fly-fishing cast; used to lengthen and shorten line, to change direction, and to dry off the fly.

**Leader:** The section of monofilament line between the fly line and the fly.

**Mending Line:** Method used after the line is on the water to achieve a drag free float. It constitutes a flip, or series of flips with the rod tip, which puts a horseshoe shaped bow in the line.

**Nymphing:** Fishing flies representative of the nymph stage of insects.

**Streamer:** Fly tied to imitate the various species of baitfish upon which game fish feed.

**Wet Fly:** Any fly fished below the surface of the water.

### How to Read the Water

**Stream:** Trout hold in pockets of slower water where they can watch swifter water and dart out, or just slide over, to grab insects floating by. There is a calm pocket just in front of and behind rocks. A bubble line in the water marks a seam where faster water meets slower water. A seam lies on the inside of an oxbow, and where current hits a cut bank and then is deflected back into the stream's center.

**Lake:** If a lake is deep enough, there is a thermocline eight feet or more below the surface where warm surface water meets colder water. Fish will often hang on the thermocline. Underwater structures like fallen trees and rock piles will always hold fish. Lakeside docks and fallen trees will often have bass under them.

**Ocean:** Many charter captions make a living by fishing over submerged wrecks. Outside of these and other structures, it's important to realize all the water is moving. In some places the ocean moves like a river churning north or south along the Gulf Stream or another path. These ocean currents carry food for many fish and are often different temperatures than the water just a few miles away.

## Make a Fish Trap

If you're ever lost in the wild and need to catch a fish, you can fashion a hook out of a pin, needle, or piece of wire and use thread from your clothing as line. Indians sometimes carved fish hooks, but their preferred method was to make a fish trap. Cut a lot of green saplings. Build a wall by pushing the saplings into the stream bottom going out into a stream. From its ends, build walls going downstream. Then build a large "V" facing downstream and pointing into the downstream side of your trap. Fish will swim in, and most will try to get out by going upstream. You can also bait the trap if there is no current and construct a spiraled entrance that fish can't get out of.

## Fishing's Most-used Knot

**Improved Clinch:** To tie on a lure or fly, put the line through the hook/lure's eye and spin the lure four times. Put the end of the line through the bottommost loop (just above the hook's eye) and then put it through the big loop you just formed. Wet the knot and tighten it.

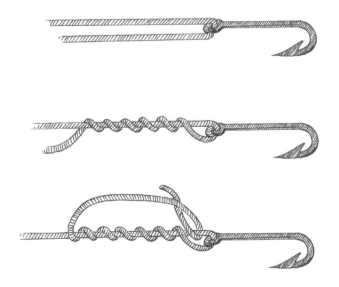

# PART 3

"*Sport is where an entire life can be compressed into a few hours, where the emotions of a lifetime can be felt on an acre or two of ground, where a person can suffer and die and rise again on six miles of trails through a New York City park. Sport is a theater where sinner can turn saint and a common man become an uncommon hero, where the past and the future can fuse with the present. Sport is singularly able to give us peak experiences where we feel completely one with the world and transcend all conflicts as we finally become our own potential.*"

—GEORGE A. SHEEHAN

A man steps into a ring or field and his reality shrinks to the ropes or lines. His allotted time begins to tick audibly. His life struggle is simplified to the rules of competition. The yards gained or lost, blows struck or received of every play or round are felt as profoundly as life's jolting tragedies and joyous triumphs. He knows the game, match, or race can make a humble man bold, a sinner a saint. He grits his teeth for the finish line, the goal, the last bell, the checkered flag. All along spectators cheer or jeer and he knows he'll walk off the field, or be carried off, a loser or a winner; though, either way, he'll retain his pride only if he fights like the game is a real struggle of life and death. And in the end, if he's more than just an athlete, he'll know to leave his blood and ego on the field, because men don't gloat or point fingers, they walk away tall, content they tried, knowing they'll strive again on and off the court.

Such is why we love sports, and should. Life is never so simple and clear, and rarely as heroic, as in competition. But it's also why some don't love sports, and why some will question their inclusion here among the necessary parts of an ultimate man. They'll point to the jock who struts arrogantly on college campuses. They'll say we revere this part of man too much, that sports stars can be downright idiotic when thrust behind a microphone, even though they're godly on the field or court. They'll say too many athletes have an excess of what the Greeks called "hubris," a word best defined as "outrageous arrogance." They'll say athletic stars too often don't have enough of the other qualities espoused in this guide. They'll scoff that modern spectator sports nurture and reward displays of unsportsmanlike bravado, because though rule-bound, sports are poor teachers of ethics. So then, ask the anti-jocks, the nerds, the intelligentsia, is being an athlete really a good and necessary part of being a man?

Playing is. Being a sports star isn't. Here's the difference: athletics is a segment of a man's education that is lacking without the others. This is why the Greeks combined poetry, rhetoric, and other contests along with their athletic Olympic events. This is why, though being the star of a team offers an opportunity to be everything a man should, if a man is fooled by his fame into thinking being a sports star is all there is, the athlete will be just another clichéd, blockheaded jock, a punch-drunk egotist who ages and suddenly finds himself lost in a stupor on the sidelines.

Men need to be well-rounded. But ignoring this part of an education can leave a man without the physical confidence earned from the toil and triumph of competition. This is why the Greeks used sport to teach a boy to push his body, to take his stamina to new limits. They saw it as training for battle and for manhood. They knew the human body is capable of much more than someone who has never really pushed their body realizes. It's a necessary step on the path to manhood to harness the confidence and self-knowledge that comes from this understanding of one's body. Whether big or small, strong or weak, young or old, a person who has learned what his body can and can't do is more likely to tackle life's conflicts with quiet confidence—and that is manly.

The athlete is also more likely to deal well with physical discomfort. Complaining about pain and injury is never manly; learning to cope with your body's weakness is. The best athletes seem to rise above their physical limitations to a higher plain. Many athletes are injured on the field of competition, but the best play through their ailments and still astound. Whether it's a tight muscle, a bruised rib, a strained tendon, or worse, the great players shrug off pain and play like they're immortal even when they feel mortality straining in every sinew. Despite a broken hand, Floyd Patterson defeated Tommy "Hurricane" Jackson in 1956, and won a chance at the title, a chance he took and won. In 2004 Boston Red Sox pitcher Curt Schilling pitched the sixth game of the American League Championship series despite an ankle injury. The images of his bloody sock carried him to fame as Schilling threw everything he had and won.

As for the injuries that can't be overcome, like when a football player sacrifices his body to make a tackle and destroys his knee, well, such are the times when true champions rise. When they're taken off the field in a stretcher, and they're grimacing in outrage at their body's frailty, we sympathize. The athlete trained his body, honing it into peak condition as all great athletes do, and finally lost, as he inevitably must, sooner or later. But if he's a well-rounded man, such an athlete can grow to even larger proportion if he grits his teeth and transitions his life to its next chapter without bitterness. An athlete can lament publicly about a disabling injury and get true pity just once; if he does so twice people will turn away, knowing intuitively that the athlete should move on. Life is a journey, as Shakespeare penned, "One man in his time plays many parts...."[1] We grow and strive and learn, but we can't knock out opponents forever. To be men we must try until the signs are clear, and then move on without remorse.

This is why Ernest Hemingway wrote, "Ah, Madame, you will find no man who is a man who will not bear some marks of past misfortune. Either he has been hit here, broken this, or contracted that, but a man throws off many things and I know a champion at golf who never putted so well as with the gonorrhea."[2]

The sport played isn't crucial as long as it pushes a man mentally to overcome pain and weariness and to concentrate on the objective, while at the same time, developing his body with his mind. Most sports do that. Football violently tests speed, stamina, and skill, and forces a man to learn to catch the ball despite the impending collision with the 300-pound linebacker nicknamed "Steamroller." Tennis pits one man against another in a contest of power, speed, and skill. Boxing is a crushing sport of skill, stamina, and strength, but has more to do with courage and confidence than most know. Team sports teach more than just individual fortitude, but also leadership and sacrifice.

Sporting teams as we know them today didn't begin until the nineteenth century, after the incorporation of regular sports and exercise into school regimes. Modern spectator sports were the result of an urbanization of industrialized societies. Suddenly, a growing percentage of boys weren't pulling plows, working in factories, hiking, riding, or hunting. To keep them active and knowledgeable about their strengths and weaknesses, sports were invented that could be played in urban areas. Baseball, whose origins are unsettled, solidified in the nineteenth century, as did American football and European football (soccer). Basketball was perhaps the most deliberate attempt to keep boys fit and to encourage them to push themselves.

In December 1891, Dr. James Naismith, who was a Canadian physical-education instructor at a YMCA Training School in Springfield, Massachusetts, wanted to find a sport that would keep his students occupied and in shape during the New England winter. To do so he needed a sport that could be played in a gymnasium. He developed an idea, wrote the basic rules of basketball, and nailed a peach basket onto a 10-foot elevated track. In contrast with modern basketball nets, this peach basket had a bottom. Balls had to be retrieved manually after each basket. Later, some smart boy thought to cut a hole in the basket. Peach baskets were used until 1906 when they were finally replaced by metal hoops with backboards. The first official game was played in the YMCA gymnasium on January 20, 1892.

Men have benefited ever since.

# Athletic Skills Every Man Should Know

## Baseball

> *"If it wasn't for baseball, I'd be in either the penitentiary or the cemetery. I have the same violent temper my father and older brother had. Both died of injuries from street fights in Baltimore, fights begun by flare-ups of their tempers."*
> —BABE RUTH[4]

> **"You gotta be a man to play baseball for a living, but you gotta have a lot of little boy in you, too."**
> ROY CAMPANELLA[3]

### FOUR-SEAM FASTBALL

Place your index and middle fingertips on the perpendicular seam of the baseball. The horseshoe-shaped seam should face into the ring finger of your throwing hand. Put your thumb directly beneath the baseball on the

smooth leather in the center of the horseshoe seam. Grip the ball softly in your fingertips. There should be a space between the ball and your palm, as a loose grip minimizes friction between your hand and the ball.

### CURVEBALL

With your middle and index fingers together, grip the ball along the right seam (for right-handers). Maintain a tight grip, but don't let the palm of your hand touch the ball, as this will reduce the topspin that is essential to an effective curve. Go through your normal wind-up, taking care not to change your typical arm speed. When your arm comes forward, the palm of your hand should be facing your head (like you're throwing a football). Keep your wrist cocked, and as you release the ball, turn your wrist and snap it down.

### CIRCLE CHANGEUP

Make a circle (an "okay" sign) with your throwing hand. Center the baseball between your three other fingers with the baseball tucked against the circle. Throw this pitch with the same arm speed and body mechanics as a fastball, only slightly turn the ball over by throwing the circle to the target.

### THE PHYSICS OF THE PERFECT SWING

#### Step 1: Loading

There are many different stances used by Major Leaguers; choose one that suits you, just make sure you get to a simple, proper load position. The key points to a good load are: Your weight moves primarily onto the inner portion of your back leg and foot; your front shoulder closes slightly, loading your hands and tilting the bat head forward toward the pitcher; your front knee kicks in.

# HENRY LOUIS "LOU" GEHRIG
# 1903–1941

He was born "Ludwig Heinrich Gehrig" and raised in New York City. He later earned the nickname "The Iron Horse" for his durability with the New York Yankees during the 1920s and 1930s, playing in 2,130 consecutive games. The record stood for more than half a century before being broken in 1995 by Cal Ripken Jr. During his career Gehrig batted in 1,995 runs and achieved a lifetime batting average of .340, a lifetime on-base percentage of .447, and a lifetime slugging percentage of .632. He was a seven-time All-Star and won the American League's Most Valuable Player award in 1927 and 1936, and was a Triple Crown winner in 1934, meaning he led the American League in batting average, home runs, and RBIs. Yeah, he was one of the greatest ever. But it's the courage of his farewell from baseball at age thirty-six that made him a legend.

When dying of amyotrophic lateral sclerosis (ALS), now known as "Lou Gehrig's Disease," he stood hat-in-hand before over 60,000 fans in Yankees Stadium on July 4, 1939 and said:

> Fans, for the past two weeks you have been reading about the bad break I got. Yet today I consider myself the luckiest man on the face of the earth. I have been in ballparks for seventeen years and have never received anything but kindness and encouragement from you fans.
>
> Look at these grand men. Which of you wouldn't consider it the highlight of his career just to associate with them for even one day? Sure, I'm lucky. Who wouldn't consider it an honor to have known Jacob Rupport? Also, the builder of baseball's greatest empire, Ed Barrow? To have spent six years with that wonderful little fellow, Miller Huggins? Then to have spent the next nine years with that outstanding leader, that smart student of psychology, the best manager in baseball today, Joe McCarthy? Sure, I'm lucky.
>
> When the New York Giants, a team you would give your right arm to beat, and vice versa, sends you a gift, that's something. When everybody down to the groundskeepers and those boys in white coats remember you with trophies, that's something. When you have a wonderful mother-in-law who takes sides with you in squabbles with her own daughter— that's something. When you have a father and a mother who work all their lives so that you can have an education and build your body—it's a blessing. When you have a wife who has been a tower of strength and shown more courage than you dreamed existed—that's the finest I know.
>
> So I close in saying that I might have been given a bad break, but I've got an awful lot to live for. Thank you.

In that moment Lou Gehrig became immortal, an icon of what a man should be. He accepted his destiny, after giving life his all, and he did so selflessly, with grace and respect for those who helped him along his path.

### Step 2: The Step

The load stage gets the hitter in time with the pitcher. The step stage gets the hitter in sync with the ball. Step short—six to twelve inches—toward the ball, and keep your weight primarily on your back leg. Be sure to keep your head in the same position, because when your head moves, you have to recalculate the ball's speed and movement.

### Step 3: Launch the Hips

Turn your hips toward the pitcher as you keep the bat back. This creates torque. Keep your head still as your lower body rotates. Keep your rear elbow tucked, but don't drop your hands. By keeping your hands back you'll be able to react to the speed of the pitch.

### Step 4: Launch the Hands

Now uncoil your upper body as you keep your eyes on the ball. Be aggressive. Move your weight to your front leg as the bat comes through.

### Step 5: Extend

Power through the ball and allow the bat to complete its swing. Shooters call this "follow through." It helps to prevent you from pulling off target.

# Basketball

## SHOOTING A BASKETBALL

Since basketball shots can be taken from on the floor or in the air, there is no one "right" stance, but the "triple-threat position" offers the most advantages. This is a low, balanced stance that allows a player to either shoot, drive, or pass. After bending at the knees, square yourself with the basket by turning your feet and torso to face the basket. Keep your hands close together on the ball with the fingers of your shooting hand spread and under (not behind) the ball. The ball should be resting on your fingertips and the upper portion of your palm. Now shoot the ball by throwing your hand and the ball (not your elbow) in line with the basket. Your other hand should stabilize the ball only in the first few inches of extension. Your shooting hand should be under the ball and your other hand on the side of the ball to stabilize it. By keeping your shooting hand under the ball you'll be forced to use your wrist to aim and spin the ball. Your elbow should be close to your body (not jutting out) as you throw. Lastly, good follow-through is critical. Your arm should be pointing toward the basket as the ball arcs to the net and your wrist should be bent down.

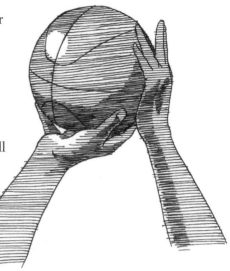

# Boxing

*"When I was a young fellow I was knocked down plenty. I wanted to stay down, but I couldn't. I had to collect the two dollars for winning or go hungry. I had to get up. I was one of those hungry fighters. You could have hit me on the chin with a sledgehammer for five dollars. When you haven't eaten for two days you'll understand."*

—JACK DEMPSEY[5]

### THE JAB-RIGHT-HAND COMBINATION

Most people throw roundhouse punches, falling forward as they swing. The roundhouse punch, though it can be powerful, is telegraphed and awkward. Boxing's jab and right hand are straight punches that gain power from speed and from the weight behind turning hips and shoulders.

> **Stance:** Face 90 degrees away from your opponent with your dominant hand directly away, then turn so your toes are 45

# HERB BROOKS
# 1937–2003

In an exhibition match at Madison Square Garden a week before the 1980 Winter Olympics, the Soviet hockey team trounced the Americans 10–3. In the week after the game and leading up to the Olympics, the American team's coach, Herb Brooks, knuckled down and pushed his players harder. While the Soviet coach, Viktor Tikhonov, rested his players for the sure-thing match and let them study plays rather than practice them, Brooks made the American team perform hard practices and rifled what later became known as "Brooksisms"[6] at them: "Gentlemen, you don't have enough talent to win on talent alone." "Boys, in front of the net it's bloody-nose alley." "Don't dump the puck in. That went out with short pants."

Although Brooks pushed his boys to the limit in practice, they arrived at the Olympics with an unmatched intensity. In their first game against favored Sweden, the U.S. earned a dramatic 2–2 tie by scoring with thirty seconds left after pulling Sweden's goalie from the net for an extra attacker. Next, they earned a stunning 7–3 victory over Czechoslovakia, widely considered the second best team in the world behind the Soviet Union. With their two toughest games in the group phase out of the way, the U.S.

team won three more times to go 4–0–1 and advance to the medal round from their group along with Sweden. In the other group, the Soviets steamrolled over their opposition, creating a match Hollywood couldn't have dramatized more effectively. Enemies in the Cold War became adversaries on the frozen pond.

Brooks' and his team's hard work paid off, and just thirteen days after being whipped by the Soviets, the Americans were set to face them again—this time in the first game of the Olympic medal round. Despite their gritty path to the finals, the Americans were still considered heavy underdogs. The day before the game, *New York Times* columnist Dave Anderson wrote, "Unless the ice melts, or unless the United States team or another team performs a miracle, as did the American squad in 1960, the Russians are expected to easily win the Olympic gold medal for the sixth time in the last seven tournaments."

Born in St. Paul, Minnesota, Brooks helped his high school hockey team win the state's 1955 championship and later played hockey at the University of Minnesota and was a member of the 1964 and 1968 Olympic teams. When he turned to coaching, he led the University of Minnesota's Golden Gophers to three NCAA championships. He knew how to play and coach. Now he had to try and defeat the topped-ranked "amateur" team in the world. The United States team was composed entirely of college players and amateurs, while the Soviets possessed the age and experience of professionals. In the year leading up to the Olympics, the Soviet team had gone 5–3–1 against NHL teams.

It was to be a Cold War mock battle in Lake Placid, New York. The fans waved American flags and sang "God Bless America." But outside the country was waiting, as ABC decided to tape the game and replay it in primetime. Inside the arena it didn't matter . . . until Soviet star Vladimir Krutov scored on American goalie Jim Craig. Brooksisms began to emanate, and the audience was gyrating. Then American Buzz Schneider scored to tie the game. Pandemonium.

Like answering vollies on a battlefield, the Soviets responded quickly with a goal by Sergei Makarov. Down 2–1, the American goalie Jim Craig began to defend the goal like a shot in the net would slay him (the Soviet team had 39 shots on goal in the game to the Americans' 16). In the closing seconds of the first period, American Dave Christian fired a slap shot on the goal, the Soviet goalie deflected the shot but misplayed the rebound, and American Mark Johnson fought it past with one second remaining in the period. Amazingly, the two teams found themselves at a deadlock going into the first intermission.

To start the second period, the Soviet coach put in his backup goalie. The new goalie allowed no goals in the second period, and Soviet Aleksandr Maltsev scored on a power play to make the score 3–2 for the Soviets. The audience didn't lose hope; then Johnson scored again for the U.S. at 8:39 into the final period. Then, just a few shifts later, U.S. captain Mike Eruzione fired a shot past the Soviet backup goalie giving the U.S. a 4–3 lead with exactly ten minutes left to play.

On came the Russians. Craig withstood another barrage of Soviet shots as minutes ticked away until the crowd began chant the last seconds. Hearing the crowd, Sportscaster Al Michaels, who was calling the game for ABC, shouted his famous call: "Eleven seconds . . . you've got ten seconds . . . the countdown going on right now! Morrow, up to Silk . . . five seconds left in the game . . . do you believe in miracles? Yes! Unbelievable!"

Brooks' intense and punishing style of coaching was sometimes questioned and even condemned, but the results were unquestionable. His crushing practice sessions, however, produced more than a gold medal. His unrelenting work-outs accomplished more than cementing his own place in American sports lore. Most importantly, out of a group of boys he forged a battalion of men, who proudly brought glory to their beloved country.

degrees towards your opponent. Keep your feet just wider than your shoulders, bend your knees slightly, and stay on your toes. Keep your elbows tucked into your chest. A right-handed fighter should look over his left hand, with his right by his right ear. It takes months of practice before you'll be comfortable with this stance, but it keeps you balanced and protects your head and body from punches.

**The Jab:** A jab starts with your hand, not your arm. It goes straight out and straight back. Keep your hand and arm loose, and extend fully. Tighten your grip just before you strike and extend again through your target. Then snap your hand straight back. When you've learned how to jab, it should attain a whiplash effect as you try to jerk your hand back just before full extension.

**The Right Hand:** Like the jab, this punch begins with your hand. As your hand begins to move, plant your front foot and pivot on your back foot. Don't lean, just turn your hips and your shoulders. Keep your arm and body loose. Tighten your fist just before striking and punch through the target. Then pivot back and pull your hand straight back as fast as possible.

# Football

*"The difference between the impossible and the possible lies in a man's determination."*

–TOMMY LASORDA[7]

## THE PERFECT PASS

The tight spiral and controlled arc required to throw a football downfield and into the hands of a receiver is a blend of skill, strength, and confidence. Throwing a football well means you have to control your mind and body despite the pressure from oncoming linebackers.

1.  **A Good Grip:** Your fingers should be spread lightly across the laces, your thumb and forefinger forming a "U" that cradles the tail of the ball. The strength of your grip should come primarily from your thumb, middle, and ring fingers.

2.  **Stance:** Stand with your feet directly beneath your hips and your left hip (for right-handed throwers) facing the target. Grip the ball solidly.

3.  **The Throw:** Turn your hips toward your target while keeping your upper body back like a batter loading for a swing. Uncoil your hips, torso, and then your shoulders. As your arm moves from the cocked position to over-head, your forearm should cross over your head in the direction you wish to throw.

4.  **The Release:** The ball's spiral depends on your release. Let go with your thumb as you throw, then let the ball rotate as the laces move off your fingertips. This will allow your hand and wrist to turn over and give the ball its spin. Do this by flicking your wrist. Your fingertips should give the ball its spin. Like a fastball, a tight palm grip will only slow the ball.

## HOW TO TACKLE ANYONE

With the increasing speed and athleticism of the players, the form tackle has sadly gone out of style in the NFL, but it's still the best and most reliable

# FLOYD PATTERSON

He had a lip of hair in front he said he wouldn't recognize himself without. He stood six feet tall and his fighting weight was a cruiserweight's 190 to 200 pounds, yet he fought heavyweight because that's where the money and fame was. His license plate read "FP1" and he was proud of his world boxing titles, but he'd never say so. He called Don King "a brilliant rogue" and Mike Tyson a "talented puncher who would be jabbed to death when he slows." Prophetic words spoken at Tyson's peak. But then Floyd knew about slowing down.

Born into a poor family in North Carolina, Floyd was the youngest of eleven children. They moved to Brooklyn, New York, and like many poor boys, he skipped school and became a petty thief. He was caught and sent to the Wiltwyck School for Boys, a reform school in Upstate New York, when he was just ten. He spent two years there, and for the rest of his life said it taught him he could be anything. At age fourteen he started to box. His trainer was Cus D'Amato at the Gramercy Gym. When he was just seventeen years old, Floyd won the middleweight boxing gold medal in the 1952 Olympics.

At about 190 pounds, he was too small for a heavyweight, but that didn't stop him. When Rocky Marciano retired undefeated in 1956, Floyd was ranked by *Ring* magazine as the top light-heavyweight contender. But with D'Amato's influence, he gained entry into an elimination tournament that would decide heavyweight champ. After beating Tommy "Hurricane" Jackson, Floyd KO'd light-heavyweight champion Archie Moore to become the youngest world heavyweight champion at age twenty-one. After defending his belt several times, Floyd squared off with Ingemar Johansson of Sweden. Ingemar knocked Floyd down seven times before a ref stopped the fight. But Floyd refused to accept defeat and won two rematches with Ingemar, both by knockouts, and became the first man to recover the world's undisputed heavyweight title. After a few more defenses of the title, Floyd lost it to Sonny Liston in 1962. Floyd would stay in boxing for another decade, and though he beat tough fighters like Eddie Machen and George Chuvalo, losses to Jimmy Ellis and twice to Muhammad Ali finally forced him to retire at age thirty-seven.

After retiring, Floyd and Ingemar became good friends; in fact, in 1982 and 1983 Floyd ran the Stockholm Marathon with Ingemar. Floyd became chairman of the New York State Athletic Commission and was inducted into the International Boxing Hall of Fame. During this time he ran a gym next to his home in New Paltz, New York, because retiring was no better than dying. He eventually adopted a young boy named Tracy Harris, who had been hanging around his gym. In the 1990s, Tracy Harris Patterson became a world champion boxer after training under Floyd's tutelage.

Late in Floyd's boxing career, a snide reporter asked him, "So Floyd, what's it like to be the heavyweight knocked down the most times?" Floyd simply replied, "Pretty good. Because I'm also the heavyweight champion who got up the most times."

That was the hardworking, positive nature of the man.

way to bring down your man. Here's how to do it (and if you're looking for a demonstration—and thirty real men engaging in battle—check out a rugby match).

Get your shoulders lower than the person you're tackling and drive with your legs as your arms encircle the person with the ball. Keep your head up, as tackling with your head down can result in a serious neck injury. Aim for your opponent's hips. As you make contact, drive your shoulders into your opponent's stomach. This is why coaches say, "Get your head on the player's numbers." Then squeeze your opponent into your body as you lock your hips into his and use your legs to push him up. Judo fighters call this the "hip throw." Done right, it results in a clean tackle and reduces the chance of injury.

# Golf

## THE ULTIMATE GOLF SWING

**Stance:** The key to consistency is to maintain your balance and use a smooth rhythm. Good ball-strikers are rarely off-balance at impact, and their rhythm bonds their positions and movements. Great rhythm allows you to properly sequence your body motion and arrive at impact in a position of leverage and power. Although your spine is tilted away from the target at address, you should have your weight evenly balanced between your right and your left foot with your middle and long irons.

**Back Swing:** As you pivot to the top of the back swing, your weight moves into the inside of the back foot. You should feel approximately 75 percent of your weight on your back foot and 25 percent on your front foot. Your weight must never move to the outside of your back foot.

**Swing:** By the time you arrive at impact, approximately 70 to 75 percent of your weight should be shifted onto your front foot. Your back foot should pivot on the ball of your foot (your toes) and you should stop shifting your weight and pivot just as the club hits the ball.

**Follow Through:** At the completion of the follow through, you should have the majority of your weight on the outside of your front foot. Continue your swing to the finish and keep your eye on the departing ball.

# Golf Drill

**S**et up ten teed-up balls and make a full swing in slow motion. The balls should only travel ten to fifteen yards. Think of this speed as 10 percent of your normal swing speed. Every ten balls, increase your body rotation speed by 10 percent. By the time you reach 80 percent, you will arrive at your optimum rhythm and balance speed.

# Soccer

**PUSH PASS:** Put your supporting foot about six inches to the side of the ball with your toes pointed in direction of your target. With your ankle locked at about 90 degrees, bring your kicking leg back and swing through the center of the ball. Contact the ball with the arch of your foot and follow through in the direction of your target. When well executed, the ball will roll smoothly rather than bounce or skip.

**OUTSIDE KICK:** When planting your supporting foot next to the ball, your toes have to be directed about 15 to 30 degrees outward from your target. This will let you drive your other foot straight at the target, hitting the ball with the outside of your laces.

**INSTEP DRIVE:** Place your supporting foot in line with the ball and toes aimed at your target. Bring your kicking foot back and swing it forward in one swift motion. Strike it with the inside of your shoelaces and follow through in the direction of your target.

**MAN FACT**

Hitting a jump shot in pool is easy—and when done right it always impresses the ladies. Make the angle of your cue steep, aim for the bottom of the ball, and shoot the cue smoothly into and through the cue ball.

**OUTSIDE CURVE:** If you're kicking the ball with your right foot, put your left (supporting) foot on the left side of the ball. The toes of your supporting foot should be aimed at your target or slightly to the side. Bring your kicking foot back and swing forward, aiming for the inside part of the ball.

**VOLLEY:** The volley is a kick used when the ball is in the air. Concentrate on when to kick rather than where to hit the ball. Make sure you're well balanced prior to actually kicking.

## Track and Field

### HOW TO THROW A SHOT PUT

**The Circle:** Step into the circle. Start with your back toward the direction you'll throw.

**Set Up:** Place the shot-put on your neck right by the jaw line with your elbow bent. The shot put should never come off your neck until the release or it will be disqualified. Next, bend down so that your right leg (if you're right-handed) is at a 90-degree angle, with your other leg straight out behind. This sets up the glide.

**The Glide:** Stay low and drive across as much of the circle as you can, using your legs to push you. Your legs will land so that they are still facing the back of the circle in a heel-toe position. Now you're set up for the power throw.

**Power Throw:** You begin by pivoting your right foot while moving your hips toward the front of the circle. You want your hips to move forward before your shoulders do to create torque. When you feel your side stretch completely, bring your shoulders around. Swing your left arm forcefully so that you get a whiplash effect. With your hips in front of your body, you can now come up and over them.

**Release:** Stretch out your arm so that the shot leaves when your arm is at its longest stretch, giving you the most time to push. At the very last moment, flick your wrist to add a tiny bit more momentum. Look up and end with your chest in the air to give good follow-through. After the shot is thrown, turn back into the circle.

# Climbing

## HOW TO BELAY UP A FACE

Climbing is a two-person operation—each climber needs to be protected by a belayer who remains on the ground. The basic setup is called a "top-rope system," meaning the rope is tied to the climber, goes up and over a pulley at the top of the wall and then down to the belayer. As the climber goes up, the belayer is responsible for taking up slack and catching the climber if they fall. The climber ties into the rope using a figure 8 knot. The belayer attaches to his end of the rope using a "carabiner" and a "belay device." Belay devices work by friction; if the rope is pulled up, it will slide easily through the belay device. If, however, the rope is pulled downward toward the hip, the friction between the belay device and the rope is enough to lock off the rope completely.

## CLIMBING KNOTS

### The Figure 8 Follow-through

This is the most important knot to learn as a climber. It is the best knot to tie the rope into your harness since it is the strongest climbing knot.

1. Grab a loose end of the rope and tie a single figure 8 knot between two and three feet from the rope's end.
2. Thread the end of the rope through the harness loop between your leg loops and pass it up through the harness tie-in point on the waist belt (same waist loop that the belay loop is attached to).
3. Snug the figure 8 against the leg loops.
4. Retrace the original figure 8 with the loose end of the rope, carefully following each part of the original knot.

5. Tighten and dress the knot by neatening the separate parallel strands and making sure they don't cross over each other.

6. You should have a leftover tail of about eighteen inches for tying a backup knot. Now tie a Fisherman's Backup knot by wrapping the tail rope twice around the climbing rope, passing the free end through the coils, and tightening it against the figure 8.

## The Bowline Knot

This knot can be tied with one hand, making it a versatile knot. The bowline is commonly used to tie into a climbing harness.

1. Start by making a loop in the line with a foot or more of the end.

2. Pass the end of the rope through the loop—over then under.

THE
BOWLINE
KNOT

**MAN FACT**

The deadliest sport of all time is arguably the Aztec sport of "Ullamaliztli." Players on two teams donned large stone belts or hip paddles. These paddles were used to bounce a rubber ball back and forth down a narrow court with inclined stone walls. The players' goal was to bounce the ball into a small stone ring high above mid-court. The game ended when either side scored a goal. The game enjoyed long popularity among the native peoples of Mexico and Central America before the Aztecs played it, including the Maya. But the stakes were a little higher when the Aztecs adopted the game. In some games, the losing captain was sacrificed to the gods.

3.  Pass the end around then back through the original loop. Tighten the knot evenly by hand and secure the end using a stopper knot.

### The Stopper Knot

This knot is used to prevent the rope from pulling through a belay or rappel device.

1.  Start the knot by making a loop, and wrap the short end of the rope around itself twice.
2.  Send the short end through the knot.
3.  Tighten the stopper knot evenly.
4.  Secure the end using a stopper knot.

# 50 Sports Facts Every Man Should Know

1.  Fishing is the biggest participant sport in the world.
2.  Soccer is the most watched sport in the world.
3.  In 1927 the archaeologist Dr. E. A. Speiser discovered a 7,000-year-old stone tablet in Baghdad, Iraq, that shows two men preparing for a boxing match.
4.  In 1975 the Japanese climber Junko Tabei became the first woman to reach the top of Everest.
5.  The record for the most complete games pitched is 749, by Cy Young.
6.  Ancient Greek athletes practiced in the nude to the accompaniment of music. They also performed naked at the Olympics.
7.  The first Olympic race, held in 776 BC, was won by a chef.

THE
STOPPER
KNOT

8. The first modern Olympics was held in Athens, Greece, in 1896. There were 311 males, but no female competitors.

9. The high jump method of jumping head first and landing on the back is called the "Fosbury Flop."

10. Before a game Major League Baseball teams have to have 90 new baseballs on hand; Major League teams collectively use about 850,000 balls per season; each ball lasts an average of 6 pitches.

11. About 42,000 tennis balls are used in the plus-minus 650 matches in the Wimbledon Championship.

12. A baseball has exactly 108 stitches and a cricket ball has between 65 and 70 stitches.

13. A soccer ball is made up of 32 leather panels, held together by 642 stitches.

14. Basketballs and rugby balls are made from synthetic material. Pigs' bladders were once used as rugby balls.

15. In 1900, owners in the National League changed the shape of home plate to a pentagon. They theorized this would stop the arguments on called strikes.

16. Golf is the only sport that was played on the moon—in 1971, astronaut Alan Shepard hit two golf balls using a six-iron on the moon's surface.

17. The oldest continuous trophy in sports is the America's Cup for sailing. It began in 1851. Americans won each year until Australia took the Cup in 1983.

18. Volleyball was invented by William George Morgan of Holyoke, Massachusetts, in 1895.

19. Babe Ruth was the first baseball player credited with ordering a bat with a knob on it.

20. Boxing was filmed for the first time in 1894 in a match between Mike Leonard and Jack Cushing.

21. If a horse wins a race "hands down" it means the jockey never raised his whip during the race.

22. Until 1859, the umpire in baseball sat behind home plate in a padded rocking chair.

23. Even though it was outlawed in 1920, the last legal spitball was thrown by New York Yankee Hall-of-Famer Burleigh Grimes in 1934. When the rule was changed, anyone already using a spitball was allowed to continue.

24. Official baseball rules state that an umpire may not be replaced during a game except if he becomes ill, injured, or if he dies.

25. In bowling, three strikes in a row is called a "turkey." The term originated in the nineteenth century when at holiday time, the first member of a team to score three strikes in a row won a free turkey.

26. On October 23, 1945, Jackie Robinson signed a Major League contract with the Brooklyn Dodgers, thereby breaking the color barrier.

27. The Boston Red Sox sold Babe Ruth to the New York Yankees on January, 1, 1920, for $100,000 to finance a Broadway play produced by Boston owner Harry Frazee. At the time of the deal, the Red Sox had won five world championships. The Yankees had only been around for seventeen uneventful years and didn't even have a ballpark to call their own.

28. In front of an infuriated Adolf Hitler, on August 9, 1936, Jesse Owens, son of a sharecropper from Oakville, Alabama, set three world records and one Olympic record.

29. In 1954, Roger Bannister became the first man to run a mile in less than four minutes.

**30.** In 1969, Joe Namath stood up at a podium in Miami, Florida, and predicted his team's win. The New York Jets and Namath did convincingly defeat the Baltimore Colts by a score of 16–7.

**31.** At the age of twenty-one, Tiger Woods was the youngest golfer to win a Masters.

**32.** In 1976, Romanian Nadia Comaneci was the first gymnast to achieve a perfect 10.

**33.** In 1971, in perhaps the most anticipated and watched sports event ever, Joe Frazier beat Muhammad Ali, but Ali got him twice more in spectacular rematches.

**34.** In 1989, Wayne Gretzky became the NHL's all-time leading scorer when he surpassed Gordie Howe's total of 1,850 points.

**35.** In 1928, "Win one for the Gipper" became a popular saying after Knute Rockne's famous halftime speech inspired Notre Dame to rally and beat Army 12–6.

**36.** On September 5, 1972, terrorists murdered eleven Israeli athletes at the Munich Olympics.

**37.** In 1938, Joe Louis knocked out Germany's Max Schmeling in 124 seconds.

**38.** In 1919, eight Chicago White Sox agreed to throw the World Series, and were later deemed the "Chicago Black Sox."

**39.** In 1962, Wilt Chamberlain scored 100 points in a single basketball game.

**40.** In 1984, Mary Lou Retton needed a perfect 10 to win the gold in the floor exercise, and she nailed it.

**41.** In 1986, 46-year-old Jack Nicklaus became the oldest man to win the Masters.

42. In 1975, John Wooden, the NCAA's most prolific coach, won a tenth consecutive title with an incredible .813 career winning percentage.

43. In 1938, Johnny Vander Meer pitched 18 innings without surrendering a hit.

44. On September 21, 1970, Monday Night Football was born as Howard Cosell gave his first nasal soliloquy.

45. In 1956, Don Larson pitched a perfect game in the World Series.

46. In 1991, Nolan Ryan pitched his seventh no-hitter when he was forty-four years old.

47. In 1997, Mike Tyson took a bite out of Evander Holyfield's ear.

48. In 1972, the Soviets beat the USA in basketball on a controversial "third try."

49. On September 14, 1994, Bud Selig and baseball owners shut down baseball, letting a monetary dispute achieve what two world wars and the 1919 Chicago White Sox couldn't.

50. In 1956, at the ripe old age of thirty-one, Rocky Marciano retired as the reigning heavyweight champ with a record of 49–0.

# PART 4

*"Cowards die many times before their deaths;
the valiant never taste of death but once."*
—WILLIAM SHAKESPEARE[1]

**"I**'m not a hero," said Special Forces Sergeant 1st Class Greg Stube just before he carefully sipped from the first beer he'd tasted since being admitted to the Walter Reed Army Medical Center a year before. After a long pull, he added, "No . . . I'm just a patriot."

I wasn't so sure. Stube had been blown apart while attempting to save a man he didn't know, a man fighting for another country's army. He'd volunteered to risk his life to free a nation and to destroy a terrorist movement, the great evil that crashed planes loaded with Americans into the World Trade Center, the Pentagon, and, while American heroes struggled to take the cockpit, a farm field in Pennsylvania. I'd been in audiences where Stube gave speeches that pragmatically outlined the noble traits a man should struggle to embody—showing he philosophically understands why he chose to fight. I've heard him declare his wife is the "real hero" for sticking by his side even when, as pain exploded through his guts and bones, he said things a hero wouldn't. I knew he volunteered a considerable amount of time helping wounded veterans readjust to American civilian life. So I pondered, *If not this man, then can anyone be a living hero in this cynical, relatavist age?*

Today we think of a hero as someone who selflessly risks their life to save another, but we don't see the person as being heroic outside their selfless act or role. We don't think of heroism as being premeditated, or as a complex figure struggling for justice, or even as a noble characteristic exposed by tragedy. Today heroism is more often viewed as just a mad moment when someone forgets their own mortality long enough to save someone's life; today we refuse to intertwine a heroic act with a fallible individual; as a result, today's men can't be heroes, but can only briefly do heroic things.

It used to be that our heroes were men of action and piety. Their entire lives were heroic and not merely isolated to a single battle or a catastrophe. The heroes of history subscribed to a code of honor, and they strove to uphold that code in every thought, action, and deed. That's why Cincinnatus was still a hero while living quietly on his farm, long after he saved Rome from destruction. That's why Sir Galahad is remembered for his enduring purity and faith rather than the number of rival knights he defeated.

But the image of the hero has shifted in our modern age to a man who is flawed, dark, and mysterious. We are reluctant to accept a heroic calling. These days purity and virtue are, to say the least, questionable. Cincinnatus, Galahad, and Roland have been replaced by anti-heroes such as Dirty Harry, Jason Bourne, and Rambo.

As I listened to Stube's infectious small-town sincerity, I began to wonder: *Why can't a man still be heroic? Are we so disillusioned that we can't revere heroism when we see it? Isn't it a good thing for boys and men to look up to someone who manifests the heroic ideal, even if such heroes err as mortals? Are we so lost in relativism that we can no longer clearly believe in role models?*

Then Stube broke my cynical train of thought by conceding, "Well, perhaps a hero did save my life." He next told me the epic story of his last day of battle, and I began to find answers from his experience to those troubling questions.

Stube told me about Staff Sergeant Jude Voss, a Special Forces team member who drove Major Jared Hill's vehicle at the center of an attacking convoy Stube was with in September 2006. They were fighting in the battle of Sperwan Ghar, just one part of what the coalition forces called "Operation Medusa." An estimated 2,000 Taliban fighters had gathered to retake Kandahar, and Special Forces teams, Canadian soldiers, and Afghan fighters mobilized to stop them. Suprisingly, the Taliban didn't run to bomb another day, but dug into strategically strong ground.

On the fifth day of the battle—the allied forces had to pull out several times after running out of ammo—Stube and the other Special Forces soldiers were making good progress up the hill despite intense enemy machine fire and constantly falling rocket-propelled grenades. But then a report that an Afghan soldier had stepped on a mine three-quarters of the way up the hill crackled over the radio, and Stube and Sergeant 1st Class Sean Mishra were ordered to take a truck up the hill to rescue the wounded Afghan.

Stube gave Voss a thumbs up from the truck's turret, Mishra hit the gas, and they drove over an embankment into the fray.

*Boom!*

The truck was rocked by an improvised explosive device (IED). The explosion was so catastrophic that Major Jared Hill, the operational commander positioned with Voss, who was hundreds of feet away, was thrown to the ground. Hill regained his feet just in time to see Voss rushing heedlessly into the smoke and flames. The bomb had detonated under the truck's right front wheel, setting the gas tank afire and blowing the driver, Mishra, through the door. Stube was trapped in the turret, his legs burning off.

Stube tried to climb out, but his barely attached leg caught on something and he collapsed. Voss fought through the smoke and fire and found Stube lying over the roof. Bullets slammed into the vehicle and ricocheted off rocks as Voss pulled Stube to the ground. Stube was on fire, so Voss burned his hands in an attempt to put out the fire, then took handfuls of sand and smothered the flames.

*Crack, crack* ... the ammunition in the burning truck began to cook off.[2] Voss started dragging Stube toward a ditch. Stube remembers feeling something peppering his face, and as the shock wore off, he realized sand was being blown into his face from machine gun bullets landing all around him.

Voss then yanked Stube into a ditch and began to treat his wounds. Hill found Mishra, the driver of the truck, dazed from the blast and placed him head-to-head with Stube. Mishra, somehow, wasn't seriously injured.

When asked if Stube would make it, Voss shook his head and frowned. Stube had a gaping wound on his side and his right leg was barely connected to his body. But Stube wasn't ready to die. As he choked on his own blood, he talked Voss through the first aid: "This is leaking," Stube managed. "Here, check this."

Somehow, perhaps in part because of his unbelievable composure, Stube was still alive when Special Forces medics arrived. "I shouldn't have lived," Stube said as we talked at the Washington, D.C., pub. "My wounds were too severe. I should have bled out."

After Stube was evacuated, the battle raged for another eight hours before U.S.-led forces took the hill. In the end the Taliban lost about 900 fighters during the fight for Sperwan Ghar, though the pivotal battle received little attention back in the States.

Stube had been through all that and still refused to think of himself as a hero, which is part of what defined Stube as a hero. Fame is not something a modern hero seeks or is even comfortable with. So, despite the contemporary point of view, I could accept Stube's flaws and view him as a living hero, a shining example of a man.

Stube credits his military training and moral background with guiding his actions in battle, which isn't hard to accept; after all, firemen and police officers also fall back on training and well-thought-out responses when thrust into violent situations. Training and codes of conduct are the basis of heroism, not just timing or disposition. With this in mind, the modern conception of heroism seems overly simplistic and cynical. Heroism can be premeditated, prepared for both morally and mentally. Men can harbor a heroic value even though they're human. Heroes can try and fail and try again. Indeed, fostering the heroic aspect within yourself is fundamental to becoming a man, though it's not necessary to be proven in battle. Men need to develop their skills and fortitude and to look within, as Ray Bradbury wrote, to "find out what your hero or heroine wants, and when he or she wakes up in the morning, just follow him or her all day."[3]

# Heroic Codes

eroic codes are the basis for just action. They are the beginning of a hero's moral foundation and a guide through the volatile events of tragedy. Here are a few of the best heroic codes ever devised. Think about how such rules apply to the real-life situations you face and find the rules that define justice for you, then you'll know how to be a hero. After all, simply acting is easy; acting rightly is tough.

# Texas Ranger Code of Conduct

1. To advance the objective of the department in preserving order and protecting the lives, rights, privileges, and property of the people in the State of Texas to the best of my ability and in an entirely impartial manner.

2. To practice at all times the motto of this organization: "Courtesy, Service, Protection."

3. To keep myself clean and presentable, and in good physical, mental, and moral health.

4. To know and obey orders and instructions at all times.

5. To keep all state equipment entrusted to me fully accounted for and in proper condition.

6. To qualify as a voter, and to vote my convictions as a citizen on all public questions and political races, but to take no other part in any public politics or campaigns.

7. To conduct my business in a straightforward manner, relying upon poise, competence, and discretion rather than threats and argument to carry out my duties.

8. To take up matters affecting me and my position with my immediate superior and through proper channels.

9. To submit through proper channels constructive suggestions for the betterment of the department and its service.

10. To conduct myself at all times, both on and off duty, in such a gentlemanly manner that I may merit the voluntary commendation of all law-abiding citizens and visitors with whom I come in contact, both those with whom I meet in carrying out my duties and those I shall live among as a citizen in order that credit may be reflected upon the Texas Department of Public Safety.

# The U.S. Marine Corps Creed

**Article I:** I am an American, fighting in the forces which guard my country and our way of life. I am prepared to give my life in their defense.

**Article II:** I will never surrender of my own free will. If in command, I will never surrender the members of my command while they still have the means to resist.

**Article III:** If I am captured I will continue to resist by all means available. I will make every effort to escape and to aid others to escape. I will accept neither parole nor special favors from the enemy.

**Article IV:** If I become a prisoner of war, I will keep faith with my fellow prisoners. I will give no information nor take part in any action which might be harmful to my comrades. If I am senior, I will take command. If not, I will obey lawful orders of those appointed over me and will back them in every way.

**Article V:** When questioned, should I become a prisoner of war, I am required to give name, rank, service number, and date of birth. I will evade answering further questions to the utmost of my ability. I will make no oral or written statements disloyal to my country or its allies or harmful to their cause.

**Article VI:** I will never forget that I am an American, fighting for freedom, responsible for my actions, and dedicated to the principles which made my country free. I will trust in my God and in the United States of America.

# The Seven Virtues of Bushido

The Japanese code of Bushido, which translates to the "way of the warrior," is the code of moral principles that Samurai were required to follow. During the Tokugawa Shogunate (1603–1868) the seven rules of Bushido were formalized into Japanese feudal law.

1. **Yuki (Courage):** A Samurai must possess the bravery/courage to face all of life's challenges with a strong and moral heart.

2. **Jin (Benevolence):** This is a magnanimous and compassionate state of mind that embraces the idea that all people are fundamentally the same and should be treated with the same respect regardless of station or situation.

3. **Rei (Etiquette):** A Samurai must respect himself and others by being a gentleman.

4. **Makoto (Honesty):** Honesty and integrity must be sought at all times.

5. **Chugi (Loyalty):** Duty to family and country is a fundamental aspect of this virtue.

6. **Gi (Rectitude):** Gi is a rightness of principle or practice, exact conformity to truth, integrity, honesty, and justice.

7. **Meiyo (Honor):** Meiyo is the sum of the previous six virtues, as someone who practices the code of Bushido would certainly be honorable.

# Embrace Your Heroic Quality

Finding and developing a moral code to your conduct is a fundamental step to becoming a hero; developing your heroic quality is next. Here is how two very different men found courage and justice—every man has his own path, but each begins by facing himself.

## G. Gordon Liddy's Heroic Method

G. Gordon Liddy argued in his autobiography, *Will,* that men develop their heroic potential when they face down their fears. Liddy went to jail after the Watergate scandal, but kept his manhood by staying loyal and by accepting accountability for his actions. Liddy mastered himself, took the worst the American legal system could throw at him, and walked out of jail a better man. He's now an iconic author and radio show host. So I asked Liddy to explain how he attained his legendary fortitude.

"I thought I had invented facing fear to grow as a man," Liddy said, "but then I found that psychologists call it the 'process of desensitization.' It doesn't work immediately, but each time you face a fear the fear diminishes. It also isn't something you only have to do once. A man will have to confront his weaknesses throughout his life to grow as a man, a potential hero.

"When I was a boy I learned to face my fears to overcome them and achieve anything; for example, when I was eight there were these freighters along the New Jersey shore that frightened me, so I worked up the courage and slipped by security guards and climbed the monstrous things. I was detected and chased, but got away. Afterward I was proud of myself. I was like a boy who'd faced a dark night and realized he was strong enough inside to overcome such things.

"It never ends. You have to face your fears all your life to grow. For example, when I first went to prison I knew I'd better stand up and fight at the first opportunity, despite the odds of getting seriously hurt. So I did. I wound up in the hospital along with the inmate I fought, but it was worth it. My fear

> "When heaven is about to confer a great responsibility on any man, it will exercise his mind with suffering, subject his sinews and bones to hard work, expose his body to hunger, put him to poverty, place obstacles in the paths of his deeds, so as to stimulate his mind, harden his nature, and improve wherever he is incompetent."
>
> MENCIUS, 3RD CENTURY, BC[4]

**121**

dissipated and one of the old convicts, a gang leader, said to me, 'Well, we found out your heart don't pump no Kool-Aid.'

"I'm seventy-eight years old now, and there are a whole new set of things I have to face, as we all do as men," said Liddy. "Certainly, men need to use good judgment when facing their fears, but to be heroes they must continually master themselves. This is why I still think men should join the armed forces. The military will teach you that it's not all about you; that we're in something together. A man needs to learn selflessness or he'll just become selfish, and there's nothing manly or heroic about selfishness."

## Juan Macho's Guide to Running with the Bulls

There are many ways to find your rite of passage to manhood, says Juan Macho, an American of Cuban ancestry who has been running with the bulls in Pamplona, Spain, for more than thirty years. "Only with the knowledge and confidence in your ability to act wisely in a crisis will you be ready to be a hero any time you're called upon," Juan explained. "That's what running has done for me."

Macho's a philosopher and hero, who is recognized on the streets of Pamplona by people who revere him. I was privileged to spend the week of a San Fermin festival with him. We walked the course, went through the rituals to purify ourselves as men facing our own mortality on our terms, and ran with other men drawn from every part of the planet to the most misunderstood festival on earth.

One warm afternoon we stopped in front of the Plaza de Torres, and Juan looked up at the ancient arena and said, "I fear men are losing their way today. Bull fighting and with it running might be gone soon. You see, attacks on masculinity are pervasive in modern society." He paused as his mind ran over the dilemma, then said, "I've run over eighty times. I no longer have the compulsion to be in the streets when the rocket goes off. But since 1988, when a young man stopped me on the street and asked for guidance to run, I saw that my role during the Fiesta needed to develop into initiating potential runners into the rituals of the *encierro*. Men need tests like this to become men."

During the course of the festival I asked many questions. Here are the answers that may help you.

### What did your first run teach you?

**Juan Macho:** *Like most life-defining moments, the event is difficult to put into words. But it was like a first sexual experience. One can read the books and watch the movies, but this is the real thing.*

### What have subsequent runs developed in you?

**JM:** *An existential feeling of what is real and what life is about. I've learned that the trappings of modern consumer life is just a lot of crap; that facing death in a form of 1,800 pounds of dark fury coming at you and then passing you by is real. Everything else is bull (pardon the pun) shit. The experience gave me a new perspective on the meaning of life.*

### Why did you choose the hardest part of the course, the "suicide run"?

**JM:** *I read somewhere, perhaps in one of Michener's books, that for time immemorial, a group of men who knew how to handle bulls were allowed the privilege to run toward the gates at the bottom of Calle Santo Domingo where the bulls are held before they are released into the streets. On rare occasions other men who distinguish themselves in the encierro are trusted in this section with the veterans. I wanted to try it, and with humility, I can say I managed to master this most dangerous of the segments of the encierro.*

### How does a first-timer do the run?

**JM:** *On the first day, watch: Get a ticket to the Plaza de Torres (the bull-fighting arena) and watch the bulls and runners come in to gauge how the crowd flows and the bulls move. After the bulls trample through and into the gates, where they'll wait to fight that evening, the gates are closed and steers are loosed among the runners in the arena. The scene is violent and more fun to watch than the bloodiest UFC match.*

*On the second day, stand: Get through the barriers by 7:30 a.m. on the street and find a "safe" spot, such as the inside of a bend, to watch the bulls run by you.*

*On the third day, run: Find a good, open path and run when you hear their hooves. Watch the crowd, as other runners will knock you down, and try to be at a full sprint when the bulls reach you. If your position is good, stay with the bulls as long as you can. But if they're directly behind you or there are so many people you can't tell, run until you spot an opening and dodge into it. Running is actually safer when you're out in the street because it gives you more options. If you're knocked down, stay down and roll away from the bulls if you can. Do this and you'll be a different person, you'll be ready to be a hero.*

# The Skills of a Hero

s you find and develop your heroic code of conduct and face yourself honestly, you must then learn the skills of a hero. Here are some fundamentals.

## Put Out a Fire

First, be prepared. Purchase a multipurpose, dry-chemical extinguisher rated for Class A, B, and C fires and keep one in an easily accessible place away from the stove. Next, know the basics. The four basic types of fire extinguishers are:

> **Class A:** This type of extinguisher is used for fires that involve wood, paper, trash, rags, or cloth. It controls the fire by wetting down and cooling the flames.
>
> **Class B:** This type puts out fires that involve gases or flammable liquids by cutting off oxygen or reducing flame.
>
> **Class C:** Suited for electrical equipment and wiring fires, this type contains carbon dioxide or a dry chemical (since water conducts electricity).

**Class D:** This type is used for combustible metal fires such as aluminum, sodium, magnesium, or zinc.

Assess the situation quickly and determine if you need to evacuate the property of all people and, if possible, pets. Life is more important than any property. If you're not sure, evacuate, then call 911. If the fire is oil-based, don't use water. Use baking soda or a cover if it's in a pan. For fires on wood, paper, and cloth, use water or a "Class A" extinguisher to douse the flames by spraying the base of the fire. For electrical fires, throw baking soda over the flames or use a "Class C" extinguisher. If you have a fire in your oven, close the oven door and turn off the heat to smother the flames.

PURCHASE A MULTIPURPOSE, DRY-CHEMICAL EXTINGUISHER RATED FOR CLASS A, B, AND C FIRES

## Stand Up for Justice

A hero has the internal fortitude and understanding of right and wrong not to join the pack of kids bullying the class wimp and instead to help the weaker person. Such actions don't end with adolescence. Every office and construction yard has the less popular, the bullied, and those who were wrongly overlooked for promotion. A hero sees these things for what they are and stands up compassionately for justice even in everyday things.

## Make Up for Someone's Weakness

We all have weaknesses and blind spots. Some people nervously say inappropriate or otherwise harmful things; others have addictions; still more have physical limitations. A hero sees these problems and quietly and humbly helps other people fit in or exceed despite them.

**MAN FACT**

Don't turn on your stove's exhaust fan if there's a fire, as this can spread the fire up into the walls.

## Prevent a Tragedy

A hero must be cognizant enough of a situation to see that someone is placing their life in harm's way, and then to prevent their mistake. This means taking the keys from a drunk, stopping a child from crossing a street improperly, and making sure a new climber is tied into his harness correctly. It means always being aware of others and not being afraid to act. Only one person will know you're a hero after such an action, but they'll still be alive.

## Ford a Stream

Jon Krakauer's book *Into the Wild* records the last days of Chris McCandless, a young man who, in April 1992, hitchhiked to Alaska and walked alone into the wilderness north of Mount McKinley after giving $25,000 in savings to a charity, abandoning his car, and burning his cash. Four months later, his body was found. McCandless is thought to have starved to death because he couldn't ford a raging river for help.

Here's what he could have done: Water that moves at seven miles per hour carries over a hundred pounds of pressure per square foot; as a result, it doesn't take white water to wash you to your death. Water temperatures below 72 degrees Fahrenheit are too cold for a person to stay warm in by swimming. So McCandless was right to be cautious; however, if the terrain is mountainous, as it was for McCandless, following a stream upriver will find tributaries that split and reduce a stream's size. Following a river downstream is more likely to lead to civilization. Rivers also can rise and fall quickly after a storm (sometimes a storm upstream), so it's wise to cross

# Someone Is Being Electrocuted

If you can quickly identify and access the source of electricity, turn it off. If not...

### FOR HOUSEHOLD GRADE CURRENT (about 120 volts)

1. You can pull the person away from the current using heavy rubber gloves or by wrapping your hands in a thick cloth (a heavy blanket should do the trick).

2. If this doesn't work, using a long, non-metallic object (like a 2x4), hit the person in the back or the butt to knock them off the current. DO NOT hit their head or their legs.

### FOR HIGHER CURRENTS (10 to 20 kilovolts)

1. Use a dry tire or inner tube to pull or knock the person off the current.

2. Even though you're insulated, you will probably still get shocked a bit, so keep your feet close together or hop from one foot to the other.

**In both cases:** After you have knocked the person off the current, call 911, as being electrocuted for a prolonged time (no matter the voltage) can cause serious injury.

when you can. Natural crossings, such as downed trees, boulders, riffles at the end of pools, and so on offer ways across.

## Keep Her Dry/Warm

In an emergency or just a downpour, a hero gives a woman—even his mother in law—his coat, shirt, or whatever he can so she can stay warm.

## Basic Baby Care

Here's another example illustrating that men have lost the battle of the sexes: a modern hero needs to be able to hold, feed, and change a baby.

**Hold:** Support the baby's neck with one hand and hold its bottom in the other.

**Feed:** Hold the bottle if necessary, but just do so carefully and patiently.

**Change:**

1. Lay a fresh diaper on a changing table, or on a towel or mat on the floor.
2. Place the baby belly side up on the clean diaper.
3. Unfasten the diaper tabs on the soiled diaper.
4. Hold your baby's feet together and very gently lift them up, raising the baby's bottom. Use the clean part of the diaper to wipe away any excess stools, then fold over the soiled section of the diaper and set the old diaper aside.
5. Wipe your baby with baby wipes.
6. Lower the baby's bottom onto the clean diaper.
7. Pat the area dry with a towel and use diaper-rash cream as necessary.

8. Position the front of the diaper just under the baby's abdomen.

9. Bring the tabs around from the back of the diaper and fasten them to the front.

# Stop a Dog Fight

A dog fight is a dangerous situation, and if you don't handle it correctly, you could come away with serious injuries. Whatever you do, do not get in between the two dogs—they will bite you.

### If you are with someone else:

1. Stand behind one dog, while the other person stands behind the other dog.
2. At the same time, each person should grab the hind legs of their respective dog.
3. Hold on tight.
4. Walk backwards to separate the two dogs.
5. As you walk backward, move in a circular motion. This way, the dogs will have to struggle to maintain their balance using only their front legs.
6. Find a barrier (fence, cage, etc.) that will separate the two dogs.

### If you are alone:

1. If you have access to water, spray or dump water on the dogs. This will sometimes break their concentration.
2. If there's no water handy, or if it doesn't work, try to wedge something in between the two dogs like a trash can lid or a square of plywood (not yourself!).

> **"**I would rather be beaten and be a man than to be elected and be a little puppy dog. I have always supported measures and principles and not men. I have acted fearless[ly] and independent[ly] and I will never regret my course. I would rather be politically buried than to be hypocritically immortalized.**"**
>
> DAVY CROCKETT[6]

# Fix a Flat

1. If you can, get the auto on a level, hard surface that's safely off the road.

2. Put out road flares or cones if necessary.

3. To prevent the vehicle from rolling, put a rock or like object behind the back and front wheels on the opposite side from the flat.

4. Place the jack on solid ground (use a piece of wood or flat rock if you're on mud or snow) and underneath the vehicle's frame.

5. Loosen the lug nuts.

6. Raise the vehicle.

7. Undo the lugs and pull off the tire.

8. Put on the spare and hand tighten the lugs.

9. Lower the jack.

10. Tighten the lugs as much as you can with a lug wrench by tightening a little on one side and then the other so it tightens evenly.

## Take the Hit

Boxers learn to stay loose and roll back with a punch. Football players spin their bodies when they get hit to reduce the blow and avoid being tackled. Here's how to do it:

1.  Don't face your assailant head-on. Direct your shoulder toward him to face him at an angle.
2.  Keep your elbows close to your midsection as they can absorb a hit better than your ribs.
3.  As you're getting hit, move with the direction of the hit to soften the blow, but be careful not to jerk too fast or you may lose your balance and make yourself even more vulnerable.
4.  If you can't move with the punch, lean into your attacker. This will reduce the power of the hit.

## Break Up a Fight

Don't get between the two combatants. Grab the back of one of their collars and pull the person downward. If you can't get the person down, try to pull him away. As you pull, kick them behind the knee and they'll fall backward.

## Make a Citizen's Arrest

Hero beware: some state laws permit you to make a citizen's arrest if you catch a person committing a felony, but if you're mistaken in the facts or the law, you could be sued for false imprisonment. Laws vary from state to state. In Massachusetts you can be sued by your detainee for kidnapping, while in Kentucky you're actually allowed to harm your suspect if he tries to flee.

## Respond to a Car Accident

1. Quickly assess the situation and, unless someone is in need of life-saving assistance, first work to prevent more injury by putting out road flares and getting someone to direct traffic.
2. Call 911 and get an ambulance and the police coming.
3. Check for injuries.
4. If the accident is minor and there are no serious injuries, move cars to a safe place, rather than risk being in moving traffic.
5. Notify your insurance agent.
6. Don't sign any document unless it is for the police.
7. Make immediate notes about the accident, including the specific damages to all vehicles involved. If the name on the auto registration and/or insurance policy is different from the name of the driver, jot it down. Get witness information, if possible, as well.
8. Be polite, but don't tell the other drivers or the police that the accident was your fault, even if you think it was. Likewise, do not accuse the other driver(s) of being at fault.
9. If you have a camera handy, and it is safe to do so, photograph the accident scene.
10. If possible, do not leave the accident scene before the police officers and other drivers do.

## Defend the Weak

*"The weak can never forgive. Forgiveness is the attribute of the strong."*
–MAHATMA GANDHI[7]

A hero fights, but only when his back is against a wall, to defend the weak or to selflessly fight for justice. A hero can never be a bully. Even Sun Tzu, credited with authoring *The Art of War*, a Chinese text on the craft of war that scholars date between the second and fourth centuries BC, wrote that the greatest victory is won without fighting. Along this theme, Theodore Roosevelt used the slogan, "Walk softly and carry a big stick; you will go far."[8] To be a man, fighting is a last resort, but knowing how is integral to being a man.

## HOW TO FIGHT OFF WILD ANIMALS

### Alligator and Crocodile

When A. J., a reformed alligator poacher, was asked how he was able wade at night in Louisiana's alligator-infested swamps yet never get eaten, he answered, "Always keep your arms by your sides."[9] If you don't keep your appendages close to your body, he explained, even a small alligator will bite them and spin its body to rip them off. However, if an alligator or crocodile is really big, say over ten feet, it may bite you anywhere and then take you down for a death roll—only luck will save you then, as you'll have to go for its eyes. But most will grab an arm or a leg and spin their bodies to rip your limb off. If this happens, grab the gator or croc and spin with it. Lock your legs or arms around it, then shove your thumbs in its eye sockets and fight like you've never fought before, because if you lose, you'll never fight again.

### Bear

First decide if the bear is predatory. If it's a black bear, fight. If it's a grizzly, it depends. If a bear attacks you at night in your tent or if it approaches you slowly, seemingly feeling you out, and you can't get away, you'd better fight with a gun, knife, or just your will to live if it gets you. But if a grizzly, especially a sow with cubs, charges when you happen upon it, use bear spray and hit her in the mouth and eyes. If possible get up a tree. If not, lock your hands behind your neck and pull your knees to your chest and play dead. Loud noises can also dissuade a bear attack. Bang pots together. Shoot a gun in the air. Above all, be ready in bear country with bear spray and know how to use it.

### Cougar

Always fight back if a cougar attacks. People live through cougar attacks because the cats don't always know how to kill erect prey. They've been trained by their mothers to go for a quadruped's neck and throat. If a cougar bites you, go for its eyes. Punch it. Scream at it. Use any weapon you have. Just don't give up.

### Lion

Unless you or someone in your party has a firearm, you'd better climb a tree fast. Lions still kill people. They kill more than 100 people each year in Tanzania alone.[10]

> I like a man who grins when he fights.
>
> WINSTON CHURCHILL[11]

### Snake

The only snake you might have to fight—you don't fight poisonous snakes, you get away from them—is a constrictor. If you have a knife or firearm, kill it if necessary. If you don't, control the head, and stay erect as you work its coiling body off you.

### Shark

Sharks have sensitive noses. Punch a shark with all your might right on the tip of its nose. Get out of the water. Sharks typically bite and then circle back for another mouthful. Though most shark attacks are instances of a shark misidentifying you as a fish or a seal—meaning they won't be back.

# How to Fight

**M**att Hughes is a nine-time World Welterweight Champion of the Ultimate Fighting Championship® (UFC). With a record of 43–7, Matt earned his reputation with mixed martial arts fans. He became a well-rounded fighter by learning wrestling, jujitsu, and boxing. Hughes says, "Training to be a fighter gave me confidence. I see it gives other men and women confidence every time a new person comes to my gym. It also taught me how to read people and to avoid bad situations. This is why people should know a little about self-defense. It disciplines you and keeps you ready for trouble."

Here's what Hughes says every man should know about self-defense.

## Five UFC Moves Every Man Should Know

### 1. Wrist Lock

When a person grabs you or pushes you, this is an easy way to take him down and get away.

1.  Grasp your attacker's palm by placing your thumb on the back of his hand and your fingers around the base of his thumb.
2.  Pull your attacker's hand into your body.

3. Turn his hand palm up and use your subdominant hand to help and add leverage.

4. Turn your body as you twist.

5. Take your opponent to the ground.

6. Get away.

## 2. Boxing's Slip/Left Hook

If you have to hit someone, this is the best counter-punch in boxing. Most people use their dominant hand to throw a big, looping roundhouse punch. When they do, their weight falls forward and they lose balance.

1. Raise your hands to your ears and bend your knees to drop your head below the shoulders of your attacker.

2. As the roundhouse goes over your head, bend slightly at the waist toward your enemy.

3. As his punch fully extends, straighten your knees as you pivot your body toward him.

4. Throw your hand as your shoulders rotate behind your hips and aim for your opponent's jaw.

## 3. Knee Sweep

When a person grabs your arm or shirt and begins pushing you back as he tries to take you down or hit you, use this tactic.

1. Grab his arm or arms and go with him as you keep your balance.

2. Turn your hips toward your dominant foot and kick that foot into the top of his knee.

3. As you kick, pull him in the direction he is pushing you and he'll lose balance and fall.

4. Let him fall past you.

5. Get away.

## 4. Groin Kick

Men are reluctant to use this tactic, but it's the first thing self-defense instructors teach women. Remember, if you're being attacked, there are no rules.

1. The most important thing is to act first. The second is not to telegraph your attack. Throw your arms up to distract your attacker if necessary, but don't let him see your kick coming.

2. Don't hold back. Halfway might not be good enough.

3. Kick straight up like you're punting a football and follow through.

4. Get out of there.

## 5. Choke Hold Break

When someone comes from behind you and attempts to put a chokehold on your neck, do this:

1. When you see the arm coming around, turn 90 degrees toward the person's arm.

2. Use your hand closest to your attacker's choking arm to hold that arm.

3. Swing your other arm up and over your attacker's opposite arm, between his arm and neck.

# TECUMSEH

"Show respect to all people, but grovel to none."

–TECUMSEH

We remember Geronimo and Sitting Bull because they fought valiantly and lost in an age when the Indian had already become a romantically tragic figure. But we've forgotten Tecumseh, a man who almost held back what was later deemed "Manifest Destiny," a charismatic Indian leader who united tribes in defense of an ancient way of life.

Tecumseh was Shawnee. He was born in 1768 in the forests of Ohio to Pucksinwah, a war chief who was killed in Lord Dunmore's War in 1774, and Methoataske, who left Tecumseh when he was eleven years old and moved west to avoid trouble on the frontier. Tecumseh stayed in Ohio and was raised as a warrior by his eldest brother, Cheeksuakalo. His education started young. While in his teens Tecumseh fought bravely at the battle of Fallen Timbers—and saw Cheeksuakalo die there. Tecumseh fought with the British in the American Revolution because he believed the English would keep the Americans from moving west.

After the Americans won their freedom, Tecumseh refused to parlay. He went west into the forests of what is now Indiana and began to gather followers, warning them of the coming tide of settlers. Around 1800 he became friends with a woman named Rebecca, a blonde, blue-eyed settler, who taught him the Bible, Shakespeare, and world history.[12] He asked her to marry him, and she consented with the condition he give up being

Shawnee and work a farm as the white settlers did. Tecumseh thought about her proposition for a month, then refused.

His life had another purpose. Around 1805 he began to argue that no one tribe could make treaties or sell land to the Americans. He developed his younger brother, Lalawethika, once a drunk, into a prophet and fed him things to say to sway the tribes. Lalawethika claimed that a great spirit told him to change his name to "Tenskwatawa." His charisma, backed by Tecumseh's words, began to draw followers. The two brothers founded a community on the Wabash that became known as "Prophetstown." Tecumseh then traveled to distant tribes to create an alliance. "The only way to stop this evil," he said, "is for the red man to unite in claiming a common and equal right in the land, as it was first, and should be now, for it was never divided."[13]

In 1809 the future U.S. president William Henry Harrison, then governor of the Indiana territory, summoned Indian chiefs while Tecumseh was away, reportedly got them drunk, and bought 3 million acres from them for $7,000 and some other concessions. Tecumseh raged when he heard of this. Outrage from the purchase brought him more followers. Fearing war all along the frontier, in 1810 Harrison invited Tecumseh to parlay. Tecumseh came with 400 warriors. When Harrison invited Tecumseh to sit, Tecumseh declared, "The Earth is my mother and on her bosom I will recline." Their opposing wills and visions couldn't come to terms.

Harrison later showed he understood Tecumseh's power when he wrote that Tecumseh was "one of those uncommon geniuses which spring up occasionally to produce revolutions and overturn the established order of things." So, to outflank his worthy opponent, in 1811, Harrison declared that the murder of some settlers in Illinois had been committed by followers of Tecumseh's brother, and demanded that Tecumseh hand over the killers. Seeing the brewing trouble, Tecumseh told his brother not to fight Harrison and left on a massive journey to gather an army. During his journey a frontiersman, Captain Sam Dale, heard Tecumseh speak and wrote, "His eyes burned with supernatural luster, and his whole frame trembled with emotion. . . . I have heard many great orators, but I never saw one with the vocal powers of Tecumseh."

He shouldn't have left. Harrison moved on Prophetstown with 1,000 soldiers. Tenskwatawa sent followers to ask Harrison to parlay, so Harrison camped and waited. Tenskwatawa then told his followers magic would make the Americans' bullets as harmless as rain, and they followed him in a night attack. It failed. Harrison's men stood down waves of screaming warriors, and Harrison burned Prophetstown to the ground. Tecumseh returned in 1812, his chance for a united front slipping away.

The War of 1812 began and Tecumseh felt renewed; he again joined the British. As a brigadier general, Tecumseh led a large force of Indians in the siege of Fort Meigs and covered General Henry Procter's retreat after the American victory on Lake Erie. But Harrison was to win the struggle. Tecumseh fell in the battle of the Thames as Harrison led the Americans to victory. Harrison's men searched for Tecumseh's body, and upon finding what they believed to be Tecumseh's corpse, they celebrated by skinning it. But they were mistaken. The Indians had removed Tecumseh's things and put them on another dead warrior. They then took Tecumseh's body to a secret place and buried him—and so passed Tecumseh, a man who stood for his people and way of life, and lost.

Tecumseh once summarized his vision of how to be a man this way:

"Live your life that the fear of death can never enter your heart. Trouble no one about his religion. Respect others in their views and demand that they respect yours. Love your life, perfect your life, beautify all things in your life. Seek to make your life long and of service to your people. Prepare a noble death song for the day when you go over the great divide. Always give a word or sign of salute when meeting or passing a friend, or even a stranger, if in a lonely place. Show respect to all people, but grovel to none. When you rise in the morning, give thanks for the light, for your life, for your strength. Give thanks for your food and for the joy of living. If you see no reason to give thanks, the fault lies in yourself. Abuse no one and no thing, for abuse turns the wise ones to fools and robs the spirit of its vision. When your time comes to die, be not like those whose hearts are filled with fear of death, so that when their time comes they weep and pray for a little more time to live their lives over again in a different way. Sing your death song, and die like a hero going home."[14]

4. Pivot away and down as your arm comes through and he'll fall off-balance and to the ground.

5. Get away.

## Matt Hughes' Five Rules of Self-defense

1. **Be Confident:** If you exude strength, few will mess with you.

2. **Stay Aware:** Watch people, especially in bad neighborhoods or bars, and be ready.

3. **Control the Situation:** Don't just react to an aggressor; you should act instead.

4. **Hurt Them First:** If a fight is unavoidable, take the initiative.

5. **Get Away:** As soon as you can, get away. There is nothing unmanly about not fighting a thug.

## What Matt Hughes Would Do

**Situation:** A mugger moves toward you

**Tactic:** Keep an object between you and get away, says Hughes. Fighting is a last resort. If you can't get away, give him what he wants. It's not worth your life. But if he attacks, don't go hand to knife. Grab a trashcan, a rock, a stick, or just take off your jacket and use it to distract and make him give you an avenue of escape. If you can't avoid him, control his weapon and disarm him by turning the knife or gun toward his thumb.

**Situation:** A man grabs you from behind

**Tactic:** Lower your center of gravity by bending your knees, says Hughes, then attempt to roll to one side. If he is able to stop you, suddenly spring up using your legs in the direction he is pulling to stop you. He'll then fall over. Get up and get away.

**Situation:** A single assailant is attacking another person

**Tactic:** A punch right behind the ear is a very effective way to drop or stun someone, says Hughes. Another good tactic is to tackle his legs. Try to take out a knee. Use your advantage and don't hesitate.

**Situation:** More than one person corner and attack you

**Tactic:** Stay on your feet. If you drag someone down, the others will only kick you. Use any object in reach. Grab some-one's ear or use a wrist-lock to control one person and to keep them between you and the others as you maneuver to escape.

**Situation:** A home intruder comes after you

**Tactic:** This is a worst-case scenario, because if he was only a robber he'd just want to get away. Fight like a wild animal and scream for help, advises Hughes. Use lamps, chairs... anything as weapons. If he gets his hands on you, go for his groin. Don't hold back. Hurt him first, then get away and call the police.

# PART 5

*"The flowering of civilization is the finished man, the man of sense, of grace, of accomplishment, of social power—the gentleman."*
—RALPH WALDO EMERSON [1]

This is the age that killed the gentleman by deeming chivalry to be sexist; by deciding a code of honor is foolishly idealistic; by determining a gentleman's agreement is antiquated; by holding youth in greater esteem than wisdom; by defining courage as not getting the "super-size" value meal; by convincing men to dress like boys; by believing refinement is eating a vegan diet; by cheering when sports stars throw tantrums; by empowering politically correct do-gooders to censure the gentlemanly vices (poker, tobacco, manly talk, an evening drink).

Even the Puritans weren't as authoritarian as today's politically correct police. The Puritans tolerated drinking, smoking, and cursing when done in moderation.[2] They agreed with Aristotle, who defined a virtue as the mean between extremes—drinking to intoxication is an extreme, as is prohibition, but a beer or martini now and then with a few pals was considered moderate, the sign of virtue and self control. But today the gentlemanly vices are no longer guilty pleasures regulated by common decency; instead they've been deemed offenses, increasingly even misdemeanors.

Such is just the beginning of why today's gentleman has become a stuffed suit. Why people now use the word "gentleman" to compliment a polite man, yet fail to appreciate that the term was once a well-defined archetype men struggled to emulate. Once referring to a man from the upper class, the word "gentleman" came to define a man with a noble demeanor. Indeed, in 1714, Sir Richard Steele wrote in London's *Tatler* (No. 207), "The appellation of Gentleman is never to be affixed to a man's circumstances, but to his Behaviour in them."

Only a few generations ago, a gentleman was a man who was chivalric, just, learned, refined, honest, courageous, and upstanding; a man who followed a code of honor; who was an icon that could actually be visualized; who was a man with refined vices, but with vices nonetheless; who was a figure men wanted to be. Sure, the downside to the old-school gentleman was that he could be an elitist, racist, and sexist snob. However, America's apathy for the European-style class structure expunged the hierarchical snobberies from the pedigree of what a gentleman was supposed to be by morphing him into the New World's self-made man. Early-twentieth-century American men of earned wealth and position, or even those without wealth or power, could be gentlemen if they followed the gentleman's code of honor and refined their actions accordingly.

Such men wore collared shirts at home and wouldn't go to church without a tie. They may have owned a funny-looking smoking jacket, maybe even a cigarette case or a pipe. Most had a little liquor cabinet that opened into a bar for guests, they knew how to mix a dozen or so drinks, and they certainly enjoyed an evening drink, a martini perhaps, or a little rye after a day of toil. Such men weren't embarrassed to drink around children, but you'd never see them drunk. They knew a dozen card games, like gin rummy, bridge, and pinochle. They preferred conversation to watching television, which they disdainfully dubbed the "noise box." They loved a good joke, and probably told the same ones a million times, but people didn't mind because boy could they tell them. They'd have an evening and go to bed at a reasonable hour because they knew when to stop, how to moderate themselves. They knew what hard times were really like, and were thankful for the chance to earn a living. They wouldn't take charity, but they gave what they could. They never cursed around women, though they sure knew how to use four-letter invective. They weren't bullies, but knew how to stand up for themselves. They seemed to be having a hell of a time. They'd traveled some and had fought bravely in the Big One, even though they'd rather not talk about what happened in those bloody wars. Such men might not have been outdoorsmen, but they certainly were adventurous. They could change a flat tire, fix a faucet, fell a tree, dance formally, and set a leg. They were men.

But today, just after the gentleman was finally cleansed of his racism, his snobbery, and his elitism, we've decided he isn't politically correct enough to live amongst us. Contemporary American culture is now only okay with vices when they're kept out of sight. You know, "what happens in Vegas stays in Vegas," and all that nonsense. Just don't kick back with a scotch or a martini when the kids are around. It's now perfectly acceptable for the state to run lotteries and the churches bingo halls, but a man can't play poker for money at his local pub. It's perfectly acceptable nowadays to toss around vicious insults under the protective anonymity of the internet, but quite illegal for a man to challenge another to step outside. It's now acceptable for a man to wear jeans and a pull-on shirt to most fine restaurants, though two generations ago a man of any means would have thought going out without a tie to be shameful. Strangers commonly sue one another for having an icy doorstep, but before someone plays Good Samaritan at an accident, they'd better consult an attorney and review their liability insurance. This is what happens when legalism trumps honor, when a gentleman's vices and virtues are scrubbed with political correctness into relative mediocrity that insults no one.

Incredibly, it took a Soviet-era Russian to point out America's modern gutting of the gentleman's code of honor. Alexandr Solzhenitsyn, a Nobel Prize-winning author who'd exposed Stalin's prison camps and other atrocities at his own peril, gave a speech at Harvard in 1978 in which people thought he'd simply sing the praises of Western democracy; he did, but he also shocked his audience by pointing out the shortfalls of overzealous Western legalism by saying things such as, "Whenever the tissue of life is woven of legalistic relations, there is an atmosphere of moral mediocrity, paralyzing man's noblest impulses."

It's this deterioration of the noble impulses that is leaving young men bereft of good role models to show them how to be gentlemen—how to treat ladies and themselves, or even how to drink moderately, smoke, cuss, and gamble. As a result, young men increasingly have few opportunities to cultivate a gentleman's moderation; they only know boyish excess, as booze, tobacco, and cards don't make boys into men—only learning how to control such vices does. But instead, men are taught that the best thing is to live a bland life.

Certainly some men should abstain; after all, if a man can't handle his vices, whether for physiological or psychological reasons, the manly thing to do is to give them up, and to seek help if necessary. But rather than let individuals refine and moderate themselves, and thereby grow into men, today's do-gooders have decided men can't handle their vices, even though little good comes from society chasing man's vices underground where they can't be moderated. In fact, given this modern manner of treating vices, it's not surprising that so many men today treat alcohol, gambling, and tobacco like a fourteen-year-old boy who just found the key to daddy's liquor cabinet. Which is part of the reason why men need their vices—at least a little. Men need to blow off steam, to male bond, to moderate themselves, to learn what is too much and what is just right.

Mark Twain understood this. "The idea that no gentleman ever swears is all wrong," said Twain. "He can swear and still be a gentleman if he does it in a nice and benevolent and affectionate way."[3] Mark Twain smoked cigars, cussed, and drank, but moderated them as a gentleman of his time was supposed to—and knew he'd gone too far when his wife told him so, as women once moderated men, instead of emasculating them. So to combat today's lack of a clear moral code of conduct, our age's adherence to legalism over honor, and the modern practice of disinfecting virtues and vices into relative mediocrity, here's how to regain some of the fading skills, honor, and disposition of a gentleman.

## Gentleman's 20 Rules of Conduct

1.  **Always Be Polite:** Even if someone is in your face, don't stoop to their level. Being polite and courteous shows that you're the better man.

2.  **Don't Curse around Ladies:** Swearing in front of women or children means you don't have the vocabulary to express your thoughts appropriately.

3. **Don't Shout:** Shouting, or talking over others, raises the stress level and implies you don't have the intellect to garner attention.

4. **Don't Lose Your Temper:** When you lose your temper, you are showing everyone that you can't control yourself, which is never manly.

5. **Don't Stare:** Ogling a woman is poor form.

6. **Don't Cheat:** A relationship is a pact a man doesn't break; if it isn't working and can't work, end it; if you do that before accepting other companionship, you'll be an honorable man.

7. **Don't Spit:** Spitting in public went out with the spittoon.

8. **Respect Your Elders:** Always be polite; use "sir" or "ma'am" when speaking to an elder you're not on familiar terms with.

9. **Don't Laugh at Others:** If someone spills a drink or trips, help them. Don't chuckle unless they do.

10. **Take Off Your Hat Indoors:** Remove your hat when you enter a building or sit down to eat, and don't put it on the table.

11. **Wait for Everyone:** When sitting down for a meal, you should wait until all the guests are properly seated and served before eating.

12. **Always Open Doors:** Whether she is about to enter your car or a restaurant, you should always hold the door.

13. **Always Help a Lady with Her Coat:** This is a simple but profound action.

14. **Help Her with Her Seat:** If an unaccompanied lady is sitting next to you, help her be seated by pulling out her chair and gently pushing it back into place.

15. **Give Up Your Seat:** If a lady arrives at the table, bus, train…and there are no available seats, you should stand up and offer her yours.

16. **Stand for a Lady:** During formal occasions, stand when a lady enters or exits the room or table.

17. **Give Her Your Arm:** When escorting a lady to and from a social event, you should offer her your arm.

18. **Ask If She Needs Anything:** When at social events, make sure to ask the ladies if you can get them something to drink, a seat, or whatever.

19. **Dress Better Than the Occasion:** A man who dresses slightly better than the crowd gains a little moral superiority.

20. **Have Impeccable Hygiene:** You can have dirty nails when you're splitting wood, but not when you take your lady's hand.

# The Chivalric Code of the Round Table

The American Heritage Dictionary defines chivalry as "the qualities idealized by knighthood, such as bravery, courtesy, honor, and gallantry toward women." But Sir Thomas Mallory, a fifteenth-century English writer who wrote *Le Morte d'Arthur*, defined the chivalrous man's code of conduct more profoundly:[4]

1. To never do outrage nor murder
2. Always to flee treason
3. To by no means be cruel but to give mercy unto him who asks for mercy
4. To always do ladies, gentlewomen, and widows succor
5. To never force ladies, gentlewomen, or widows

6. Not to take up battles in wrongful quarrels for love or worldly goods

## Gentlemen's Agreement

The gentlemen's agreement went out of style when lawsuits came in. Such agreements used to be an informal contract between two or more parties. They were often signed via a handshake, and some can actually still be legally binding. Before you enter into one, be sure the other party is also honorable.

## The Gentlemen's Duel

Duels with swords or matched percussion pistols live on in Hollywood, but around the early nineteenth century duels became illegal in Europe and most of the U.S. With the duel went a good deal of deadly hubris, but also honor's teeth, as it's difficult for men to be completely honorable when dishonor can't be punished physically. Declining a challenge to duel was once a concession of defeat, and of your manhood. Prominent and famous individuals were especially at risk of being challenged by someone who wanted to rise in the class structure. In fact, during the American Revolution General George Washington ordered his officers not to duel because he didn't want to lose good men senselessly. Subsequently, twenty states passed statutes outlawing the practice. Dueling today would likely be tried as murder; though it seems a shame men can't duel in some less deadly way to stop others from acting dishonorably.

> The gentleman does not needlessly and unnecessarily remind an offender of a wrong he may have committed against him. He cannot only forgive, he can forget.... A true man of honor feels humbled himself when he cannot help humbling others.
>
> GENERAL ROBERT E. LEE[5]

## Men's Fashion

*"Clothes make the man. Naked people have little or no influence on society."*

–MARK TWAIN[6]

## HOW TO BUY A SUIT

1. Bring someone: take your spouse or a friend along to give another opinion. You don't have to take their advice, but they might save you from buying something the salesman is pushing.

2. Be patient: tell the man on commission what you need the suit(s) for and ask for recommendations.

3. Squeeze the fabric: "no-wrinkle" suits are now available. If the cloth bounces back with little or no sign of wrinkling, it's good material. Tug the buttons gently.

4. The jacket sleeves should never meet the wrist any lower than the base of your thumb. The pants should almost hide your socks while standing.

5. Know what you're buying a suit for: realize that the fabric and style is determined by what season and what places/events you'll wear it to.

6. Always get fitted: one size does not fit all.

7. Determine your style: the variations in design, cut, and cloth, such as two- and three- piece, or single- and double-breasted, are determined by the social and work suitability of the garment.

## MAN'S 10 RULES OF FASHION

1. Match your socks to your trousers. With patterned socks, ideally the background color of the sock should match the primary color of the suit.

2. Ties should always be darker or brighter than your shirt.

3. If you weigh more than you'd like, wear dark colors.

> **MAN FACT**
> The best time of day to buy shoes is late afternoon, when your feet have swollen to their largest size.

# How to Tie a Windsor Knot

1. When beginning, the wide end should extend about a foot below the narrow end and, when finished, just reach your belt.
2. Cross the wide end over the narrow end.
3. Bring the wide end up through the loop between the collar and your tie, then back down.
4. Pull the wide end underneath the narrow end and to the right, back through the loop and to the right again so that the wide end is inside out.
5. Bring the wide end across the front from right to left.
6. Pull the wide end up through the loop again.
7. Bring the wide end down through the knot in front.
8. Use both hands to tighten the knot carefully and to draw it up to the collar.

# How to Tie a Bowtie

1. Make a simple knot—like you do when you begin to tie your shoes. One end (let's call it "A") should be about two inches shorter than the other end ("B"). You'll have to experiment with this difference until you find what's right for you.

2. Make a bow (a loop) with B and position it on the first knot you made.

3. Drop A vertically over the folded end of B.

4. Double back A on itself and position it over the knot so the folded ends make a cross.

5. Pass the folded end of A under and behind the left side of the knot and through the loop under the folded end of B.

6. Tighten the knot carefully. Straighten the center.

4. If you're buying one expensive suit, you want tropical wool. It's warm but breathable, so you can wear it all year.

5. Never wear suspenders with a belt.

6. Don't ever wear a color named for something you eat—red is fine, cranberry is gay; pink can work, salmon is emasculating.

7. Normally, button-down collars are reserved for casual use with a sports coat or no coat at all, though this rule has been relaxed.

8. Don't wear deck shoes with a suit. The English wear black shoes with business suits and save brown shoes to wear with tweed. To keep it simple: wear black shoes with grey or black suits, and brown with navy and non-business suits.

9. Double-breasted suit coats are almost always kept buttoned. When there is more than one to fasten, only the top one needs to be buttoned.

10. Single-breasted suit coats may either be buttoned or unbuttoned. In two-button suits the bottom button is usually left unfastened. Unfasten the button while sitting down to avoid an ugly bulge.

# On Vice

## Tobacco

*"A woman is only a woman, but a good cigar is a smoke."*
—RUDYARD KIPLING[8]

### CIGARS

Cigars are still manly, even if you increasingly can't smoke them in public. But before lighting that cigar, you should know what you're getting into. First of all, cigars naturally contain nicotine. Now most cigar smokers will tell you the nicotine is not the sole attraction; however, it is addictive, and can upset a new smoker's stomach. This is why smart smokers moderate their vice, and give it up when necessary. And it's why the best time for a new smoker to try a cigar is after a light meal. Start with a mild but interesting cigar, such as a Macanudo Baron de Rothschild Café or an Arturo Fuente Flor Fina 8-5-8 Natural. These particular cigars will cost you $3 to $5 apiece and can be found in most cigar stores. Or tell a tobacconist at your local shop that you're in need of recommendations.

> **❝** I haven't a particle of confidence in a man who has no redeeming petty vices. **❞**
>
> MARK TWAIN[7]

### Cigar Basics

Quality cigars are still handmade and often state this fact on the box or cigar band, though they might use Spanish: "Hecho a mano." An experienced cigar roller can produce hundreds of cigars per day. They keep the tobacco moist and use specially designed crescent-shaped knives called "chavetas" to form the filler and wrapper leaves. Once rolled, cigars are kept in wooden forms as they dry. From this stage, the cigar is a complete product that can be aged for decades if kept at about 70°F and 70 percent relative humidity. Once cigars have been purchased, proper storage is usually accomplished by keeping them in a specialized wooden box (a humidor), where conditions can be controlled; however, even if a cigar becomes dry, it can often be successfully re-humidified.

### How to Buy Cigars

Cigars are made up mostly of fillers, wrapped-up bunches of leaves inside the wrapper. Fillers of various strengths are usually blended to produce flavors, which cigar makers refer to as the cigar's "blend." Like wine makers, cigar manufacturers pride themselves on making ideal blends. The more oils present in the tobacco leaf, the stronger the filler. Types range from the lightly flavored "Volado," taken from the bottom of the plant, to the stronger "Ligero" from the upper leaves. Fatter cigars of larger gauge hold more filler, and so have a greater potential to provide a full and complex flavor. A long filler (one that uses whole leaves) is typically higher quality; whereas short-filler cigars often burn hotter and might release bits of leaves into your mouth. If a cigar is completely constructed (filler, binder, and wrapper) of tobacco from one country, it is called "puro" (pure).

Cigars should be firm but supple. If a cigar crackles when squeezed, it's too dry; it should feel like green leaves, not dead brown ones. It should also be close to the same firmness from one end to the other. If there are hard or soft spots, the cigar is filled inconsistently. Many people think that the darker the wrapper, the fuller the flavor; however, color is a poor gauge as

### MAN FACT

The word "cigar" comes from the Spanish "cigarro," which is derived from the Mayan word for tobacco, "siyar."[9] The indigenous inhabitants of the Caribbean, as well as parts of Mexico and South America, are thought to have smoked cigars since as early as the tenth century, as evidenced by Mayan archaeological evidence. Subsequently, Christopher Columbus is generally credited with the introduction of tobacco to Europe.

flavor mainly comes from the filler, and standards for cigar colors vary with manufacturers. When buying, realize the size of a cigar is measured by two dimensions: its ring gauge (its diameter in sixty-fourths of an inch) and its length (in inches). A large cigar, say 7.5-inch by 50 ring, can burn for perhaps 90 to 120 minutes.

## How to Smoke a Cigar

There are some places, such as in England, where it's considered improper to smoke a cigar with the band on; however, in the U.S. it seems to be a matter of choice. If you intend to smoke the cigar immediately, ask the tobacconist to "shoulder" (cut the cap off) the cigar for you and watch and learn. If you're going to smoke it later, have the tobacconist show you how. Cutting too far into the cigar can break the connection between the wrapper and the binder, which can cause it to unravel. Cutting too shallow can make the cigar difficult to suck air through. To start, buy a guillotine or a scissor-style cutter.

Some aficionados say lighters leave residue that affects taste. Such smokers use butane lighters or wooden matches. Before you light up, smell the cigar, note the character of the tobacco, then put the cigar in your mouth and take a few puffs through the unlit cigar to gauge the taste and smell of the unlit tobacco. Next, light the cigar by holding the flame slightly off-center on the face of the cigar and rotate the cigar with your fingers while taking very short puffs—repeat until it's evenly lit.

Don't use your lungs when smoking a cigar; lungs are meant for air, not cigar smoke. Take a puff every thirty to ninety seconds depending on how the cigar is burning. Puffing too often can cause the cigar to overheat and give it a harsh flavor. Puffing too infrequently will allow the cigar to go out. Tipping the ash of a cigar should be done only when necessary, as a well-made, hand-rolled cigar can easily hold a half-inch of ash. If you have to let a cigar go out, blow through it before it goes out to remove the smoke inside the cigar before it has a chance to become stale. This can improve the taste of a relit cigar.

### Types of Cigars

There are two main types or shapes of cigars: Parejo and Figurado. Further, there are many different sub-sets under these two categories. Here are the main ones:

> **Parejo:** The most common shape. This type of cigar is cylindrical with straight sides; it has one open end and a closed, or capped, end that must be cut. Parejos are available in two general types, of which there are many variations: Coronas and Panatelas. Coronas are what people normally picture when they think of a cigar, while Panatelas are generally longer and thinner than Coronas.

> **Figurado:** Irregularly shaped cigars, often known for their higher quality because they are more difficult to make. Some of the most common types of Figurados are Presidente, Perfecto, Pyramid, and Torpedo.

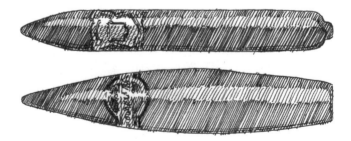

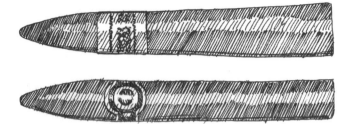

## PIPES

The charming thing about pipes is their aroma offends fewer non-smokers. The majority of pipes sold today, whether hand- or machine-made, are fashioned from briar because it has a natural resistance to fire and absorbs moisture well. Briar is cut from the root burl of the tree heath. Pipe smoke, like cigar smoke, should not be inhaled. It is normal to have to relight a pipe periodically. Excess moisture can produce a gurgling sound in the pipe and make it difficult to relight. A pipe cleaner can be used to dry it out. The bowl of the pipe can also become uncomfortably hot, depending on the material and the rate of smoking.

Pipe tobacco can be purchased in several forms, which vary widely in flavor. There are a lot of blends to experiment with, and you can blend your own. Most pipe tobaccos resemble cigarette tobacco, though they are more moist; to keep them this way, they must be kept in airtight packaging. In the most common method of packing, tobacco is added to the bowl of the pipe in several batches, each one pressed down until the mixture has a uniform density that optimizes airflow—this is difficult to gauge without practice. If the tobacco needs to be repacked later, while it's burning, a tamper might be needed.

## CIGARETTES

Sorry, cigarettes lost their manly mojo. Cary Grant, Frank Sinatra, John Wayne, and other icons of classic American film somehow seemed more virile when puffing away; today, cigarettes' ill effects and addictiveness have clouded their coolness.

# Alcohol

*"The harsh, useful things of the world, from pulling teeth to digging potatoes, are best done by men who are as starkly sober as so many convicts in the death-house, but the lovely and useless things, the charming and exhilarating things, are best done by men with, as the phrase is, a few sheets in the wind."*

–H. L. MENCKEN[10]

## HOW TO OPEN A BOTTLE OF CHAMPAGNE

The cork doesn't have to fly across the room and potentially take your lady's eye out. Remove the foil and wire. Place a dishtowel over the cork and hold the cork with your thumb and pointer finger, then slowly turn the bottle, and the cork will come out easily.

## WINE

### The Wine Lingo

So there you are at the head of a table when some snooty waiter hands you a wine list, yet like most guys you're not a wine connoisseur. What do you do? First, ask your lady and guests if they prefer red or white. Pay attention to what they're ordering. The old rule of red meat goes with red wine and white meat (fish, chicken) goes with white holds, but isn't very important—taste trumps menu selections. In fact, pairing wine and food is a complex business, so just keep the general tastes in mind. For example, acidic foods, like a Greek salad, work best with wines that share an acidic undertone, such as a Pinot Grigio; while sweeter foods, such as chicken rosemary, pair best with wines that are a little drier than the food, like a dry Riesling.

Ask the waiter for recommendations, but watch to see whether he or she knows their wine. If they don't, ask who on staff is the resident expert. Have him or her come to the table. They'll be delighted. Present your problem, but stay assertive and don't give too much authority away. The conversation will impress your lady, as your willingness to learn is commanding and endearing. Choose some wines based on all the above, and be aware that one bottle equals four glasses of wine. Also, unless you are an expert, leave terminology such as "nutty," "fruity," "oaky," and "silky" to charlatans and experts.

### How to Let Red Wine "Breathe"

Before dinner, decant wine into glasses or a wine decanter. Let old, quality reds breathe for one hour and younger reds two to three hours. Some low-cost wines won't be improved by breathing them.

## KNOW A LITTLE ABOUT WINE

### Red Wine Grapes

- **Cabernet Franc:** This grape is often blended with Cabernet Sauvignon to add bouquet—many don't think much of it when it's by itself.
- **Gamay:** This grape produces a fruity wine, such as French Beaujolais.
- **Grenache:** This grape is often used to make rosè wine; it is a component of French Chateauneuf-du-Pape, Cotes du Rhone, and other blends from South France. There are also many good grenache-based wines from Spain (where it is called "garnacha") and California.
- **Nebbiolo:** This grape can be found in California, but is originally from the Piedmont area of Northern Italy. It's used to make wines such as Barolo, Barbaresco,

> **MAN FACT**
>
> When you serve wine, the temperature of quality reds should be 59°–65°F; lesser reds, rosés, and complex whites should be 50°–55°F; typical whites should be 46°–50°F; and sweet whites and champagne should be 43°–46°F.

Ghemme, and Nebbiolo. These are lightly colored red wines that can be tannic when young. When they age, Nebbiolo wines reveal complex aromas and flavors.

- **Syrah (Shiraz):** Syrah grapes are popular and produce deep red, tannic, and long-lived wines.

- **Cabernet Sauvignon:** Cabernet Sauvignon is originally from Bordeaux, but became one of the world's most popular reds. Its flavors are traditionally oaky with hints of tobacco, but flavors vary widely.

- **Pinot Noir:** This grape's name is derived from the French words for "pine" and "black," which alludes to its dark purple pine cone-shaped bunches of fruit. It's known as a fickle grape that needs warm days and cool evenings. Basically, Pinot Noir tends to have a light to medium body and an aroma of black cherry, raspberry, and currant.

- **Zinfandel:** This grape is now mostly grown in California. It has a great deal of fruity characteristics. Some young Zinfandels can be spicy and robust. They often have a dark color scheme, medium to high tannin levels, and high alcohol content.

- **Merlot:** The classic Merlot grape was developed in France's Bordeaux region. It makes a soft, medium-bodied red wine with fruity flavors.

### White Wine Grapes

- **Chardonnay:** This is a green-skinned grape that produces French white Burgundy and perhaps the most popular wines in the U.S.

- **Chenin Blanc:** This grape is from the Loire Valley in France. In the U.S. it is often used to make a light, fruity wine.

- **Riesling:** This grape originates from the Rhine in Germany. It often yields a floral smelling wine that tastes light and fresh. It can be a great dessert wine.
- **Sauvignon Blanc:** This green-skinned grape originates from the Bordeaux region of France. It makes a sharp but light wine.
- **Semillon:** This golden-skinned grape is one of the major varieties grown in Bordeaux. It may be dry or sweet and is often seen as an after-dinner wine.
- **White Zinfandel:** Made from the zinfandel grape, white zinfandel is a light pink color; it is sweet and uncomplicated, often favored by people who don't drink much wine.

## WHISKEY

Whiskey is a straightforward, manly drink, but its wide range of grains, flavors, and distillation processes also attracts connoisseurs. Most of the best whiskey comes from four countries, each of which makes distinctly different whiskies: Ireland (Irish Whiskey), Scotland (Scotch), America (Bourbon, Tennessee Whiskey, Rye Whiskey, blended American Whiskey), and Canada (Canadian Whiskey). This diverse market ensures that every whiskey lover can cultivate an opinionated view of types and brands. Here are the basics:

**Irish Whiskey:** This is the father of whiskey. There are several types of whiskey common to Ireland: single malt, single grain, pure pot still, and blended whiskey. Most Irish whiskey

**MAN FACT**

The word "whiskey" is an Anglicization of the Gaelic term "uisce beatha," which translates, "water of life."

# 10 Mixed Drinks
# Every Gentleman Should Know

### 1. Bloody Mary

**Ingredients:** 2 ounces of vodka, dash of red wine, dash of wine and sherry mix, pinch of celery salt, salt and pepper, 7 drops of Worcestershire sauce, 5 drops of hot sauce, 1 (6-ounce) container of tomato juice, celery stalks, cherry tomatoes

**Preparation:** Combine all of the ingredients in a highball glass containing ice; stir well; serve with a celery stick and cherry tomato. To substitute mix, add red wine and a dry sherry to the Bloody Mary.

### 2. Margarita

**Ingredients:** 1-1/2 ounces of silver tequila, 1 ounce of Cointreau, 1/2 ounce of fresh lime juice, splash of simple syrup, coarse salt for the rim

**Preparation:** Wet the lip of the glass; pour the course salt onto a plate; put the rim of the glass into the salt and turn it; add crushed ice and the ingredients to the glass; top it with a slice of lime.

### 3. Martini

**Ingredients:** 3-1/2 ounces of vodka or gin, 1/2 ounce of dry vermouth, olive or lemon twist for garnish

**Preparation:** Pour ice, vodka, and vermouth into a glass shaker; shake and pour into a martini glass; garnish with olives or lemon twist.

### 4. Old-Fashioned

**Ingredients:** 3 maraschino cherries, orange slice, 1 tbsp of sugar, 2 ounces of bourbon, 4 ounces of soda water

**Preparation:** Add two cherries and an orange slice to a glass; add 1 tbsp of sugar; mix the sugar and fruit; pour in bourbon; add ice; top it with soda water; garnish with a cherry.

### 5. Tom Collins

**Ingredients:** 2 ounces of gin, 1/2 lemon, 1 tsp of powdered sugar, club soda, lemon wedge

**Preparation:** Fill a shaker half full of ice; pour in ingredients; shake well; strain over new ice in a Collins glass; top it off with club soda and garnish with a lemon wedge.

### 6. Mint Julep

**Ingredients:** 4 fresh mint sprigs, 2-1/2 ounces of bourbon, 1 tsp of powdered sugar, 2 tsp of water

**Preparation:** Muddle mint leaves, water, and powdered sugar in a julep cup; fill with crushed or shaved ice and add bourbon; top it off with more ice and mint leaves for garnish.

### 7. White Russian

**Ingredients:** 2 ounces of vodka, 1 ounce of coffee liqueur, light cream

**Preparation:** Pour vodka and coffee liqueur into an ice-filled, old-fashioned glass; top off with light cream; stir thoroughly.

### 8. Manhattan

**Ingredients:** 3/4 ounce of sweet vermouth, 2-1/2 ounces of bourbon, dash of bitters, 1 maraschino cherry, 1 orange peel twist

**Preparation:** Combine vermouth, bourbon, bitters, and three ice cubes in a mixing glass; stir gently so as not to cloud the drink; put the cherry in a chilled cocktail glass and strain the mixture over the cherry; rub the cut edge of the orange peel over the rim and twist it over the drink, but do not drop it in.

### 9. Typhoon

**Ingredients:** 1 ounce of gin, 1 ounce of Anisette, 1 ounce of lime juice, champagne

**Preparation:** Shake gin, Anisette, and lime juice with ice; strain into a cocktail glass over ice; fill glass with chilled champagne and stir lightly.

### 10. Whiskey Sour

**Ingredients:** 1/2 tsp of powdered sugar, 2 ounces of whiskey, 1/2 lemon wedge, cherry

**Preparation:** Fill a shaker half full of ice; combine ingredients; shake well and strain over ice in a glass; garnish with a lemon wedge and a cherry.

is distilled three times, but so is some Scotch; thus it is a myth that this is the main distinction between the two varieties. Irish whiskey also differs in that peat is almost never used in the malting process, so the smoky, earthy overtones common to Scotches are not present.

**Scotch Whisky:** By tradition, Scotch whisky is the only whisky that uses the spelling for whisky without the "e." At one time, all whisky was spelled without (whisky). But in the late nineteenth century the reputation of Scottish whisky became very poor, so the Irish and American distilleries adopted the spelling "whiskey" to distinguish their higher quality products.[11] The Scotts now have their reputation back. The distinct smoky flavor of this double-distilled formula is due to its malt drying process, part of which is done over a peat-fueled fire allowing the smoke to come in direct contact with the malt. Single-malt Scotch whisky is produced by a single distillery in one season from a single batch of whisky, whereas blended Scotch whisky is mixed to reduce the harsher tones of single-malts with other whiskies.

**Bourbon:** Bourbon received its name from Bourbon County, Kentucky, and, according to a 1964 act of Congress, it must be made from a mash containing at least 51 percent corn.

**MAN FACT**

The legal blood-alcohol limit is .08 percent in some states and .10 in others. The accepted maximum to drink and stay below the limit is one drink per hour, but this varies with the alcohol content of drinks and with body size.

This straight whiskey must be aged a minimum of two years in new, charred oak barrels. No blending or additives (except water to reduce to 80 proof) are allowed in Bourbon.

**Tennessee Whiskey:** This is an American whiskey that undergoes a filtering stage called the "Lincoln County Process" wherein the whiskey is filtered through maple charcoal before being poured into casks for aging. Tennessee Whiskey need only be comprised of 51 percent of any grain, with corn being the most often used.

**Blended American Whiskey:** Like blended Scotch, various whiskeys of different ages are blended to create a balanced flavor, often at a reasonable price. Blended American whiskey is only made of about 20 percent Rye and Bourbon—the remaining percentage is comprised of industrial spirits.

**Rye Whiskey:** By law, American rye whiskey has to be made from at least 51 percent of rye grain, but wheat and barley are also often used. Rye is known as being a little more bitter than bourbon.

**Canadian Whiskey:** According to Canadian law, Canadian whiskey must be mashed, distilled, and aged for at least three years. Good Canadian whiskey is known for being light-bodied and good in mixed drinks. Made primarily of corn or wheat and supplemented with rye and often barley, Canadian whiskey is aged in oak barrels. Most Canadian whiskey is a blend of various grain whiskies of different ages.

## BEER

Beer is a manly drink; sure, some women drink beer, but these days some women also go hunting. Knowing your beers will give you an edge in bar conversations and help you moderate your consumption with your tastes. If you're just a Coors or Bud man, that's fine, but if you want a little manly sophistication, you should know these beer basics.

**MAN FACT**
The mysterious "33" printed on bottles of Rolling Rock immediately below the company motto is an accident. It's the proofreader's count of the number of words in the motto, and the printers left it in.

### A Brief History of Beer

Beer was referred to in ancient Egyptian and Mesopotamian writings. In fact, Babylon's Code of Hammurabi (circa 1760 BC) outlined beer regulations.[12] Later, the use of hops in beer was recorded by captive Jews in Babylon around 400 BC.[13] According to a 2004 study by the Kirin Holdings company, the Czech Republic was the number one beer consumer per capita, Ireland was second, and Germany third. The U.S. was down at number 13.

Beer is produced by brewing and fermenting starches, mainly from cereals, the most common of which is barley, although wheat, corn, and rice are often used. Most beer is later flavored with hops, which adds bitterness and acts as a preservative. There are two common types of beer: lager and ale.

> **Lager:** This is the most commonly consumed beer in the world. The name "lager" comes from the German "lagern" which translates to "to store," as brewers around Bavaria stored beer in cool cellars and caves during the warm summer months. German brewers noticed that the beers continued to ferment and to become clearer when they were stored in cool conditions. Lager yeast is a cool, bottom-fermenting yeast and typically undergoes primary fermentation at 45°–55°F and then is given a long secondary fermentation at 32°–40°F. During the secondary stage, the lager clears and mellows. The cooler conditions also inhibit the natural production of esters and other byproducts.
>
> **Ale (Stout, Pale Ale, Brown Ale):** Ales are normally brewed with top-fermenting yeast; however, the biggest distinction between ales and lagers is that ales are fermented at higher temperatures and thus ferment more quickly than lagers. Ale is typically fermented at temperatures between 60° and 75°F, which often produces a beer with a fruitier, sweeter taste than lagers.

### At What Temperature Should Beer Be Served?

Do the Europeans really drink warm beer? Yes and no. Warmer temperatures actually reveal the range of flavors in a quality beer. Imperial stout, for example, is served at room temperature; however, cooler temperatures are more often used with lagers. The late English beer aficionado and writer Michael Jackson proposed a scale for beer serving temperatures:

1. Serve wheat beers and pale lagers at 45°–50°F.
2. Serve strong ales, amber, and dark lagers at 50°–55°F.
3. Serve dark ales, including porters and stouts, at 55°–60°F.

# Gambling

> *"I had sooner play cards against a man who was quite skeptical about ethics, but bred to believe 'a gentleman does not cheat,' than against an irreproachable moral philosopher who had been brought up among sharpers."*
> —C. S. LEWIS[14]

### HOW TO WIN AT POKER

Poker is about being able to win the pot, not getting the highest hand. Being skilled at disguising your hand is probably your most valuable asset, but it's closely followed by the ability to memorize played cards while being constantly aware of which cards are "live."

1. First, learn to play poker. Poker is skill, experience, and then a little bit of luck—in that order.
2. Most beginners have trouble with the hard-to-remember middle range of the hand hierarchy; to remember it, memorize this phrase: A full house beats a

> **MAN FACT**
> Cassius Marcellus Coolidge (1844–1937) painted the poker-playing dogs. The name of the painting is "No Monkeying."

flush beats a straight. To give you something to visualize, picture a house surrounding a flush toilet that has a straight piece of something floating in it.

3. Before you ante up, set your budget and have the fortitude not to change it.

4. If you can, leave while you're ahead.

5. Never borrow money to gamble, and don't lend either, as lending money to a friend who is losing is a sure way to kill a friendship.

6. Whether you're winning or losing, always keep a low profile.

7. Before you gamble online, read the rules, know the terms, and check if the online casino is a member of a known association.

8. Take a break of at least three hands after a bad beat to avoid tilting.

9. Your gambling stake should be between ten and twenty times your average bet.

10. Learn to lose: men lose gracefully, but not foolishly.

## HOW TO PLAY A CRAPS TABLE

When you place a basic craps bet, you are betting on how lucky the person with the dice is. This is why there's often a lot of camaraderie around a craps table. Begin at a craps table on the area marked "Pass Line." The Pass Line

**MAN FACT**

Poker's "dead man's hand" (aces over 8's) earned its name because they are the cards "Wild Bill" Hickok is said to have been holding when he was shot dead.

bet is a series bet, meaning that the person shooting the dice may have to roll the dice multiple times before you win or lose. The first roll in a series is called the "come-out" roll, and it is different from the rest of the rolls in the series. On the come-out roll, the numbers 7 and 11 are automatic Pass Line winners and the series ends; 2, 3, or 12 (known as "craps") are automatic Pass Line losers; any other number rolled (4, 5, 6, 8, 9, or 10) becomes the shooter's point and the series continues. The object of the game now becomes for the shooter to roll their point number again before they roll a 7. If any number other than the point or a 7 is rolled, nothing happens and the shooter rolls again. If the point is rolled, Pass Line bets win and the series ends; however, if a 7 is rolled, Pass Line bets lose (known as a "seven out") and the series ends.

## THE BEST BET IN VEGAS

In the long run, the best game to play is blackjack—learn the odds of each hand and the house edge is only half a percent. The worst bet is slot machines.

## WHEN TO SPLIT CARDS IN BLACKJACK

To maximize your odds at blackjack, memorize every splitting scenario on the probability-based basic strategy chart, which is available in books and on pocket cards wherever gambling's legal. If you aren't so serious, these four rules are a good cheat sheet to splitting situations.

1.	Always split 8's or aces. Why: You rid yourself of those bust-friendly 16's or 12's.
2.	Never split 10's (or face cards). Why: Only a fool gives up 20.
3.	Never split 4's or 5's. Why: You shouldn't trade in your good chances at 18's or 20's for pairs of crappy 14's or 15's.

4. Split any other pair when the dealer has a visible 4, 5, 6, or 7. Why: You should never miss a chance to double your bet when the dealer's likely to bust.

# A MAN'S GUIDE TO PROFANITY

*"If I cannot swear in Heaven I shall not stay there."*
—MARK TWAIN

A gentleman never swears when a lady is present. But a gentleman should know how to use profanity, as it is sometimes a male bonding ritual.

Some rules are easy: a gentleman should never swear in anger, as cursing in anger makes a man a fool; a man should never use profanity around children. The other rules can be more subtle, but here are some basics to keep in mind.

## HOW MUCH SHOULD A GENTLEMAN SWEAR?

Sparingly. A gentleman's profanity should be imaginative and never overused. George Carlin grew famous for using four-letter invective so much it became humorous by overuse, but it lost its punch—and besides, it required the right audience. In general, gentlemen should only use four-letter observations with wit and class.

## WHERE CAN YOU LEARN TO CURSE POETICALLY?

The armed forces, for starters. They really foster the ability to use expletives graphically. Check out films like *Full Metal Jacket* for some great examples. Another place to learn to curse with flare is the rural South. Southern men have turned the use of profanity into an art form.

# WINSTON CHURCHILL

**W**inston Leonard Spencer Churchill was born into the English upper class at the height of the British Empire, but he still had to earn his reputation as an iconic gentleman. Churchill described himself as having a "speech impediment" when he was a child; it was a defect he overcame so well he is as much known today for his speeches as he is for standing steadfast before Adolf Hitler in World War II. In fact, Churchill cultivated his speaking ability so well some of his comebacks are still repeated. One famous example tells of Churchill entering a men's room at the House of Commons to find his political rival Clement Attlee standing at the urinal. Churchill took a position as far as he could from Attlee, only to hear Attlee jab, "My dear Winston, I hope that despite being adversaries in the House, we could be friends outside of it." Churchill answered, "Ah Clement, I have no quarrel with you, but in my experience, when you see something big, you tend to want to nationalize it."

Churchill became so synonymous with the gentlemanly vices that a cigar size is named after him. His dinner parties were don't-miss, raucous affairs. Legend has it that one evening when Churchill had been drinking heavily at a party, he bumped into Bessie Braddock, a Socialist Member of Parliament. "Mr. Churchill, you are drunk," Braddock censured. Churchill replied, "Bessie, you are ugly. And I'll be sober in the morning."

As time buries a man as large as Churchill, his aura, his persona, and his witty lines become his popular definition. We forget about the boy who needed three attempts to pass the admittance exam into Sandhurst (The Royal Military Academy), the man who deserves a share of blame for the disastrous landings at Gallipoli in 1915, and the man who said, "It is alarming and also nauseating to see Mr. Gandhi, a seditious middle temple lawyer, now posing as a fakir of a type well known in the east, striding half-naked up the steps of the viceregal palace … to parley on equal terms with the representative of the king-emperor." But perhaps Churchill's now-popular reputation is as it should be; after all, Churchill was larger than life. He'd been tested under fire. As prime minister of England, he stood down Hitler and was his nation's spine. He made mistakes, but he changed and grew with the times.

From 1895–1899, Churchill served his country as a cavalry officer in India and elsewhere. Then, to garner fame and fortune enough to dress as a gentleman of his time, Churchill worked as a war correspondent. While covering the Second Boer War for the *Morning Post,* he acted so bravely during the ambush of an armored train that some speculated he'd be awarded the Victoria Cross. He wasn't, but he did become famous when he escaped from a Boer prison camp and traveled almost 300 miles through enemy territory to Portuguese Lourenço, Marques in Delagoa Bay.

From his first book in 1898 until he became Britain's prime minister in 1940, Churchill's income was almost entirely earned via his pen. His most famous newspaper articles appeared in the *Evening Standard* from 1936 and warned of the rise of Adolf Hitler and the danger of the policy of appeasement. His six-volume memoir *The Second World War* and his book *A History of the English-Speaking Peoples* are still popularly read. Churchill was awarded the Nobel Prize in Literature.

At a speech in Dundee, Scotland, in 1908, Churchill summed up his view of what a gentleman should be this way: "What is the use of living, if it be not to strive for noble causes and to make this muddled world a better place for those who will live in it after we are gone? How else can we put ourselves in harmonious relation with the great verities and consolations of the infinite and the eternal? And I avow my faith that we are marching towards better days. Humanity will not be cast down. We are going on swinging bravely forward along the grand high road and already behind the distant mountains is the promise of the sun."

## DO YOU HAVE TO CURSE
## WHEN THE SITUATION IS RIGHT?

No. Sometimes the power of understatement trumps a full flush of profanity. For example, I was in the backseat of a pickup one snowy October day in Montana when the driver, who'd never driven in snow before, lost control. We went careening for a snow fence; he jerked the wheel again and we went sliding for a semi; he again over-corrected the wheel and the truck spun around three full times before stopping in a snow bank. Now I could have cursed, but instead I just said in a very calm voice, "Would you quit playing in the snow, Jim? I'm trying to get some sleep."

## DO YOU HAVE TO CURSE
## AT SOMEONE WHO DESERVES IT?

No, but you can't let them get away with disparaging you, either. So consider using humor, as insults can be more effective when they're funny. One of the best lines in *Monty Python and the Holy Grail* is the most absurd: "Your mother was a hamster, and your father smelt of elderberries!" If someone stupidly or selfishly endangers themselves or others, you could simply say, "I find it hard to fathom that out of millions of sperm, you were the fastest."

A great example of the humorous-yet-clean retort occurred when John Wilkes, an eighteenth-century English journalist and politician, parried insults with John Montagu, the Fourth Earl of Sandwich. "Sir," Montagu started, "I do not know whether you will die on the gallows or of the pox." Wilkes responded, "That, sir, depends on whether I first embrace your Lordship's principles or your Lordship's mistresses."

# PART 6

# ROMANTIC

"*A man's face is his autobiography. A woman's face is her work of fiction.*"
—OSCAR WILDE[1]

Since Eve beguiled Adam men have been struggling to answer the question: "What do women want?" Today, however, men have largely concluded that the ancient feminine riddle is a paradox. Even that ultimate ladies' man, Frank Sinatra, professed, "I'm supposed to have a Ph.D. on the subject of women. But the truth is I've flunked more often than not. I'm very fond of women; I admire them. But, like all men, I don't understand them."[2] And the man who invented psychoanalysis, Sigmund Freud, opined, "The great question that has never been answered, and which I have not yet been able to answer, despite my thirty years of research into the feminine soul, is 'what does a woman want?'"[3]

Back in the fourteenth century, Geoffrey Chaucer provided a plausible answer in his Canterbury Tales. "The Wife of Bath" spins a yarn about a knight in King Arthur's court, who raped a woman and was subsequently caught. He would have been killed for the crime, but the queen interceded by asking the king to turn the knight over to her for judgment. The king complied, and the queen gave the knight a year and a day to find out what women really want. She told him if his answer failed to satisfy her, she'd have him executed. The knight searched all over England for a year, but every woman he found said something different—riches, flattery, beauty, security....

On his way back to the queen after a confusing and unfruitful year, the knight stumbled upon an old hag, and asked her what women want. The hag agreed to tell him if he promised to grant her one request at a time she chose. He agreed, and the hag gave him his answer: what women want most is "to have the sovereignty as well upon their husband as their love, and to have mastery their man above." In other words, women want to be in charge.

Delighted by this perfect answer, the queen pardoned the knight. Now the hag chose to make her request: she wanted the knight to marry her in return for her answer. The marriage took place the next day. But the hag was so ghastly the knight couldn't bring himself to consummate the union. So she made him a deal: he could choose whether he wanted his wife to be ugly and faithful or beautiful and unfaithful.

Perplexed, at last he begged her to decide. She was delighted: this capitulation to her will signified her complete domination of her husband. As a result, she became both fair and faithful and lived with him happily ever after.

Granted, the idealistic days of chivalry are long over, but the takeaway still holds true: women want to be in charge.

Meanwhile, today's women still cling to most of the tenets of the old chivalric ideal, a code that requires men to treat women as ladies. Women adore chivalry, even though feminists often deem it to be sexist. Women, you see, still want the fairytale of the valiant knight in shining armor freeing them from a tower. However, though women want the dashing knight or the cowboy in the white hat to sweep them off their feet and be their hero, they also want to compete with men equally in the workplace. This is naturally confusing to men, as being both a sexless equal and a manly hero (depending on the timing, context, and relationship) is something even 007 couldn't manage. And it's why so many of today's men have given up trying to uncover what women actually want. Now men shrug as women declare they want to be both ladies and women at the same time (and sometimes even men). This is why, back in 1933, Compton Mackenzie wrote, "Women do not find it difficult nowadays to behave like men, but they often find it extremely difficult to behave like gentlemen."[4] Indeed, women now have membership in every segment of a "man's world," but they don't have to adhere to man's chivalric code.

Given this rigged arrangement, how does a man navigate today's feminist minefield and come out the other side with some working notion of what women want? First, realize that the modern spin on the Wife of Bath's tale is that women want men who are strong, yet supple to their wills—even when their wills are whimsical. Women want to be in charge, except when a spider crawls up the wall, there is a bump in the night, or a calamity strikes. So to be an old-fashioned romantic with a modern sense of equality, first, as Sigmund Freud advised, gird your loins with the realization that "a woman should soften but not weaken a man."[5] Next, as stupendous as this notion at first seems, come to understand that women don't see any contradictions in their viewpoint. To women it seems reasonable that they don't want their men to be shallow, yet they want their men to tell them they're beautiful often, even though a man can't possibly tell a woman she's beautiful without being superficial.

So the only concrete thing we can say about romanticism is that it's the acknowledgment that man has a heart. Without a heart a man becomes like the Tin Man, wandering the Land of Oz with brains and bravado, but no human compassion. This is why every male icon from Ancient Greece's Odysseus to the Middle Age's Roland to the American West's Wyatt Earp to contemporary heroes like James Bond and Superman have been confused romantics. And why every Hollywood action hero is a cliché without humanizing scenes, such as when Lethal Weapon character Martin Riggs cries at the grave of his dead wife. Don't fret too much if you don't know what women want; just know that a man who isn't a romantic isn't a complete man.

How do you be a romantic? By becoming, as much as you can, the strength behind her will. When you're wrong—and you will be—reaffirm her power over your heart with an honest romantic gesture.

Now, to make chivalry as comprehensible as possible, the rest of the chapter is loaded with advice from successful women and the time-tested skills of ultimate romantics.

# WOMEN

## 10 GREATEST QUOTES ON WOMEN

"It upsets women to be, or not to be, stared at hungrily."
—*Mignon McLaughlin*[6]

"I have great hopes that we shall love each other all our lives as much as if we had never married at all."
—*Lord Byron*[7]

**MAN FACT**
Having trouble remembering birthdays and anniversaries? Here's a trick: write them down in a date planner and each year take five minutes and copy the dates into your new calendar—yeah, they get mad because it's really that simple.

"A pessimist is a man who thinks all women are bad. An optimist is a man who hopes they are."

*—Chauncey Mitchell Depew*[8]

"Whether they give or refuse, it delights women just the same to have been asked."

*—Ovid*[9]

"Ah, women. They make the highs higher and the lows more frequent."

*—Friedrich Wilhelm Nietzsche*[10]

"One should never strike a woman; not even with a flower."

*—Hindu proverb*[11]

"Do you not know I am a woman? When I think, I must speak."

*—William Shakespeare*[12]

"You should never say anything to a woman that even remotely suggests that you think she's pregnant unless you can see an actual baby emerging from her at that moment."

*—Dave Barry*[13]

"You treat a lady like a dame, and a dame like a lady."

*—Frank Sinatra*[14]

"When the candles are out, all women are fair."    —*Plutarch*[15]

# THE SKILLS OF AN ULTIMATE ROMANTIC

## HOW TO BE JANE AUSTEN'S ULTIMATE ROMANTIC MAN

Elizabeth Kantor researched and wrote *The Jane Austen Guide to Happily Ever After* (2012) to determine how women today can find the type of man the English author Jane Austen (1775–1817) said women should marry. I spoke with Elizabeth Kantor, who has the following advice for men who want to be a Jane Austen-style hero:

- Always consider the emotional effect of what you say to the opposite sex, says Kantor. "Self-control in a man is the greatest aphrodisiac," she says. Don't say whatever comes to your mind. "Be mature with what you say and how you say it because whatever your intentions are, hers are probably much more serious than she'll even admit."

- Kantor's book is designed, among other things, to help women sniff out the guys who say they're gentlemen, but who are really just playing the field. But how can a man show his intentions are honorable? "A man needs to find a clear way to show his principles are good," says Kantor. "Be sincere and courteous, but also look for ways to show, not just tell, her what you're made of."

**MAN FACT**
Know the return policy before you buy jewelry. You never really know if she'll like it or not, so make sure she can return it or trade it in.

# How to Buy Jewelry

**Gold:** Pure gold is known as 24k gold, but most jewelry is made from either 18k gold, 14k gold, or 10k gold. By mixing gold with other alloys, jewelers can create stunning golden shades. White gold, pink gold, rose gold, orange gold, and even green gold are just some of the many colors of gold.

**Diamonds:** The diamond is the birthstone for April. Diamonds are the recommended gift for couples celebrating their 10th, 60th, and 75th wedding anniversaries. When shopping for a diamond, keep in mind that the value of a stone is determined by the "Four C's": cut, color, clarity, and carat weight. "Cut" refers to the perfection of the design and the overall symmetry of the stone. "Color" is easy: the whiter the stone, the greater its value. Most diamonds are graded on the GIA color scale that begins with "D" for colorless and continues all the way down to "Z." "Clarity" refers to the presence of surface or internal flaws within a diamond. External marks are known as "blemishes," while internal ones are called "inclusions." And "carat weight" refers to the size of the stone. When you give her a stone, explain the Four C's and tell her why this particular one is special.

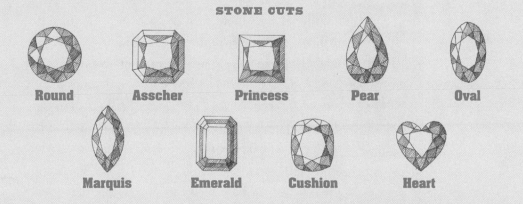

**STONE CUTS**

Round    Asscher    Princess    Pear    Oval

Marquis    Emerald    Cushion    Heart

**Gemstones:** Some peoples attributed magical, mystical powers to gemstones and believed the stones could cure specific ailments. From a man's perspective, the great thing about gemstones is that some wise marketer designated a birthstone for each month. They're a great and easy gift for a first anniversary.

**January:** Garnet

**February:** Amethyst

**March:** Aquamarine

**April:** Diamond

**May:** Emerald

**June:** Pearl

**July:** Ruby

**August:** Peridot

**September:** Sapphire

**October:** Opal

**November:** Citrine

**December:** Blue topaz

- "Jane Austen is famous for not describing her characters, but she was also realistic about the importance of looks," says Kantor. She advises men to show they're serious about a woman by being serious about themselves—yes, this means good hygiene, a clean shirt, good posture, and exercise.

- "Jane Austen wanted women to see men as they really are," says Kantor, "not as some romantic fantasy a woman has built up in her mind." To help women do this, Kantor gives a lot of advice for how women looking for a Jane Austen-style hero can investigate a man on social media and by networking. The point is, she'll be checking, so be careful how you're seen on Facebook and elsewhere.

- "To be a Jane Austen hero, a man needs to have a good temperament," says Kantor. He can't lose his cool when a waiter is rude or when a tire goes flat. He must be manly, especially when things go wrong.

- Jane Austen was very aware of reputation, notes Kantor. The women in her books are always evaluating where a man stands in society. Likewise, women today wonder about the same things. So your reputation matters. Women will talk. If you want to be taken seriously by a nice girl—a girl with a dog-eared copy of Pride and Prejudice—you have to be an upstanding individual with a good reputation.

- Jane Austen's heroines don't always marry the man with the fortune, but they're practical about a man's prospects, explains Kantor. She advises that when a woman asks what a man does, he should proudly answer without egotism or hyperbole. If she judges you poorly for it, then she isn't the woman for you anyway.

## HOW TO FIGHT FOR HER

Sorry, fisticuffs are a last resort. Men show they are separate from the animals by being the only creatures on earth that strive to make asses of themselves to win the opposite sex's adoration. Lions fight, often to the death, as do bears, cougars, and wolves to win a mate. Bucks slam antlers together in brutal shoving matches. Rams smash horns together. Wild turkeys fan their plumage, but also fight by swinging spurs on their legs. Prairie chickens dance, springboks prance and spar, and falcons soar and dive. But a human male eagerly emasculates himself by blushing with daisies in his hand, bumbling out lines of poetry in public, and producing boxes of chocolate as bribes to win a woman's affections. Ever notice that the women in the modern movies always go off with the guy who got the bloody lip, not with the one who won the fight?

## HOW TO MEET THE WOMAN OF YOUR DREAMS

"Do what you love," says Anne Sorock. Bars have probably worked for millions, but a better way is to get out there and do what you love to do. If that's rock climbing, great, join a local rock climbing club and network. Whether it's gardening, skiing, swimming, or cooking, there are classes you can take and clubs you can join where you'll meet people who have this common interest. C. S. Lewis wrote: "Friendship must be about something, even if it were only an enthusiasm for dominoes or white mice.... When the two people who thus discover that they are on the same secret road are of different sexes, the friendship which arises between them will very easily pass—may pass in the first half-hour—into erotic love."[16]

# Women Aren't Attracted to Metro-Sexuals

Urban sophisticates losing their masculine traits—the males who know how to accessorize—now have their own language in fashion circles. "Manties" are all the rage with these half-men; the new word is, of course, a contraction

# Women's Top Five Tips for the Manly Romantic

- **Too Much Is Too Much:** The age-old advice is to make the person you're pursuing want more. Women do this by playing hard to get. Anne Sorock, who runs a nonprofit called The Frontier Lab that does marketing research for various companies, says, "We want a man with depth; not just a Rambo." She says a man should leave a woman wanting to "know more."

- **Use a Touch of Humor:** Humor is huge, said all the women asked. Humor shows confidence. With humor you have to go out on a limb and be daring. Just be careful not to be crass or insulting.

- **Be Handy:** An old Canadian television comedy called "The Red and Green Show" used to advise men: "If the ladies don't find you handsome, they should at least find you handy." Every woman interviewed for this book said men should know how to fix electronics, change flat tires, and so on. And that they shouldn't brag about being able to do these things, but should just take care of the task in a manly, stoic way.

- **Drop the One-liners:** One-liners are over-rated, said every woman interviewed. So then, when meeting a woman, how can a man present himself quickly so she won't think he's just another jerk? With a romantic gesture or a short, funny anecdote, said the women interviewed.

- **Remember to Wash:** There should only be dirt under your nails when you're actually splitting wood. Your breath shouldn't smell like a roadside ditch, your clothes shouldn't have sweat stains on them, and your cologne must be manly, but not so strong that it floods a room. Think James Bond. He's fighting international crime syndicates one minute and looking debonair in a tux the next.

of "man" and "panties" and defines silky, revealing undergarments for metro-sexuals—how they keep their manhood literally in the right place is hard to say. Metro-sexuals also have "mandals," "mewelry," "murses," "mantyhose," and "mankinis." The *Wall Street Journal* recently reported that the Oxford English Dictionary is even considering including these words in the lexicon.[18] Nevertheless, now that you're aware of these words, don't use them. A real man wouldn't use them except in a joke. Most of the women interviewed for this book said they'll be friends with metro-sexuals, but they don't find them sexy.

> **MAN FACT**
> Clark Gable was into fancy sports cars. So Carole Lombard, on their first official date in 1936, gave him an old, beat-up Model T Ford painted white with red hearts all over it. She also had it delivered with a note saying, "You're driving me crazy."[17]

## Back When Men Were Men

Instead of emulating some emasculated pop-culture icon (despite what Hollywood often characterizes, women still love masculine gentlemen), look back to when men were allowed to be men. Humphrey Bogart's character Rick in Casablanca is the epitome of a man. He's confident, stoic, sophisticated, not showy, crass, or loaded with cheap boyishness and even cheaper lines. He's secure and debonair, but not cocky or narcissistic. He's painfully in love with a woman he can't have but is a man about it. In other words, it's not your pick-up line, but your demeanor that counts. Bogart's character is wildly inviting, even mysterious, which leaves women wanting to know more. This is precisely what most women want.

In Casablanca, here's how he breaks off a relationship that just isn't working:

**Yvonne:** Where were you last night?

**Rick:** That's so long ago, I don't remember.

**Yvonne:** Will I see you tonight?

**Rick:** I never make plans that far ahead.

## What's Romantic?

What a woman sees as romantic depends on where she is in life; for example, one wise woman who has two kids and works a time-consuming job said, "Cleaning the house and fixing a romantic dinner while bringing me a nice chardonnay while I am sitting in front of the fireplace reading a book." Meanwhile a woman just out of college said, "A man who takes me out and only looks at me." True to form, every woman interviewed for this section did say something different. But the theme was the same: romance is doing the unexpected gesture, a physical statement that lets the woman in your heart know how much you appreciate her and how sexy and special she is.

# How to Set a Table to Impress

1. Above the plate from left to right: Bread plate with butter knife (top left of dinner plate); coffee cup (top right of dinner plate); water glass; wine glass; liqueur glass.

2. Tableware from left to right: Salad fork; dinner fork; dessert fork; dinner plate with salad or soup bowl on it; knife; small spoon; soup spoon.

3. The napkin can be placed in the water glass, folded on the dinner plate, or beside the flatware on the left.

Such things are particularly romantic when there is some effort involved in lighting up her life and some sacrifice to your life.

Another woman put it this way: the ultimate romantic man has "sexy eyes, a warm smile, a good sense of humor, a quick wit, a high intellect, a fun spirit, and is a lover of adventure." But then she smiled and said, "Just kidding. Actually, the single most important approach a man can do to make a woman feel romantic, is to show her his admiration, respect, trust, and love. Women function much more on a cerebral level. When we perceive the man does not have any hidden agenda and that he truly wants us as human beings, most of us women respond beautifully."

"I agree," said another woman, "It's not flowers and candy, as they are superficial. Mind you, it's still a nice afterthought, but certainly not the essence. You can be showered with gifts and still not feel the way you would want to feel. For women it is emotional and cerebral. Anything that can touch us that way works. I hate to say it, but we are truly sappy. And if men were half as smart as women, they would have figured that out a long time ago, and then acted on it."

## HOW TO LOOK AT WOMEN

In the eyes! You'll find it a lot easier to talk to any woman if you look her in the eyes. This is what women do when they speak to someone. Men, when their eyes aren't wandering, tend to look at a person's mouth. That's fine, but concentrate on her eyes without looking intense. Look away casually, as you would normally do, but when you bring your eyes back around to her, go right to her eyes.

Many of the women interviewed for this section said that the way a man looks at a woman is half the battle. Women said they feel romance from a man who looks at them softly, yet intently, in their eyes, concentrates on what they're saying and gives them the feeling that at times they are the only one in the world who counts.

## HOW TO TALK TO WOMEN

One woman interviewed explained, "One thing would be to actually listen with interest when a woman speaks, showing respect and appreciation. Have you noticed that men tend to hear approximately every other word?" Another said, "To hear what a woman's needs are is rather simple: If you hear what she says it becomes so much easier to satisfy her." Ask an innocent question. Then listen, keep your eyes above her neck, and reply with wit and warmth.

## HOW TO SAY GOODBYE

"With a sweet memory of you," said one woman I asked. Leave something—a card, a poem, a gift—in a place they'll find it the first evening after you've left on a business trip. It'll pay more dividends than diamond earrings.

## HOW TO SAY WELCOME BACK

Make a big deal of homecomings, but don't do too good of a job taking care of things. You want them to feel as needed as they really are. Tell them you can't do it without them.

# Seven Ways to Say, "You Are Beautiful":

**Spanish:** "Usted es hermosa." (oo-sted ess er-mo-sa)

**Portuguese:** "Você é bonita." (vo-say eh boo-nee-ta)

**French:** "Vous êtes belle." (voo zayt bel)

**Italian:** "Siete bella." (see-ay-tay beh-la)

**German:** "Sie sind schön." (zee zint shurn)

**Japanese:** "Anata wa utsu ku shii." (anata-wa-utsu-ku-she)

**Chinese:** "Ni hen mei." (knee-hen-may)

## HOW TO STAY ON A WOMAN'S MIND

Remember the old-fashioned post office, all towns still have one. Go there and send a letter or even a post card when you're away. Yes, call, text message, and email too, but send the letter. Put a poem in it—no matter how bad or cheesy—or just a funny anecdote, just let her know she's on your mind.

## HOW TO MAKE AN ENTRANCE

It's easy to forget about the entrance, but it may be the only time all night she really looks at you. Dress well. Control your image as much as she does hers. Move with care. Keep your back straight and be a man. Show up with flare. Ring her doorbell and lighten the mood by being a little over the top. Whatever you do, do it intentionally.

## HOW TO MAKE WOMEN SMILE

Self-effacing stories that are endearing, such as an anecdote of how you tried to help an old lady across the street who was waiting for the bus, will not only make her smile, but will tell her something about your good character. Be witty, not sarcastic; light, not derisive. Whenever you don't know what to say, tell a short, true story about something that happened to you earlier that day or a related and light anecdote that's related to something raised in the conversation. When you begin telling a story you'll find you're speaking easily and well, because the narrative takes over.

## HOW TO BUY CANDY

Find a knowledgeable salesman and ask where the chocolate came from and why it was made the way it was. If you can tell a woman you bought fine Belgium chocolate from Leonidas, Neuhaus, Godiva, or Nirvana because their famous pralines are still made by hand in small shops using original equipment, and that this particular flavor is made only in the spring with fresh hazelnut and was impossible to find, you'll give her an impression of you she'll never relinquish.

## HOW TO BUY FLOWERS

Flower arrangement is actually a Japanese art Samurai used to master. But few have the time to know what flowers are perfect for each season and event. Find a local shop that delivers, where the florist has time to talk. Tell the sales person what you're sending flowers for in a revealing way, so they'll be personally involved in the arrangement. Roses are good, but the second time a woman gets roses from you, she'll be half as impressed.

## HOW TO SERENADE A FAIR LADY

The custom of serenading dates back to the Renaissance or before, but it's thankfully dead outside of rare Hollywood appearances. However, it still works. Just make sure she's not the type who deplores being the center of public attention and chose a song even you can sing. Unless you have an outstanding voice, use a little self-effacing comedy.

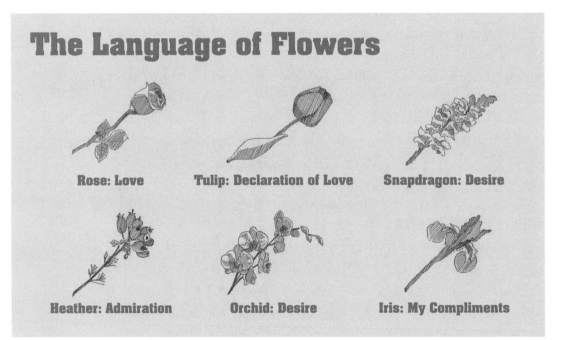

# The Language of Flowers

**Rose: Love**

**Tulip: Declaration of Love**

**Snapdragon: Desire**

**Heather: Admiration**

**Orchid: Desire**

**Iris: My Compliments**

> **MAN FACT**
> In Japan, women give men the cards and candy on Valentine's Day.

## HOW TO DO VALENTINE'S DAY

The first recorded association of Valentine's Day with romantic love is found in Geoffrey Chaucer's *Parlement of Foules* ("For this was on seynt Volantynys day Whan euery bryd comyth there to chese his make.") Mark February 14 on your calendar and plan something simple or intricate, just make sure you make her feel special and let her know she rules your heart. The U.S. Greeting Card Association estimates that about one billion valentines cards are sent each year worldwide—only Christmas has more cards sent. The association also estimates that women purchase 85 percent of all valentines, which shows they're making up for a lot of fools.

## 10 MOST CHIVALROUS GESTURES

- **Open the Door for Her:** This should be a habit, not something you have to think about.
- **Help Her into the Car:** There is something very masculine about a man who makes an effort to help a woman into a car, onto a train….
- **Get a Chair for Her:** When you take her to dinner, pull out a chair for her and push it in.
- **Hang Up Her Coat:** This is an endearing thing to do and provides an opportunity for physical contact.
- **If She Stands, Get Up:** This used to be reflexive, but today men don't bother.
- **Carry Stuff for Her:** No matter how successful, every woman loves the notion of a masculine man carrying heavy things for her.

# CARY GRANT
# 1904-1986

*"To succeed with the opposite sex, tell her you're impotent. She can't wait to disprove it."*

—CARY GRANT

He was born "Archibald Alec Leach" in 1904. Never did a name more poorly suit a man. He was raised in Horfield, England, a working-class neighborhood that literally translates to "filthy open land." His father placed his mother in a mental institution when he was ten years old. She was never to come out. His father told him she'd gone on a "long holiday." He was in his thirties when he discovered his mother alive, still living in an institutionalized care facility.

He acted up and was expelled from grammar school. He joined the "Bob Pender stage troupe" and thereby made his first trip to the U.S. as a stilt walker in 1920. He decided to stay in the U.S. After some hard-earned success on and off Broadway, he went to Hollywood in 1931, while still in his twenties. He changed his name to "Cary Lockwood." Paramount Pictures didn't like "Lockwood" and rechristened him "Cary Grant." A star was born. In 1933 he starred alongside Mae West in "She Done Him Wrong" and "I'm No Angel." But after Paramount put Grant in a series of apathetic films until 1936, he signed with Columbia Pictures.

Grant began to star in screwball comedies, such as, "Arsenic and Old Lace" with Priscilla Lane and "Bringing Up Baby" with Katherine Hepburn. Known today as a lady's man, he actually did more comedy than drama. In 1940 he co-starred in "The Philadelphia Story" with Hepburn and James Stuart and his debonair persona was solidified. Howard Hawks said Grant was "so far the best that there isn't anybody to be compared to him."[19] Alfred Hitchcock said Grant was "the only actor I ever loved in my whole life."[20]

In 1940, when Adolf Hitler was threatening England, Grant volunteered to join the Royal Navy, but, at thirty-six, he was over the age requirement. During the war years, Grant donated entire salaries from several movies to British war charities. He was accused of sidestepping the war, but was vindicated. Throughout his life his sexual orientation was questioned. He fought the unsubstantiated rumors. In 1980, when Chevy Chase joked that Grant was homosexual, Grant sued him for slander. They settled out of court.[21] In a 2004 interview for Turner Classic Movies, Grant's third wife, Betsy Drake, said, "Why would I believe that Cary was homosexual when we were busy f---ing?"[22]

Though he was his generation's definition of sex appeal, Grant was a poor romantic. He married his first wife, Virginia Cherrill, on February 10, 1934; they divorced thirteen months later. Grant then married the well-to-do Barbara Hutton. They were unkindly nicknamed "Cash and Cary." They divorced in 1945. Grant wouldn't take penny from Hutton and they remained lifelong friends. Grant next married actress Betsy Drake in 1949. He appeared with her in two films. They lasted until 1962. His fourth marriage, to actress Dyan Cannon—who was thirty-three years younger than Grant—took place in 1965. At the age of sixty-two he fathered a daughter with her. Cannon left him in December 1966 and custody fights over their daughter went on for a decade. Ever the optimist, Grant married again in 1981 to British hotel PR agent Barbara Harris—she was forty-seven years younger than Grant. Harris was by his side when he died.

**MAN FACT**

Cowboys aren't too manly to read poetry. Cowboy poetry was born in Elko, Nevada, in 1985. Hal Cannon, a musician and the author of a dozen Western books, with money from the National Endowment for the Arts, organized a "Cowboy Poet Gathering." From that event, cowboy poetry began to gather momentum as rhyming cowboys emerged from bunkhouses all over the West. Although many had been writing for years, it seems they were embarrassed to admit they liked a sissy thing like poetry—now you know why "Brokeback Mountain" touched a nerve.

- **Help Children:** Show children how to do something, talk to them, not down, and take a lively interest in them.

- **Be Good to Her Mother:** No matter what a woman says about her mother, she still wants you to be a gentlemen to her.

- **Restrain Your Temper:** No matter how rude a waiter is or how obnoxious someone is in a theatre, approach them with humor and show them by example what they should be doing.

- **Defend Her Against All:** Stand up for her. Always take her side in public.

# PART 7

## PAL

*"A friend loveth at all times, and a brother is born for adversity."*
—PROVERBS 17:1

**W**here would we be without pals? Could Trey Parker have created the comedy *South Park* if he hadn't met Matt Stone in college? Would quarterback Steve Young have won three Super Bowl rings with the San Francisco 49ers without the receiver Jerry Rice? Had Bill Hewlett and David Packard not teamed up in a one-car garage in the late 1930s to complete a fellowship, would we have had Hewlett-Packard's innovations? Where would the world be if Paul Allen and Bill Gates didn't happen to be childhood friends who teamed up to begin Microsoft? Or what if Steve Jobs hadn't had Steve Wozniak's genius to start up what became Apple? Would we have anything like Google if Sergey Brin and Larry Page hadn't hit it off at Stanford? Would John Lennon's cynicism have inhibited his most creative works without Paul McCartney's optimism? Could Mick Jagger have become a rock star without the quiet fortitude of Keith Richards?

We need our pals. And not just for great accomplishments. Friends keep us sane, they keep us grounded, they laugh with us, not as us—as you grow older you realize how big a thing that is—they share our triumphs, and are there like deep foundations to help us weather failures and tragedies.

Friendship, though an abstract thing, is so important to us even the scientists have extolled its merits. For example, numerous studies indicate friendship can make us healthier, and even increase our lifespan.[1] Granted, studies on friendship should generally be treated as intoxicated strangers: they may be interesting, but they're just as likely full of it. One recent study determined that the number of pals someone has in school is an indicator of how much money they'll make.[2] ("Each extra school friend added 2% to the salary," reported the BBC.) Another study linked the number of friends we have to our "brain density."[3] Yet another says it found a link between the number of friends we have and how much physical exercise we get.[4] For all the absurdity, though, such studies agree on a crucial point: we need friends, and we need them for more than just socializing. Friends stand behind us, help us accomplish our goals, and—if they're the right kind of friend—help us become who we should be.

The trouble is, we're losing our pals. A 2006 study published in the *American Sociological Review* determined that 25 percent of Americans have no close friends. Even worse, while in 1985 the average guy had four pals, by 2006 the average man had just two. "You usually don't see that kind of big social change in a couple of decades," said the study's co-author Lynn Smith-Lovin, professor of sociology at Duke University in Durham, North Carolina.[5] So why are we losing our friends?

Lots of factors are affecting our ability to make and keep pals.

First of all, once widely accepted manly events are now inhibited by political correctness. Tuesday night card games with the guys, men-only social clubs, hunting trips, and other such activities used to be viewed as necessities so that men could be men. People used to appreciate the reality of the differences between the sexes, and men and women enjoyed separate activities. No one considered men sexist or chauvinistic for wanting to shoot pool or go fishing with other men and without the ladies present— any more than the men would have dreamed of whining about the ladies getting together for tea or quilting bees.

> " Without friends no one would choose to live, though he had all other goods. "
>
> ARISTOTLE, *NICOMACHEAN ETHICS*

**MAN FACT**

The best way to drink with pals isn't to thump down a bottle of Jack Daniel's and ask, "On the rocks or straight up?" That's the quickest way to get drunk with pals. Instead, see if someone knows how to make something you don't know how to mix. Try a martini, old-fashioned, or even a typhoon (see the "Gentleman" section of this book for the recipes). Making these drinks is an art. People have their own techniques and tastes, so try something new. Or maybe try a new micro-brew or wine. Learn how to make the mixed drink, or learn facts about the beer or wine. Then drink slowly. Alcohol should be savored, not gulped. Do it this way and drinking will become a bonding experience, not a scene from the 2009 film *The Hangover*.

But these days men-only gatherings are considered politically incorrect. Popular culture rarely portrays manly get-togethers as mature events. Instead they're depicted as frat-house flashbacks. Sitcom writers seem to think "man rooms" (which they've deemed "man caves") are only for men who secretly want to be John Belushi in the 1978 flick *Animal House*. In general, men are treated as adolescents, needing to be under the watchful eye of adults (read: women) at all times.

This is a philosophical shift. Men, to be men, once had to man up to crises, to work every day for the welfare of their family, to take on real responsibility. Those few times when they got away to hunting camp were earned—they were even the mature expression of their manliness. A man who didn't shoulder responsibility wasn't manly. A man who over-drank or went on the dole was embarrassed because he put his manliness in question. None of that is as true as it once was. Now the very definition of manliness is murky, and that has affected male friendships. Men rarely have the chance to speak only to men, out of the presence of women, that is also negatively affecting the state of male friendship.

This isn't to say men can't be friends with women, or that we shouldn't enjoy co-ed activities—we should. But there's an important place for

## MAN FACT

Women can certainly be a part of a group of pals if they don't censor the manliness from the conversation or make the scene all about themselves. For example, in 1955, after a long party in Las Vegas in which Humphrey Bogart, Frank Sinatra, Judy Garland, David Niven, and others had a hell of time, Lauren Bacall surveyed the damage and declared, "You look like a ... rat pack."[6] Legend has it this comment prompted them to form the "Rat Pack." Sinatra became "Pack Leader" and Bacall "Den Mother." The group famously became an exclusive group of pals—gals included.

men-only activities (just like women should have their girl time), and sacrificing this to political correctness cheapens our friendships and is causing us to lose profound connections with our pals.

Man's never-ending confusion with women aside, men today are also letting egotism kill their friendships. Maybe this is some kind of Hollywood "action-hero syndrome." Today we're told to be John Wayne, 007, or maybe some sappy, chick-flick metro-man. We're told this so much that our sidekicks have become not just expendable but often nonexistent. Have you noticed how unnecessary Robin has become in the latest Batman movies? Bruce Willis only had paper-thin characters to help him in the *Die Hard* movies. Spiderman has his villains to fight, but is really on his own. There are exceptions. The cop team—like in the *Lethal Weapon* movies and many more—is a Hollywood formula, but even these cop teams are rarely two different types of people; more often they're two one-dimensional parts of the same two-dimensional character. Such flimsy facsimiles of male heroes don't inspire friendship.

Perhaps this is a big part of the reason why study after study is finding that our society is becoming increasingly narcissistic.[7] If we're not careful in this culture, we can become obsessed with ourselves. This makes us bad friends, as nobody wants to hang out with a guy who can't shut up about his own accomplishments, or who's completely caught up in how great he is. When so many of us are busy looking after number one, our friendships become more and more one-sided and eventually fade away altogether.

In this ego-centric universe it's easy to forget that the star quarterback is useless without a receiver who can sprint and catch. It's easy to overlook the players who get on base before the homerun hero comes to bat, or the corner man giving the champ instructions, or the player who got the assist. And this tendency goes far beyond sports. Just consider that the best man at a wedding is forgotten as soon as he finishes speaking. Friends, pals, confidants, amigos, co-pilots, and first mates right the ship while the captain sleeps, tell famous men when they're wrong, and are steady when the political winds change, yet rarely get credit. Sergeants, editors, agents, coaches, managers, teachers, parents, priests, and senseis are somewhere behind every man who has ever achieved anything, but they typically remain anonymous. And we forget these people in our own lives, too. When you accomplish a goal or make it somewhere in your life, do you take the time to turn around and see who helped you get there?

So look around. Who has stood behind you?

Who has told you when you're being stupid and picked you up when you're down? Who has laughed with you? Who has slapped you on the back when you've really achieved something? Who are the pals who shared ballgames, a beer or two, and life-changing advice? They shouldn't be taken for granted. Even the Bible says we need pals: "Two are better than one; because they have a good reward for their labor. For if they fall, the one will lift up his fellow: but woe to him that is alone when he falleth; for he hath not another to help him up."[8]

Finally, the mobility of today's workforce plays a big role in taking us away from our friends. People are no longer tied to a neighborhood or town. We move. According to the U.S. Census Bureau, 37.1 million people moved in the U.S. in 2009. Of those, 67.3 percent stayed within the same county, 17.2 percent moved to a different county in the same state, 12.6 percent moved to a new state, and 2.9 percent moved internationally. The Census Bureau says, "Nearly 3/4 of the U.S. population moves an aver-

## MAN FACT

The one place we do see the best man at a wedding is at the wedding toast. Movies often use the best man's speech for a cheap laugh by having the old pal say something crass. Don't do that. The best toast you can give is one that's not just honest and from the heart, but also one that characterizes the groom as the man he tries to be, the man he is at his best, the man his bride has fallen in love with.

age of once every 5 years."[9] When we're not with our pals, our friendships tend to fade away. Social media can help keep friends in touch, but "Facebook friends" are a paper-thin wrapping over very little at all unless backed up by real card games, ball games, fishing trips, or whatever blows your hair back. (Some studies even indicate that Facebook friendships can be unhealthy. A study titled "Narcissism on Facebook: Self-Promotional and Anti-Social Behavior"[10] that was published in the journal *Personality and Individual Differences* established a link between the number of Facebook friends someone has and how narcissistic they are.)

So how do we keep the pals we've got and make new friends? In his 1960 book *The Four Loves*, C. S. Lewis argued that without a shared experience, a passion for a hobby or really anything that interests us that we share with another, a friendship doesn't grow or last. Friendships that aren't about something lasting are shallow and easily ended. This is why some high school or college pals fade away after graduation, as the shared experience of school is over.

Friendships need to be about something other than ourselves. C. S. Lewis noted that while lovers are often pictured looking at each other, friends are always seen looking in the same direction, as if they're headed for the same goal. So keep your friendships in constant repair by looking for passions in common. And remember, the more solid the passion, the more solid (and lasting) the friendship is likely to be. A mutual passion can be as simple as stamp collecting, as adventurous as rock climbing, or as studious as a shared scholarly interest.

The next step is to make plans for these activities. A bowling night (if that's your thing) or a Saturday ball game if you both root for the same team … whatever it is, think ahead and make plans.

After all, even in this social media age we need pals to tell us when we err, to congratulate us when we succeed, and to pick us up when we fall. We need friends to help us be the best men we can be. This why Lewis wrote that true friendship grows from virtue—is in fact "the school of virtue"—because the two people are striving together to become the best versions of themselves.

# How to Make a Pal

Lost pals aren't easily replaced, but they must be. The English author Samuel Johnson (1709–1784) put this best: "If a man does not make new acquaintances, as he advances through life, he will soon find himself left alone. A man, Sir, should keep his friendship in constant repair."[11] Finding new pals as we move and mature is all about following our passions. Whether you're into wine, cigars, fly-fishing, or the Boston Red Sox, here are five things to do.

- **Join a Club:** Older guys get together to play soccer, chess, and softball, as well as to bird watch and shoot birds—this way you'll meet people who are into the same things.
- **Leave Your House:** As men get older they're less inclined to go to the bar or a barbeque.
- **Try Something New:** If your life seems smaller, it just might have shrunk. You're never too old to try a new thing. If you like it, you just might make friends along the way.
- **Travel:** Go to the place you grew up or, better yet, go wherever your bloodline originally came from. Ask questions and introduce yourself. Friendships will follow.

- **Renew Old Acquaintances:** Reach back into the past and see what happened to all those guys. You might be surprised who you find.

## The Greats on Friendship

**Aristotle:** In *Rhetoric*, Aristotle (384–322 BC) used the term *philía* to define friendship as platonic, virtuous love. Aristotle said philía is "wanting for someone what one thinks good, for his sake and not for one's own, and being inclined, so far as one can, to do such things for him."[13] In ancient texts, philos denoted a general type of love, used for love between family, friends, and combined with a desire or enjoyment of an activity. Aristotle defined this characteristic to show the importance of true friendship between pals.

**Cicero:** In the first century BC, Marcus Tullius Cicero (106–143 BC) took Aristotle's philía a bit further. He wrote a book titled *On Friendship* after the death of his close friend Titus Pomponius Atticus. Cicero determined that in order to have a true friendship you must be honest, as this permits

## Best Friends Creed

I will stand up for my pal, whether he's right or wrong.

I will privately tell my friend when he is wrong.

I will let no woman come between us, but will be a gentleman with all.

I will be honest in all things, though never judgmental.

I will pick my pal up when he's down.

I will watch my pal's back.

I will not gossip about my pal's shortfalls.

I will be loyal.

I will keep the friendship alive with common interests.

I will be mirthful, portentous, and only occasionally doleful.

someone to trust you completely. Cicero found that we must do things for a pal without the expectation of reward. He also believed if a friend is about to make a mistake, you shouldn't compromise your own moral code to help him; instead, you must explain why you think he is wrong. Cicero thought that without virtue, true friendship couldn't exist.

**C. S. Lewis:** C. S. Lewis (1898–1963) noted modern society's deficit of friendship in his 1960 book *The Four Loves*: "To the Ancients, Friendship seemed the happiest and most fully human of all loves; the crown of life and the school of virtue. The modern world, in comparison, ignores it. We admit of course that besides a wife and family a man needs a few 'friends.' But the very tone of the admission, and the sort of acquaintanceships which those who make it would describe as 'friendships,' show clearly that what they are talking about has very little to do with that Philía which Aristotle classified among the virtues or that Amicitia on which Cicero wrote a book." C. S. Lewis was using a Christian perspective to again give meaning to the views Aristotle once outlined for Ancient Greeks and Cicero pontificated to Romans. Like Cicero, Lewis also argued that true friendship grows from virtue and shared passions.

## Best 10 Business Friendships

- **Thomas Edison and J. P. Morgan:** In the 1870s and 1880s, Morgan and others financed Edison's achievements.

> **MAN FACT**
> George Washington said, "A slender acquaintance with the world must convince every man, that actions, not words, are the true criterion of the attachment of friends; and that the most liberal professions of good-will are very far from being the surest marks of it."[14]

- **Bill Hewlett and David Packard:** They teamed up in 1939 to form Hewlett-Packard.
- **James D. Watson and Francis Crick:** They co-discovered DNA in 1953.
- **Gordon Moore and Bob Noyce:** In 1968 they started Intel.
- **Eugene Kleiner and Tom Perkins:** In 1972 they started Kleiner Perkins.
- **Paul Allen and Bill Gates:** In 1975 they started what became Microsoft.
- **Steve Jobs and Steve Wozniak:** In 1976 they began Apple.
- **Herbert Boyer and Robert Swanson:** In 1976 they launched Genetech.
- **Len Bosack and Sandy Lerner:** In 1984 they started Cisco.
- **Sergey Brin and Larry Page:** In 1998 they founded Google.

# Be a Pal

A pal should know when his friends are up or down. When they're up—they've gotten the promotion, won an award, had a child—congratulate them. When they're down, quietly help them. The manly way to do this is to help and then never talk about it again, not to him or anyone else. If he wants to talk, he will. In the 1954 classic *Magnificent Obsession*, Rock Hudson, a spoiled playboy, learns a new philosophy that changes his life after he causes a tragedy. He learns that helping others without letting them know you've helped them builds character. It's an empowering idea. In this case, your pal can know, but no one else.

# Best Pals of All Time

## Meriwether Lewis and William Clark

We learn in grade school that President Thomas Jefferson commissioned the Corps of Discovery in 1803 to explore the Louisiana Purchase. We also learn that U.S. Army Captain Meriwether Lewis and Captain William Clark led the mission. However, most don't learn that when Jefferson chose Lewis to lead the expedition, Lewis then selected Clark as his partner and insisted that Clark be treated as his co-captain.

Lewis had joined the Army in 1794. He'd served in the Ohio Valley and the Old Northwest Territory, where he became friends with Clark. In 1801, Lewis was appointed as President Thomas Jefferson's private secretary. A few years later, Jefferson chose Lewis to be the commander of the expedition.

Meanwhile, Clark had served in the U.S. Army for four years—participating in the campaigns of General Anthony Wayne in the Northwest Territory—before resigning his commission in 1796. Because of the Army's seniority system, Clark received a second lieutenant's commission instead of a captaincy when he joined Lewis. But he and Lewis chose to conceal this from the members of the expedition. Lewis insisted on referring to his friend as "Captain Clark."

Together, Lewis and Clark hired trappers and other woodsmen to join the party. Their friendship helped glue the group together as they explored west up the Missouri River and finally over the Rocky Mountains, looking for a northwest passage to the Pacific Ocean. The equality of their friendship was critical, because though Lewis and Clark had a shared love for the outdoors, they had very different personalities. Lewis, a scholar of cartography and natural science, was said to be moody and introverted. In contrast, historians say Clark was a gregarious extrovert with natural leadership abilities. Like two friends should, they made up for each other's weaknesses and complemented each other's strengths. Though they forded rivers, met undiscovered Native American tribes, and had to hunt for their food across vast expanses of high plains, snow-capped mountains, and dense forests, they only lost one man along the way. Sergeant Charles Floyd died on August 20, 1804, from what is generally thought to have been a ruptured appendix. The tight and complementary friendship between Lewis and Clark is a central reason why they were able to cross a continent and come back with only the loss of one member of their expedition.

## Larry Bird and Magic Johnson

Larry Bird and Earvin "Magic" Johnson were fierce rivals, but they developed a strong friendship off the court. There's even a Broadway play (*Magic/Bird*) about their combative path to friendship. In the 1980s, the Boston Celtics and the Los Angeles Lakers dominated basketball. In the book *When the Game Was Ours*, Bird says, "We fought like hell for the same thing for 12 years, and through it all, the respect was always there. For the rest of our lives, we're connected. I used to mind. I don't anymore."[15]

Johnson once explained, "We're so competitive anyway that there was a dislike there. I even hated him more because I knew he could beat me."[16] But then in 1985, a shoe company asked Johnson and Bird to tape a commercial together in French Lick, Indiana—Bird's hometown. At that point they'd yet to even have a conversation. During the shoot, the two didn't speak to each other. But after the shoot they had lunch together at Bird's house. "His mom gave me the biggest hug and hello, and right then she had me," Johnson says. "Then Larry and I sat down for lunch, and I tell you, we figured out we're so much alike. We're both from the Midwest, we grew up poor, our families [are] everything to us, basketball is everything to us. So that changed my whole outlook on Larry Bird."[17]

After the lunch the friendship didn't grow until they'd retired. Then, on November 7, 1991, Johnson called Bird and told him he had been diagnosed with HIV. Bird has said he'll never forget the moment he got the call. In a new adversity, they became close pals.

## Thomas Jefferson and John Adams

In these partisan times it's worth remembering the two who got the fight started: Thomas Jefferson and John Adams. Jefferson and Adams met in the Continental Congress and worked together on the committee to draft the Declaration of Independence. They grew closer in Europe while serving as ambassadors to France and England. John and his wife Abigail consoled Jefferson over the loss of his wife.

Joseph Ellis wrote about Adams and Jefferson in his book *Founding Brothers*: "They were an incongruous pair, but everyone seemed to argue that history had made them into a pair. The incongruities leapt out for all to see: Adams, the short, stout, candid-to-a-fault New Englander; Jefferson, the tall, slender, elegantly elusive Virginian; Adams, the highly combustible, ever combative, mile-a-minute talker, whose favorite form of conversation was an argument; Jefferson, the always cool and self-contained enigma, who regarded debate and argument as violations of the natural harmonies he heard inside his own head."[18]

Their political differences became apparent in the 1790s as they served in President George Washington's cabinet. Jefferson wanted a weak federal government. Adams believed a strong federal government was necessary. In 1796 and 1800, Jefferson and Adams competed for the presidency. Adams won the first time. Jefferson became Adams' vice president, as the person who had the second most electoral votes became vice president in those days. Jefferson could be vindictive. He secretly hired newspaperman James Callender to defame the Adams administration. While on Jefferson's payroll, Callender wrote "The Prospect Before Us," a pamphlet that alleged political corruption in the Adams administration. Adams responded by using his newly passed Alien and Sedition Acts to prosecute Callender. The trial was presided over by Supreme Court Justice Samuel Chase, who was later impeached partly because of his handling of the Callender trial. Callender was jailed until the last day of the Adams administration.

Meanwhile, partly because of the unpopularity of the Alien and Sedition Acts, Jefferson beat Adams in the next presidential election. Afterwards, Jefferson and Adams didn't have a civil communication for twelve years.

After Benjamin Rush worked to reunite them, Adams finally wrote a letter to Jefferson on January 1, 1812. At first their correspondence was stiff, but after a while their letters became less formal. In a letter that John Adams wrote to Jefferson on July 15, 1813, Adams wrote: "You and I ought not to die, before We have explained ourselves to each other."[19]

They corresponded about a variety of topics, both personal and political. They disagreed on a lot. You can read their letters in the book *The Adams-Jefferson Letters* (University of North Carolina Press, 1988). After fifteen years of resumed friendship, on July 4, 1826, Jefferson and Adams died within hours of each other. Their deaths occurred on the fiftieth anniversary of the signing of the Declaration of Independence. On his deathbed Adams uttered his last words: "Thomas Jefferson survives." But Jefferson had actually died a few hours earlier.

# Lewis Addison Armistead and Winfield Scott Hancock

This epic friendship ended when one charged across a battlefield to break the other's line at Gettysburg. Lewis Addison Armistead (1817–1863) met Winfield Scott Hancock (1824–1886) in the U.S. Army. When the Civil War began, then-Captain Armistead was in command of a small garrison in San Diego. Armistead was from North Carolina. Hancock was a Pennsylvanian. With the war between the states declared, Armistead left to fight for his state. However, before Armistead left to join the Confederacy, accounts say a farewell party between Armistead and Hancock took place. That evening, Armistead is said to have put his hand on Hancock's shoulder and, in tears, told him, "Goodbye, you can never know what this has cost me."[20]

Armistead became a Confederate brigadier general. Hancock became a general for the Union. They both had distinguished careers during the war. But then they faced off in Gettysburg. Armistead's brigade arrived during the evening of July 2, 1863. The next day he charged a line held by his old friend Hancock. Armistead led his brigade towards the center of the Union line in what has become known as Pickett's Charge. Armistead led from the front. He was seen waving his hat from the tip of his saber. He reached the stonewall that was the charge's objective. The brigade went over the wall and got farther than any other—this event is sometimes referred to as the "High Water Mark of the Confederacy."

Nevertheless, the charge was quickly stopped by a Union counterattack. Armistead was shot three times just after crossing the wall, but his wounds were not believed to be mortal. He was taken to a Union field hospital. Armistead asked to speak to Hancock, but Hancock's responsibilities and his own wounds prevented him from seeing his old friend. Perhaps Hancock thought he had time. Tragically, he didn't. Armistead died on July 5 of "secondary fever and prostration."[21]

## C. S. Lewis and J. R. R. Tolkien

We would be poorer without the fantasy worlds—Narnia and Middle-Earth—these men inspired each other to create. In 1926, when they were both young professors, C. S. Lewis and J. R. R. Tolkien met at an Oxford faculty meeting. British author Colin Duriez explained in his 2003 book *Tolkien and C. S. Lewis: The Gift of Friendship* how these two authors met, found they had a shared love for mythical tales, and later pledged to bring

> **MAN FACT**
> President Ronald Reagan and Tip O'Neill, who was Speaker of the House from 1977 until 1987, would disagree during policy debates, but would exchange jokes afterward. When Reagan was shot, O'Neill visited his bedside.

such stories to the public. Tolkien and Lewis believed myth and legend could be used (as they had been throughout history) to make the complex battle between good and evil intelligible to a modern audience. They realized it was only recently that myths had been marginalized into children's tales. In this case they wanted to make the Christian Gospel relevant to even secular readers.

In 1936, after Tolkien had written the youth novel *The Hobbit*, they had a momentous conversation about their desire to bring such stories to a wider audience. During a walk in the grounds of Magdalen College, Tolkien explained to Lewis how to use the Gospel narratives in modern tales. Lewis soon was working on the Narnia series, *The Great Divorce*, and more; meanwhile, Lewis encouraged Tolkien to finish and publish the *Lord of the Rings* trilogy.

# Of Men and Nicknames

Nicknames can be passwords into an inner circle of friends. Using some must be earned. Even knowing some requires familiarity. Getting a nickname from close pals is a badge of honor. To close friends, for example, Congressman Mike Ross's nickname is "Click." Only his hunting pals use it. He earned the nickname by forgetting to load his rifle when he was on his first deer hunt. When he saw a big buck he aimed and pulled the trigger, but only heard "click." The buck ran off and the nickname stuck.

> **MAN FACT**
>
> Frank Sinatra lamented when Dean Martin died: "Too many times I've been asked to say something about friends who are gone—this is one of the hardest.... Dean was my brother, not through blood, but through choice.... He has been like the air I breathe, always there, always close by."[22]

More often, nicknames are a little more public. They can even be tokens of esteem. They're earned. They say something about us. A Special Forces officer I once interviewed was nicknamed "Moses." I thought it was because he was wise. He said, "No, you're thinking of Solomon. I'm called Moses because I once parted a black sea in Mogadishu with a shotgun. You know, before Blackhawk Down happened."

Some nicknames begin as passwords between pals before growing to replace given names. Eldrick Woods is Tiger Woods's real name. He was given the nickname "Tiger" by his father to remind him to fight for his dreams. This custom of nicknames has been going on a long time. Plato's real name was "Aristocles." The nickname "Platon" was given to the Ancient Greek philosopher by his wrestling coach, Ariston of Argos. It means "broad."

Sports are, of course, a major source of nicknames. Tom "Flash" Gordon earned his nickname when he burst on to the scene as a pitcher in 1989 at the age of twenty-one and went 17–9. The X-Games star Shaun White earned his nickname ("The Flying Tomato") due to his acrobatic moves and his long red hair. George Herman "Babe" Ruth grew so legendary we forgot his first name. In fact, he earned a lot of nicknames: "The Great Bambino," "The Sultan of Swat," "The Colossus of Clout," and simply "The Babe." Adam "Pacman" Jones received his nickname as a young child, when it was noted that he could drink his milk as fast as the video game character. (Due to legal troubles, Jones now wants to be known as "Adam Jones." So yes, we can also lose our hard-earned nicknames when we err.)

# On Man's Best Friend

The dog has always been "man's best friend." Even Homer thought so. In his ancient epic *The Odyssey*, Odysseus returns from twenty years away fighting the Trojans and then attempting to get home only to be thwarted by the gods. Odysseus comes back disguised as a beggar be-cause he wants to see if his wife, Penelope, has been faithful. When he shows up at his doorstep he finds his old hunting dog, Argos, waiting for him. The old dog recognizes him. Argos wags his tale but is too weak to rise. Odysseus, however, can't greet his beloved dog, as this would betray who he really is, so he walks right past Argos while quietly shedding a tear. As he enters his home, Argos dies alone. Homer included that scene to touch his readers' hearts. Now, more than two and a half millennia later, dogs are still some of man's best friends.

# Brotherhood of War

*"Wars may be fought with weapons, but they are won by men. It is the spirit of the men who follow and of the man who leads that gains that victory."*[23]
—GEORGE PATTON

War ferments a unique brotherhood among men, a bond as real today as it was when 300 Spartans stood together at Thermopylae. A heart-wrenching example took place in Iraq in April 2004

# The Rifleman's Creed

The Rifleman's Creed is worth pondering in a chapter on "Pals" because, like the relationships Samurai had with their swords, a rifle for a soldier is a friend that must be taken care of and understood.

---

*This is my rifle. There are many like it, but this one is mine. It is my life. I must master it as I must master my life. Without me my rifle is useless. Without my rifle, I am useless. I must fire my rifle true. I must shoot straighter than the enemy who is trying to kill me. I must shoot him before he shoots me. I will. My rifle and I know that what counts in war is not the rounds we fire, the noise of our burst, or the smoke we make. We know that it is the hits that count. We will hit.*

*My rifle is human, even as I am human, because it is my life. Thus, I will learn it as a brother. I will learn its weaknesses, its strengths, its parts, its accessories, its sights and its barrel. I will keep my rifle clean and ready, even as I am clean and ready. We will become part of each other.*

*Before God I swear this creed. My rifle and I are the defenders of my country. We are the masters of our enemy. We are the saviors of my life.*

*So be it, until victory is America's and there is no enemy.*

when U.S. Marine Corporal Jason Dunham sacrificed himself for his brothers in arms. On April 16, 2008, LTG William B. Caldwell IV wrote this letter of remembrance:

> Four years ago Corporal Jason Dunham did the unimaginable when an insurgent tossed a grenade into the middle of his unit. In a split second, he placed the welfare of his comrades above his own. Covering the grenade with his Kevlar helmet

and his body, he saved the lives of the Marines around him. Tragically, he died of his wounds eight days later. Jason's actions may come as a shock to us, but not to the people who knew him because they reflect the character of the man he was.

Jason was always concerned for others. He had extended his term of enlistment because he wanted to stay with his squad for their entire tour in combat. His good friend Lance Corporal Mark Dean said, "You're crazy, why would you do that?" Jason's response was: "I want to make sure everyone makes it home alive. I want to be sure you go home to your wife alive." Shortly before deploying to Iraq, Lance Corporal Dean was a little short on cash and Jason bought him a phone card so he could call his wife. From his first day in the Marines, Corporal Dunham stood out for his outstanding leadership abilities. One of his leaders, Staff Sergeant John Ferguson, said he showed "the kind of leadership where you're confident in your abilities and don't have to yell about it." A fervent patriot, his father, Dan Dunham, said, "Jason believed that all men on this earth should be free."[24]

# DAVID

"I am distressed for you, my brother Jonathan;
You have been very pleasant to me. Your love to me
was more wonderful than the love of women."[25]
— D A V I D

Most people know of David as the youth who killed the Philistine Goliath. But how many people know that David went on to become a king—in part because of his friendship with Jonathan, the son of Saul, king of Israel? This is one of the Bible's greatest stories of friendship. David and Jonathan were heroic figures of the ancient kingdom of Israel, and their story is recorded in the books of Samuel.

After David killed Goliath, he returned the giant's head to King Saul, where he met Jonathan, who had also been fighting the Philistines. The Bible describes their immediate bond: "Now it came about when [David] had finished speaking to Saul, that the soul of Jonathan was knit to the soul of David, and Jonathan loved him as himself…. Then Jonathan made a covenant with David because he loved him as himself. Jonathan stripped himself of the robe that was on him and gave it to David, with his armor, including his sword and his bow and his belt. So David went out wherever Saul sent him, and prospered; and Saul set him over the men of war."[26]

David enjoyed great success in the battles he fought, and Jonathan fought right alongside him. They became brothers in arms. Eventually Saul became alarmed as David's popularity grew. After one fierce battle, the women of Israel sang, "Saul has slain his thousands and David his ten thousands."

So Saul decided to kill David. Jonathan, learning of his father's plan, warned David to hide, and went to his father to plead for David's life. Saul agreed not to kill David, but soon changed his mind. David had to flee for his life. When Jonathan learned of this, he promised to speak again to his father. Saul did not take this well—he turned his fear and wrath on his own son, saying, "You son of a perverse, rebellious woman! Do I not know that you have chosen the son of Jesse to your own shame, and to the shame of your mother's nakedness?"[27] Saul was so angry he threw his spear at his son.

Jonathan went away shaken and fasted; finally, he went to David in the wilderness and told him that his father's mind could not be changed. As they parted ways, Jonathan reminded David of their great friendship, saying, "The LORD shall be between me and you, and between my descendants and your descendants, forever."

Jonathan was eventually slain in a battle against the Philistines, on Mount Gilboa, along with his two brothers Abinadab and Malchi-shua. When David learned of the death of his friend, he wept. David's mourning has carried through the generations. He cried, "I am distressed for you, my brother Jonathan; you have been very pleasant to me. Your love to me was more wonderful than the love of women."

The story of the friendship of David and Jonathan has been repeated through the ages. The sages characterized the relationship between Jonathan and David in the following Mishnah: "Whenever love depends on some selfish end, when the end passes away, the love passes away; but if it does not depend on some selfish end, it will never pass away. Which love depended on a selfish end? This was the love of Amnon and Tamar. And which did not depend on a selfish end? This was the love of David and Jonathan."[28]

# PART 8

*"Those who nourish the smaller parts will become small men.*
*Those who nourish the greater parts will become great men."*
—MENCIUS, CHINA, 3RD CENTURY BC[1]

Today, philosophy is viewed as an arid, academic discipline. When we think of a philosopher, we think of a crotchety professor in a tweed jacket, shuffling about the university muttering to himself. His hair is tousled and if he looked up (he never does), you'd be hard-pressed to find his beady eyes behind his thick-paned spectacles.

It wasn't always so. Some of the greatest men were philosophers: Aristotle; Alexander the Great; Cicero; Thomas More; Benjamin Franklin. Such men knew philosophy wasn't a discipline reserved for socially inept eggheads, but is rather the basis of a man's belief system. Philosophy is based on the Ancient Greek word "philosophia," which means "love of wisdom." In the Classical age, philosophy wasn't seen as a dogmatic set of rules, but was rather designed to teach a man to think, to attain wisdom through truth. Classical men studied philosophy near the end of their educations to tie studies together and to thereby give them moderate, reasoning approaches to life.

Consider how Cicero's philosophy guided him after he witnessed the bloody assassination of Julius Caesar, who many Romans feared was becoming a tyrant. At sixty-two years old, Cicero, a Roman attorney, senator, and philosopher, suddenly found himself in a power vacuum with Mark Antony, a man eager to take Caesar's place and become dictator of Rome. Cicero had to decide whether to flee Rome to one of his country villas or fight to restore the Roman Constitution. When Brutus, the Roman senator who led the assassination, lifted his bloody knife over Caesar's corpse, he looked at Cicero and bellowed, "Restore the republic."[2]

Cicero decided to fight for freedom. To do so he wrote and published his *Philippics*, attacks condemning Antony's attempt to take over where Caesar left off. Cicero had the courage to act because he knew exactly what he stood for—he had thought his principles through. During that same pivotal year in Roman history, he wrote a book that outlined his philosophy. Cicero titled the book *De Officiis* (today it's often titled "On Duties") and wrote it to teach his son Marcus (who was then away studying philosophy in Athens) man's ultimate philosophy. It was a book Frederick the Great of

Prussia later called the greatest book on morality and ethics ever written. In fact, in 1531, Sir Thomas Elyot, in his *Governour*, listed three essential texts for bringing up young men: Plato's *Republic*, Aristotle's *Ethics*, and Cicero's *De Officiis*. In 390 AD, Saint Ambrose decreed *De Officiis*, though it was a pagan work, to be on par with Roman Catholic Church doctrine.

Cicero divided the book along Plato's four cardinal virtues: wisdom, justice, courage, and moderation. These virtues were Cicero's building blocks for the ultimate man's philosophy.

# Man's Ultimate Philosophy

## I. Wisdom

The first Platonic virtue, wisdom, Cicero explained is "the knowledge of truth." What is truth? Truth is what philosophers, like Socrates, devoted themselves to finding through a constant examination and questioning of evidence. This is why Plato, whom Cicero drew so heavily on, quoted Socrates as saying, "The unexamined life is not worth living for a human being."[3] Socrates felt such wisdom can only be found through truth. The Chinese philosopher Mencius agreed; he explained wisdom this way: "The feeling of commiseration is the beginning of humanity; the feeling of shame and dislike is the beginning of righteousness; the feeling of deference and compliance is the beginning of propriety; and the feeling of right and wrong is the beginning of wisdom. Men have these four beginnings just as they have their four limbs. Having these four beginnings, but saying that they cannot develop them is to destroy themselves."[4]

## WHAT NOT TO DO

Wisdom is about more than truth and knowing what to do, it's also about what not to do. Here are six no-no's from our man Cicero.

### The Six Mistakes of Man

1.  The delusion that personal gain is made by crushing others.
2.  The tendency to worry about things that cannot be changed or corrected.
3.  Insisting that a thing is impossible because we cannot accomplish it.
4.  Refusing to set aside trivial preferences.
5.  Neglecting development and refinement of the mind, and not acquiring the habit of reading and studying.
6.  Attempting to compel others to believe and live as we do.

# 2. Justice

Cicero advised his son that the second Platonic virtue, justice, can be wielded only through wisdom. To make sure you are administering true justice, Cicero cautioned to first follow what we now call the Golden Rule.

## THE GOLDEN RULE

The Bible defines the "golden rule" as, "Do unto others as you would have them do unto you."[5] In the first century BC, around the same time Cicero was writing *De Officiis*, Rabbi Hillel, a renowned Jewish religious leader, said, "What is hateful to you, do not to your neighbor; that is the whole Torah; the rest is the commentary thereof; go and learn it."[6]

## PASSIVE INJUSTICE

Cicero cautions that we need to do more than just not commit theft, murder, or adultery ourselves. It's no less wrong to stand by and allow someone else to be robbed or murdered. We cannot be hypocrites; we cannot be passive bystanders to injustice.

# 3. Courage

Cicero held that courage is fundamental to man's philosophy because it allows a man to stand up bravely for justice, which is precisely why Cicero stood up to Antony; in fact, Cicero wrote that fear must never stop a man from standing for justice, because "no man can be brave who thinks pain the greatest evil; nor temperate, who considers pleasure the highest good." Cicero tempered this point with analogies that praised the value of prudence—so that one's courage and self-sacrifice might truly serve the greater good.

Cicero lived and died by this code. About a year after *De Officiis* was completed, Antony convinced Augustus (Gaius Julius Caesar Octavianus) to send soldiers to slay Cicero. The stoic philosopher and statesman showed no fear, but told his assassin, "There is nothing proper about what you are doing, but at least make sure you cut off my head properly."[7] Cicero then stretched his neck out and waited for the end and so died for the very principles he outlined in *De Officiis*.

Thomas Paine (1737–1809), an English political writer, theorist, and activist, showed he approved of Cicero's stand for freedom when he wrote, "I love the man that can smile in trouble, that can gather strength from distress, and grow brave by reflection. 'Tis the business of little minds to shrink; but he whose heart is firm, and whose conscience approves his conduct, will pursue his principles unto death."[8]

Ayn Rand (1905–1982), an Objectivist philosopher and author, outlined man's courage this way:

> In order to live, man must act; in order to act, he must make choices; in order to make choices, he must define a code of values; in order to define a code of values, he must know *what* he is and *where* he is—i.e., he must know his own nature (including his means of knowledge) and the nature of the universe in which he acts—i.e., he needs metaphysics, epistemology, ethics, which means: *philosophy*. He cannot escape from this need; his only alternative is whether the philosophy guiding him is to be chosen by his mind or by chance.[9]

## 4. Moderation

Moderation is the last of the four virtues outlined by Cicero. The temple of Apollo at Delphi bore the inscription *Meden Agan* ("nothing in excess"). Like Plato and Aristotle, Cicero believed in finding the proper mean between two extremes—too much modesty results in over-shyness, too little in arrogance; too much humor leads to foolishness, too little results in drabness; too much courage will cause a foolish death, too little will make man a slave. Cicero agreed with Aristotle that good choices create good habits, making the extremes less undesirable, as everything falls into harmony when a man actively uses wisdom, justice, courage, and moderation to be a philosophically moral man.

Thomas More, an English philosopher and lawyer whom Erasmus called *omnium horarum homo* ("a man for all seasons"), adhered to the ultimate man's philosophy. In 1530, Henry VIII proclaimed that he (not the pope) was the Supreme Head of the Catholic Church in England. He did this so that he could procure an annulment of his marriage to Catherine of Aragon. More, as a devout Catholic, knew he could no longer serve both his king and his conscience, so he resigned his position as Lord Chancellor of England.

His resignation, however, was not accepted; as a result, More did his duty to the king insofar as it did not infringe upon his duty to his conscience or his Church. More neither supported nor condemned the king, but rather kept silent on the issue. Finally, in 1532, after failing to gain More's approval, King Henry angrily accepted More's resignation. Still, More lived on in happiness with his family, even though his wealth had almost completely disappeared after his fall from the king's graces. However, in 1534, when the Act of Succession was passed requiring all citizens to swear an oath denying "any foreign authority, prince or potentate," More was put in the position of either renouncing the Roman Catholic Church or being charged with treason. More refused to take the oath. He was imprisoned in the Tower of London and beheaded on July 6, 1535. Like Cicero, More believed, "It profits a man nothing to lose his soul for the whole world."[10] So does any real man.

# Man's Greatest Moral Codes

Here are some of the greatest moral guidelines ever written, from the Ten Commandments to the Scout's Oath.

# The Ten Commandments

The Bible's Old Testament tells us Moses brought these ten rules down from Mount Sinai, directly from God. They are still the foundation of morality in the Western world.

I.   I am the LORD your God, who brought you out of the land of Egypt, from the house of slavery. You shall have no other gods before Me.

> **MAN FACT**
> The U.S. Military Academy's creed is an easy-to-remember code of ethics: "A Cadet will not lie, cheat, or steal, or tolerate those who do."

2. You shall not make unto you any graven image or any likeness of anything that is in heaven above, or that is on the earth beneath, or that is in the water under the earth.
3. Do not swear falsely by the name of the LORD.
4. Remember the Sabbath day and keep it holy.
5. Honor your father and your mother.
6. Do not murder.
7. Do not commit adultery.
8. Do not steal.
9. Do not bear false witness against your neighbor.
10. Do not covet your neighbor's wife.

## Buddhism's Eight Precepts[11]

Buddha taught the precepts to help men live free from guilt of wrongdoing, so that people can progress more easily on their path to enlightenment.

1. I undertake the training rule to abstain from taking life.
2. I undertake the training rule to abstain from taking what is not given.
3. I undertake the training rule to abstain from sexual misconduct.

4. I undertake the training rule to abstain from false speech.

5. I undertake the training rule to abstain from malicious speech.

6. I undertake the training rule to abstain from harsh speech.

7. I undertake the training rule to abstain from useless speech.

8. I undertake the training rule to abstain from drinks and drugs that cause heedlessness.

# The Ten Precepts of Taoism[12]

The Ten Precepts are the classical rules of Chinese Taoism, a man's guide to justice and morality.

1. Do not kill but always be mindful of the host of living beings.

2. Do not be lascivious or think depraved thoughts.

3. Do not steal or receive unrighteous wealth.

4. Do not cheat or misrepresent good and evil.

5. Do not get intoxicated but always think of pure conduct.

6. I will maintain harmony with my ancestors and family and never disregard my kin.

7. When I see someone do a good deed, I will support him with joy and delight.

**MAN FACT**
Alexander the Great was the student of Aristotle, who was the student of Plato, who was the student of Socrates. Talk about a dynasty.

8.  When I see someone unfortunate, I will support him with dignity to recover good fortune.

9.  When someone comes to do me harm, I will not harbor thoughts of revenge.

10. As long as all beings have not attained the Tao, I will not expect to do so myself.

# Benjamin Franklin's 13 Rules of Improvement

Franklin sought to cultivate his character and become a wise and just man by adhering to what he ascertained to be the fundamental thirteen virtues. He first developed these when he was twenty years old (in 1726). He recorded them in his autobiography:

1.  **Temperance:** Eat not to dullness; drink not to elevation.

2.  **Silence:** Speak not but what may benefit others or yourself; avoid trifling conversation.

3.  **Order:** Let all your things have their places; let each part of your business have its time.

4.  **Resolution:** Resolve to perform what you ought; perform without fail what you resolve.

5.  **Frugality:** Make no expense but to do good to others or yourself; i.e., waste nothing.

6.  **Industry:** Lose no time; be always employed in something useful; cut off all unnecessary actions.

7.  **Sincerity:** Use no hurtful deceit; think innocently and justly, and, if you speak, speak accordingly.

8.  **Justice:** Wrong none by doing injuries, or omitting the benefits that are your duty.

9.  **Moderation:** Avoid extremes; forbear resenting injuries so much as you think they deserve.

10. **Cleanliness:** Tolerate no uncleanliness in body, clothes, or habitation.

11. **Tranquillity:** Be not disturbed at trifles, or at accidents common or unavoidable.

12. **Chastity:** Rarely use venery but for health or offspring, never to dullness, weakness, or the injury of your own or another's peace or reputation.

13. **Humility:** Imitate Jesus and Socrates.

# Miyamoto Musashi's 21 Steps to Self-Reliance

Miyamoto Musashi was a Samurai in seventeenth-century Japan who remained undefeated in more than sixty individual matches. He wrote *The Book of Five Rings* late in his life to explain his Zen philosophy on how a man should live. His final act was to write "The Way of Walking Alone," which makes up these twenty-one rules on living as a man.

1. Do not turn your back on the various Ways of this world.
2. Do not scheme for physical pleasure.
3. Do not intend to rely on anything.
4. Consider yourself lightly; consider the world deeply.
5. Do not ever think in acquisitive terms.
6. Do not regret things about your own personal life.
7. Do not envy another's good or evil.
8. Do not lament parting on any road whatsoever.
9. Do not complain or feel bitterly about yourself or others.
10. Have no heart for approaching the path of love.
11. Do not have preferences.
12. Do not harbor hopes for your own personal home.

# SOCRATES
# 469 BC–399 BC

Today we see Socrates through the writings of his student Plato. Perhaps this is why Socrates seems so perfect. Surely, the real Socrates possessed faults that his dramatized counterpart did not. Still, a man who inspired all that Socrates did must have been among the best of men. In fact, in some ways Socrates was even better than his modern reputation. Today, few know that Socrates was a trained hoplite (foot soldier) in the Athenian army. A courageous fighter, he was commended for bravery in the battle of Delium (424 BC) and saved his friend Alcibiades during a battle near Spartolus in 434 BC He was literally a warrior-philosopher.

As a young man, Socrates was taught rhetoric as part of the regimented Athenian system for teaching a boy to become a man who could defend the city, ply a trade, and debate in Athens' citizen Assembly. He then took to philosophy and stood up to the Sophists, philosophers who believed that winning a debate was more important than being right. The Sophists used half-truths and turns of phrase to win their arguments, achieving personal gain while leading others astray. Socrates tirelessly combated the Sophists and their method, all the while striving to discover truth. According to Plato, Socrates condemned the Sophists, saying, "False words are not only evil in themselves, but they infect the soul with evil." In the course of his battles with the Sophists, Socrates became known as the "gadfly" of Athens (the gadfly was said to sting horses into stampedes) because he irritated the establishment with questions that probed for the truth.

During his life, Socrates offered countless morsels of wisdom, but there are two teachings in particular that every man should take to heart. The first is that the truly wise man is the man who, paradoxically, does not consider himself wise. As told in Plato's *Apology*, Socrates' friend Chaerephon had asked the Oracle at Delphi if there was any man wiser than Socrates. The Oracle responded that none was wiser. Socrates then began to question men who were considered wise and discovered that each man believed that they knew a great deal, but they were not, in fact, truly wise. Socrates, on the other hand, did not consider himself to be wise, and therefore was the wisest of them all. This story highlights the importance of humility and of constantly striving for truth and wisdom. If a man thinks that he is wise, he will stop pursuing truth.

Finally, in his quest for wisdom, Socrates often questioned prominent Athenians and so found himself opposed by the powerful elite of the city. These enemies were the underlying reason that Socrates was found guilty of corrupting the youth of Athens. After he was sentenced to death, Socrates had an opportunity to escape when his friends bribed the prison guards. But he chose to stay and accept his death because he believed that fleeing justice would signify a fear of death, which he thought no true philosopher (or man, for that matter) has. He also believed that running away from the law would go against his own teachings. So not wanting to live out the rest of his days as a hypocrite, Socrates courageously accepted death. Socrates also realized that death was not the end. "Crito," he began his last words, "we owe a cock to Asclepius. Please don't forget to pay the debt." Asclepius was the Greek god for curing illness. Plato interpreted Socrates' last words to mean that death is a cure that gives freedom to the soul. Unwavering in his principles, Socrates lived life and accepted death as every man should.

13. Do not have a liking for delicious food for yourself.

14. Do not carry antiques carried down from generation to generation.

15. Do not fast so that it affects you physically.

16. While it's different with military equipment, do not be fond of material things.

17. While on the Way, do not begrudge death.

18. Do not be intent on possessing valuables for a fief in old age.

19. Respect the Gods and Buddhas, but do not depend on them.

20. Though you give up your life, do not give up your honor.

21. Never depart from the Way of the Martial Arts.

## Scout Oath (or Promise) of the Boy Scouts of America

"On my honor, I will do my best to do my duty to God and my country and to obey the Scout Law; to help other people at all times; to keep myself physically strong, mentally awake, and morally straight."

# 10 Most Masculine Deaths of All Time

If there's one common thread between all men, it's this: we all die. A real man accepts death as a fact of life. Just as the ultimate man lives nobly, he should die nobly. There's nothing wrong with dying in your sleep, but these guys went out with a bang.

## 10. Buffalo Bill Cody (1846–1917)

After a life lived in the saddle in the American West, touring the world with his "Buffalo Bill's Wild West" show with a revolving cast of living legends such as Sitting Bull and Wild Bill Hickok, Buffalo Bill Cody found himself at the end of his trail in Denver in 1917. Rather than die quietly in bed, he decided to go out on his terms. He called his pals together for a last card game. Cody played until he slumped onto the table. They said he died of kidney failure, a month short of his seventy-first birthday, but he really died from a life lived loudly.

## 9. The Unknown Soldier

The Tomb of the Unknowns (also known as the "Tomb of the Unknown Soldier") is a monument dedicated to American servicemen who died without their remains being identified. It is located in Arlington National Cemetery near Washington, D.C. The "Unknown Soldier" of World War I is a recipient of the Medal of Honor and the Victoria

> **MAN FACT**
> Because he was quiet and overweight while at the University of Paris, students and faculty alike referred to Saint Thomas Aquinas as "The Dumb Ox." He became one of the greatest philosophers who ever lived.

Cross. On Memorial Day in 1921, four unknowns were exhumed from four World War I American cemeteries in France. U.S. Army Sergeant Edward F. Younger, who had received the Distinguished Service Medal, then selected the Unknown Soldier from among the four identical caskets. Because the soldier is unknown, we can't point to his faults and failings as a man. Instead, he is the hero in everyman.

## 8. Davy Crockett (1786–1836)

Davy Crockett, a frontiersman and congressman from Tennessee, lost reelection to the U.S. Congress in 1831 after opposing President Andrew Jackson's Indian Removal Act, a law that forced the Cherokee from land they legally owned and that led to the "Trail of Tears." Though Crockett won when he ran again in 1833, he soon suffered another defeat. In his autobiography he wrote, "I told the people of my district that I would serve them as faithfully as I had done; but if not...you may all go to hell, and I will go to Texas."[13] Following his last defeat, he headed for Texas. He was subsequently trapped in the Alamo by Santa Anna's Mexican troops. After the battle, Ben, a former American slave who acted as cook for one of Santa Anna's officers, maintained that Crockett's body was found in the barracks surrounded by at least sixteen Mexican bodies and that Crockett's knife was stuck in one of them.[14]

## 7. Pheidippides (530–490 BC)

The story passed down over eons asserts that Pheidippides, an Athenian herald, was sent to Sparta to request help when the Persians landed at Marathon, Greece. To complete the journey he ran 150 miles in two days. He then ran twenty-six miles from a battlefield near the town of Marathon to Athens to announce that the Greeks were victorious over the Persian invaders in the Battle of Marathon in 490 BC. When he arrived in Athens he said, "Nenikékamen" ("We have won") and fell dead from exhaustion. He thereby passed into legend.

# 6. Sir William Wallace (1270–1305)

The movie *Braveheart* made Sir William Wallace a popular hero again, even though much of the Hollywood tale was factually false; however, Wallace's stand for freedom was right. Wallace evaded capture by the English until August 5, 1305, when John de Menteith, a Scottish knight loyal to King Edward, turned Wallace over to English soldiers. Wallace was transported to London and tried for treason. He was crowned with a garland of oak to suggest that he was the king of outlaws. He responded to the treason charge by saying, "I could not be a traitor to Edward, for I was never his subject." Wallace was found guilty, stripped naked, and dragged through the city behind a horse. He was then emasculated, eviscerated, had his bowels burned before his eyes, and was finally beheaded and drawn and quartered. His head was placed on a pike atop London Bridge. His limbs were displayed separately around England. His body parts were supposed to warn others of the folly of fighting for freedom. They had the opposite effect.

# 5. Spartacus (109–71 BC)

Spartacus was a Roman slave who was trained at the gladiatorial school (ludus) near Capua, belonging to Lentulus Batiatus. In 73 BC, Plutarch wrote that Spartacus and about seventy other slaves escaped from the gladiator school, seized a wagon full of weapons, and fled to the caldera on Mount Vesuvius. Other slaves began to join the charismatic Spartacus, and thus began the Third Servile War.

Spartacus' intention was thought to be to escape Italy and return home. The Senate sent Claudius Glaber with a militia of about 3,000 to stop him. Glaber besieged Spartacus on Vesuvius, but Spartacus had ropes made from vines and, with his men, he climbed down a cliff on the other side of the volcano. Spartacus and his men then launched a surprise attack against the Romans. Many of the Roman soldiers were quickly killed, including Glaber. Spartacus' success convinced more slaves to join him—soon Spartacus had an army of 140,000 escaped slaves.

The Senate next sent two consuls, Gellius Publicola and Gnaeus Cornelius Lentulus Clodianus, each with a legion, to capture Spartacus and destroy his army. Spartacus defeated them both. He then defeated yet another legion under Gaius Cassius Longinus. At the end of 72 BC, Spartacus made a deal with pirates, who agreed to transport him and his army to Sicily, but he was betrayed. Eight legions led by Marcus Licinius Crassus isolated Spartacus' army. Spartacus broke through Crassus' lines, but Pompey the Great's forces intercepted them and forced them to surrender. According to Plutarch, "Finally, after his companions had taken to flight, he [Spartacus] stood alone, surrounded by a multitude of foes, and was still defending himself when he was cut down."[15] After the battle, 6,600 of Spartacus' followers were crucified along the Appian Way from Brundisium to Rome.

## 4. George Washington (1732–1799)

Sure, George Washington died in bed of pneumonia when he was sixty-seven years old, but it was a choice he made. On December 23, 1783, when he resigned his commission as commander-in-chief of the Continental Army, Washington chose his quiet death. When he peacefully left his military command, the United States was governed under the Articles of Confederation without a president. Washington had every opportunity to make himself a military dictator. Many of his fellow officers wanted him to do just that. But Washington stifled such talk and, in emulation of the Roman general Cincinnatus, who did his duty and then returned to the plow, Washington returned to private life at Mount Vernon before he was called to lead once again. He later served for two terms as America's first president and, more importantly, ensured that there was a peaceful and democratic transfer of power. How many men in the course of history willingly gave up power and chose to die quietly as just another citizen?

# 3. Oishi Kuranosuke (1659–1703)

In 1701, Asano Takumi-no-Kami Naganori, a *daimyo* (feudal lord), was ordered to arrange a fitting reception for the envoy of the Emperor in Edo (Tokyo). Kira Kozuke-no-Suke Yoshinaka, a powerful Edo official, was told to show him how. Trouble ensued when Kira was arrogant and insulting. Some say Kira wanted bribes that Asano, a devout Confucian, wouldn't grant. Regardless, historians agree Kira's insult was great enough to prompt Asano to attack him. Asano was stopped and only managed to cut Kira's cheek. Asano was subsequently ordered to commit seppuku (ritual suicide) for attacking a member of the court. Asano's property was confiscated, his family was ruined, and his Samurai left leaderless—making them *ronin*. Asano killed himself honorably, but then Oishi Kuranosuke (also known as Oishi Yoshio), his top-ranking Samurai, vowed revenge as Samurai honor demanded. He was joined by a group of Samurai who later became popularly known as the "forty-seven ronin."

Complying with his orders, Oishi surrendered the Asano castle, but not before removing the Asano family to safety. Oishi then left his wife so that no harm would come to her after he took revenge. Oishi made a show of frequenting geisha houses and getting drunk, acting the part of a Samurai who was too weak and corrupt to seek revenge. Meanwhile, the rest of the faithful ronin gathered in Edo and, by taking jobs as workmen and merchants, gained access to Kira's house. One of the ronin (Kinemon Kanehide Okano) even married the daughter of the builder of the house to obtain the plans. Others gathered weapons and secretly transported them to Edo. In January 1703, Oishi, with the forty-six other ronin, attacked Kira at his residence in Edo. After a long battle, they found Kira and cut his head off.

After placing Kira's head on Asano's grave, they surrendered. As they knew they would be, Oishi and the other ronin were sentenced to commit seppuku. Oishi and the other ronin took their own lives as ordered.

## 2. Leonidas (around 540–480 BC)

The movie *300* brought Leonidas, a Spartan king, to a new generation of people. But his selfless act of standing with 300 Spartans in the pass at Thermopylae has kept him alive for nearly 2,500 years. He could have escaped, but he chose to stay and die because he knew his death would rally all of Greece.

Before going to the pass, Leonidas consulted the Oracle at Delphi, and legend has it he heard the following prophesy:

> Hear your fate, O dwellers in Sparta of the wide spaces;
> Either your famed, great town must be sacked by Perseus' sons,
> Or, if that be not, the whole land of Lacedaemon
> Shall mourn the death of a king of the house of Heracles,
> For not the strength of lions or of bulls shall hold him,
> Strength against strength; for he has the power of Zeus,
> And will not be checked till one of these two he has consumed.[16]

Leonidas accepted his fate, stood against tyranny, and died heroically with a sword in his hand and freedom in his heart, and thereby gave the Greeks a rallying cry they used to defeat the Persian army.

## 1. Jesus (c. 6 AD–39 AD)

Whether Christian, Jew, Muslim, or atheist, there's no denying that Jesus Christ's death on the cross was manly. Accused of calling himself the King of the Jews—which subverted the power of the Emperor—and of supposedly spreading teachings contrary to Judaism, Jesus was brought to trial. A simple denial would have saved him, but Jesus stood firm.

Crucifixion was then the most humiliating form of execution, but the Romans went even further by forcing Christ to make the long and painful trek to Golgatha after scourging and beating him. All this, even without mentioning the salvific quality of his death, would be enough for Jesus to join the pantheon of great men. But for Christians, his death was much more than manly resilience in the face of injustice. For the Christian, Christ's death means salvation. It means that Jesus offered up his life so that others might live. Beyond an acceptance of his fate and an adherence to his principles, Jesus' death was an *intended* act for the sake of others. Indeed, as Christ himself said in the Gospel, "There is no greater love than this, to lay down one's life for his friends." Surely, that is the ultimate in manliness.

# APPENDICES

CONTINUE YOUR MANLY EDUCATION

These are very eclectic lists because men from numerous backgrounds and cultures contributed to them to ensure they are well-rounded. Many great and manly movies and books are left out, as only 100 made the cut. But it's a beginning, and as such, is designed to give you more resources in your life-long quest to be all you can be.

## APPENDIX 1:
# 100 Movies Men Should See

1. *Ben-Hur*, 1959, directed by William Wyler, starring Charlton Heston: As Judah Ben-Hur, Heston is what every man should be, a figure struggling to stand for justice, his people, and his family, who rises through faith to transcend obstacles in his path.

2. *High Noon*, 1952, directed by Fred Zinnemann, starring Gary Cooper and Grace Kelly: Gary Cooper marries Grace Kelly and turns in his badge, before learning a bad guy he put away years before is arriving on the noon train to meet his old gang and get revenge. Cooper leaves town, but then stops his wagon. Grace Kelly pleads, "Don't go back, Will." Gary Cooper replies, "I've got to, that's the whole thing."

3. *The Godfather* series, 1972–1990, directed by Francis Ford Coppola, starring Robert Duvall, Al Pacino, Robert De Niro, and Marlon Brando: These movies are a male guide to honor and respect.

4. *Rocky*, 1976, directed by John G. Avildsen, starring Sylvester Stallone, Talia Shire, and Burgess Meredith: There is nothing more manly than the rags-to-riches-to-rags story of Rocky. Watch Sylvester Stallone dig for his manhood, punch a side of beef, and scream "Adrian" as he struggles to be a man.

5. *Saving Private Ryan*, 1998, directed by Steven Spielberg, starring Tom Hanks, Matt Damon, Edward Burns, and Tom Sizemore: This is a movie about men and war, and the ties that bind a band of brothers.

6.  *Good Will Hunting*, 1997, directed by Gus Van Sant, starring Matt Damon and Ben Affleck: Every man has to find his path in life. A psychologist, a girl, and his best friend force Matt Damon along his path.

7.  *Casablanca*, 1942, directed by Michael Curtiz, starring Humphrey Bogart, Ingrid Bergman, and Paul Henreid: Rick, played by Humphrey Bogart, is aloof, debonair, and hard-boiled—until his old flame Ingrid Bergman reminds him he has a heart.

8.  *The Seven Samurai*, 1954, directed by Akira Kurosawa, starring Takashi Shimura and Toshiro Mifune: Okay, guys don't like to read subtitles; drop the bias this once. A poor Japanese village begs some Samurai to fight off bandits who annually raid the village. Seven Samurai come not for pay, but for honor.

9.  *The Big Country*, 1958, directed by William Wyler, starring Gregory Peck, Jean Simmons, and Charlton Heston: Gregory Peck goes to the American West to marry a rancher's daughter he'd met in the East, but finds he has to prove he's a man to her all over again.

10. *Die Hard*, 1988, directed by John McTiernan, starring Bruce Willis, Alan Rickman, and Bonnie Bedelia: A group of European terrorists gets their worst nightmare: an American man who thinks he's a cowboy.

11. *The Shawshank Redemption*, 1994, directed by Frank Darabont, starring Tim Robbins and Morgan Freeman: This is a movie about hope. Even in prison, a man can stay a man by keeping his mind.

12. *Stand By Me*, 1986, directed by Rob Reiner, starring Wil Wheaton, River Phoenix, Corey Feldman, Jerry O'Connell, and Kiefer Sutherland: Four 12-year-old boys go looking for a dead body; what they find is a coming-of-age event.

13. *Walking Tall*, 1973, directed by Phil Karlson, starring Joe Don Baker and Elizabeth Hartman: When Buford Pusser avenges his wife's murder with a wooden club, you're proud to be a man.

14. *The Big Sleep*, 1946, directed by Howard Hawks, staring Humphrey Bogart and Lauren Bacall: A private-eye stays clean in a dirty cesspool

of mobsters and cops on the take because he stays loyal to his manly code of honor.

15. *Mr. Smith Goes to Washington*, 1939, directed by Frank Capra, starring James Stewart and Jean Arthur: A naïve, young U.S. senator goes to Washington, refuses to be corrupted, and finds himself filibustering the great political machine.

16. The "Man with No Name Trilogy" (*A Fistful of Dollars*, *For a Few Dollars More*, and *The Good, the Bad and the Ugly*), 1964–66, directed by Sergio Leone, starring Clint Eastwood: Eastwood is a bounty hunter, of a sort, who fights unflinchingly and with the cool detachment of a professional.

17. *L.A. Confidential*, 1997, directed by Curtis Hanson, starring Kevin Spacey, Russell Crowe, Guy Pearce, and James Cromwell: This just might be the best cop movie ever.

18. *The Vikings*, 1958, directed by Richard Fleischer, starring Kirk Douglas, Tony Curtis, and Janet Leigh: This classic is a how-to guide on fighting and dying like a man.

19. *The Searchers*, 1956, directed by John Ford, starring John Wayne: When Comanches abduct a little girl, they don't take into account what one relentless man can do.

20. *Full Metal Jacket*, 1987, directed by Stanley Kubrick, starring Matthew Modine, Adam Baldwin, Vincent D'Onofrio, and R. Lee Ermey: Originally made to show the horrors of war, after this manly flick you'll feel like you went to boot camp and Vietnam.

21. *Dirty Harry*, 1971, directed by Don Siegel, starring Clint Eastwood: "Do you feel lucky, punk" was repeated by every school kid for a decade after this manly flick came out.

22. *The Dirty Dozen*, 1967, directed by Robert Aldrich, starring Lee Marvin, Ernest Borgnine, Charles Bronson, and Jim Brown: This is one of the manliest casts ever gathered—misfits willing to die for a second chance in life.

23. *Terminator*, 1984, directed by James Cameron, starring Arnold Schwarzenegger, Michael Biehn, and Linda Hamilton: If you don't like this movie, you're probably a girl.

24. *12 Angry Men*, 1957, directed by Sidney Lumet, starring Henry Fonda: This is one of the greatest movies on men grappling with justice ever produced.

25. *Braveheart*, 1995, directed by Mel Gibson, starring Mel Gibson, Sophia Marceau, Catherine McCormack, Patrick McGoohan, Angus Macfadyen, Brendan Gleeson, and the musical prowess of James Horner: How to live for love, brotherhood, and freedom.

26. *Field of Dreams*, 1989, directed by Phil Alden Robinson, starring Kevin Costner and James Earl Jones: This film's underlying theme is the fulfillment of a man's dreams, no matter what mistakes he may have made.

27. *The Harder They Fall*, 1956, directed by Mark Robson, starring Humphrey Bogart, Rod Steiger, and Jan Sterling: The climax comes when Humphrey Bogart, who has sold his principles for money, has to sell out completely—or do the right thing.

28. *The Pride of the Yankees*, 1942, directed by Sam Wood, starring Gary Cooper and Teresa Wright: When Gary Cooper delivers Lou Gehrig's famous line—"Today, I consider myself the luckiest man on the face of the earth"—you choke up and know what it is to be a man.

29. *Fists of Fury*, 1971, directed by Wei Lo, starring Bruce Lee and Maria Yi: The fight scenes make this movie drip with testosterone, but Bruce Lee's battle for justice makes it an ultimate man film.

30. *Dead Poets Society*, 1989, directed by Peter Weir, starring Robin Williams, Robert Sean Leonard, and Ethan Hawke: A teacher shows boys how to find their own path to manhood and thereby unleashes a storm.

31. *Gladiator*, 2000, directed by Ridley Scott, starring Russell Crowe, Joaquin Phoenix, Connie Nielsen, and Oliver Reed: When Russell Crowe

says, "Father of a murdered son, husband to a murdered wife, and I shall have my vengeance in this life or the next," you shiver.

32. *Paths of Glory*, 1957, directed by Stanley Kubrick, starring Kirk Douglas: Douglas plays a French officer fighting in WWI who tries to save four soldiers picked at random to be executed for a poorly executed charge on German trenches.

33. *The Candidate*, 1972, directed by Michael Ritchie, starring Robert Redford and Peter Boyle: How politics can slowly, decision by decision, corrupt a man.

34. *I Am a Fugitive from a Chain Gang*, 1932, directed by Mervyn LeRoy, starring Paul Muni, Glenda Farrell, Helen Vinson, and Noel Francis: An innocent man is sentenced to ten years on a chain gang. He escapes but is slowly turned into a criminal.

35. The five early James Bond films with Sean Connery (*Dr. No, From Russia with Love, Goldfinger, Thunderball, You Only Live Twice*), 1962–1967: James Bond's creator, Ian Fleming, thought Connery was a poor choice, but after the raging success of *Dr. No,* he knew Connery was Bond.

36. *Any Given Sunday*, 1999, directed by Oliver Stone, starring Al Pacino and Cameron Diaz: Manhood is not something you earn, but something you keep fighting for all your life. Al Pacino finds this out—and keeps his manhood on and off the field.

37. *Attack!*, 1956, directed by Robert Aldrich, starring Jack Palance, Lee Marvin, and Eddie Albert: Men make the tough choices in World War II.

38. *Tombstone*, 1993, directed by George P. Cosmatos, starring Kurt Russell, Val Kilmer, Sam Elliott, and Bill Paxton: Brotherhood, courage, honor, and justice are the manly themes this Western brings alive.

39. *Hoosiers,* 1986, directed by David Anspaugh, starring Gene Hackman and Dennis Hopper: Hackman plays a hard-luck coach in this underdog basketball story and comes out a man.

40. *When We Were Kings*, 1996, directed by Leon Gast: This documentary of the 1974 "Rumble in the Jungle" between Muhammad Ali and George Foreman is about men giving their all.

41. *Eight Men Out,* 1988, directed by John Sayles, starring John Cusack, Jace Alexander, and Gordon Clapp: This dramatization of the 1919 Chicago Black Sox scandal argues that men must speak up when they see injustice.

42. *Cape Fear*, 1962, directed by J. Lee Thompson, starring Gregory Peck and Robert Mitchum: Mitchum plays a criminal who was sent to jail by Peck and now seeks revenge. The film navigates a gray area of justice: Do the ends justify the means?

43. *From Here to Eternity*, 1953, directed by Fred Zinnemann, starring Burt Lancaster, Montgomery Clift, Deborah Kerr, Donna Reed, Frank Sinatra, Ernest Borgnine, and Philip Ober: Soldiers stationed on Hawaii just before the attack on Pearl Harbor struggle to be men; some succeed.

44. *Bridge on the River Kwai*, 1957, directed by David Lean, starring Alec Guinness, Sessue Hayakawa, William Holden, Jack Hawkins, and Geoffrey Horne: The whistling of the Colonel Bogey March is unforgettable, but this is a man movie because it's about keeping honor in desperate times.

45. *Key Largo*, 1948, directed by John Huston, staring Humphrey Bogart and Lauren Bacall: Bogart, playing a WWII hero returned home, is confronted by mobsters and forced to figure out what courage really is.

46. *Lord of the Rings* (the trilogy), 2001–2003, directed by Peter Jackson, starring Elijah Wood, Ian McKellen, Sean Astin, Viggo Mortensen, Andy Serkis, and Liv Tyler: An epic tale of men fighting for good over evil.

47. *Conan the Barbarian*, 1982, directed by John Milius, starring Arnold Schwarzenegger: This muscle-bound, rags-to-riches story follows a man on a quest.

48. *Gunga Din, 1939,* directed by George Stevens, starring Cary Grant, Douglas Fairbanks Jr., and Victor McLaglen: This swashbuckling tale explores courage, honor, and masculine friendship.

49. *Bad Day at Black Rock*, 1955, directed by John Sturges, starring Spencer Tracy, Lee Marvin, Robert Ryan, and Anne Francis: This Western film

noir follows a mysterious stranger who arrives at a tiny isolated town in search of a murdered man. He confronts racism and delivers justice.

50. *The Adventures of Robin Hood*, 1938, directed by Michael Curtiz, starring Errol Flynn and Olivia de Havilland: The best cinematic retelling of this classic manly tale.

51. *All The King's Men*, 1949, directed by Robert Rossen, starring Broderick Crawford, John Ireland, and Joanne Dru: Willie Stark rises as a politician from a rural county seat and along the way becomes what he rose to stop—it's a lesson in how *not* to be a man.

52. *The Great Escape*, 1963, directed by John Sturges, starring Steve McQueen, James Garner, Richard Attenborough, and Charles Bronson: Allied soldiers in a German prison camp organize an escape and find out who is selfish and who can be selfless.

53. *The Guns of Navarone*, 1961, directed by J. Lee Thompson, starring Gregory Peck, David Niven, Anthony Quinn, Anthony Quayle, and Stanley Baker: These men are tasked with a desperate mission to take out German cannons in WWII. Selfless courage is their only weapon.

54. *The Firm*, 1993, directed by Sydney Pollack, starring Tom Cruise, Jeanne Tripplehorn, and Gene Hackman: A young attorney navigates a path to justice through mobsters, dirty lawyers, and an uncaring bureaucracy.

55. *North by Northwest*, 1959, directed by Alfred Hitchcock, starring Cary Grant, Eva Marie Saint, and James Mason: After being mistaken for a government agent, this average man finds he can be heroic.

56. *Farewell to the King*, 1989, directed by John Milius, starring Nigel Havers, Nick Nolte, Frank McRae, and Gerry Lopez: In World War II, an American POW escapes a Japanese firing squad and hides out in Borneo where he is adopted by a head-hunting tribe. Before long, he becomes king. This is the story of how power can corrupt a man.

57. *Black Hawk Down*, 2001, directed by Ridley Scott, starring Josh Hartnett, Ewan McGregor, and Tom Hardy: This true story of tragedy and heroism captures modern warfare at its most desperate.

58. *Shenandoah*, 1965, directed by Andrew V. McLaglen, starring James Stewart, Doug McClure, and Katharine Ross: A father struggles to keep his family together in the American Civil War.

59. *Sands of Iwo Jima*, 1949, directed by Allan Dwan, starring John Wayne, John Agar, Forrest Tucker, and Adele Mara: How to lead by example is what this World War II flick teaches.

60. *First Blood*, 1982, directed by Ted Kotcheff, starring Sylvester Stallone, Richard Crenna, and Brian Dennehy: A hero shunned by his people struggles for meaning in a country turned inside out.

61. *The Quiet Man*, 1952, directed by John Ford, starring John Wayne and Maureen O'Hara: A boxer accidentally kills his opponent in the ring, and then retreats to the country of his birth to find himself and his manhood.

62. *The Longest Day*, 1962, directed by Ken Annakin, starring John Wayne, Henry Fonda, Robert Mitchum, Sean Connery, and Rod Steiger: D-Day and its aftermath unfold in this epic tale of heroism.

63. *Big Jake*, 1971, directed by George Sherman, starring John Wayne, Maureen O'Hara, and Richard Boone: When a boy is kidnapped, it takes a man to get him back.

64. *Captain Blood*, 1935, directed by Michael Curtiz, starring Errol Flynn and Olivia de Havilland: A swashbuckling Errol Flynn fights to regain his freedom and his honor.

65. *The Caine Mutiny*, 1954, directed by Edward Dmytryk, starring Humphrey Bogart, José Ferrer, and Van Johnson: A classic account of the sometimes complex dividing line between legality and justice.

66. *Run Silent, Run Deep*, 1958, directed by Robert Wise, starring Clark Gable and Burt Lancaster: A thrilling portrayal of the challenges of command.

67. *The Bullfighter and the Lady*, 1951, directed by Budd Boetticher, starring Robert Stack, Joy Page, and Gilbert Roland: An American longs to be a bullfighter; he ends up learning how to be a man.

68. *The Third Man*, 1949, directed by Carol Reed, starring Joseph Cotton, Alida Valli, and Orson Welles: A man has to decide between friendship and justice.

69. *Predator*, 1987, directed by John McTiernan, starring Arnold Schwarzenegger: This man versus alien classic screams that sometimes a man can overcome anything.

70. *Hamlet*, 1948, directed by Laurence Olivier, starring Laurence Olivier, Basil Sydney, Eileen Herlie, and Jean Simmons: Olivier brings Shakespeare's greatest play to life as he shows a boy growing into a man.

71. *A Man for All Seasons*, 1966, directed by Fred Zinnemann, starring Paul Scofield, Wendy Hiller, Leo McKern, Orson Welles, and Robert Shaw: This is an exploration of the ultimate man's conscience.

72. *The Patriot*, 2000, directed by Roland Emmerich, starring Mel Gibson, Jason Isaacs, Heath Ledger, and Joely Richardson: A man who understands the horrors of war is forced to fight for his family and freedom.

73. *Spartacus*, 1960, directed by Stanley Kubrick, starring Kirk Douglas, Laurence Olivier, and Peter Ustinov: In his quest for freedom, a slave nearly overthrows Rome.

74. *Mutiny on the Bounty*, 1962, directed by Lewis Milestone, starring Marlon Brando, Trevor Howard, Richard Harris, and Hugh Griffith: A mutiny erupts to dislodge an abusive captain.

75. *Gentleman's Agreement*, 1947, directed by Elia Kazan, starring Gregory Peck, Dorothy McGuire, and John Garfield: A journalist's exploration of anti-Semitism develops him as a man.

76. *Notorious*, 1946, directed by Alfred Hitchcock, starring Cary Grant and Ingrid Bergman: Grant has to decide between duty and love as Bergman gives everything to take down a Nazi ring.

77. *The Professionals*, 1966, directed by Richard Brooks, starring Lee Marvin, Burt Lancaster, Robert Ryan, and Woody Strode: This kidnap-rescue adventure pits men who live by a code of honor against those who don't.

**78.** *The Natural*, 1984, directed by Barry Levinson, starring Robert Redford, Robert Duvall, and Kim Basinger: A man fights for a second chance.

**79.** *Raiders of the Lost Ark*, 1981, directed by Steven Spielberg, starring Harrison Ford, Karen Allen, and Paul Freeman: Indiana Jones has a schooled intellect and an adventurous spirit; more men should use him as a role model.

**80.** *3:10 to Yuma*, 1957, directed by Delmer Daves, starring Glenn Ford, Van Heflin, and Felicia Farr: A man is humiliated in front of his son—who doesn't yet realize he's doing the right thing. Both the classic 1957 version and the 2007 remake of this Elmore Leonard short story make for manly viewing.

**81.** *The Male Animal*, 1942, directed by Elliot Nugent, starring Henry Fonda, Olivia de Havilland, and Joan Leslie: A pure jock and a total intellectual compete for the same woman, and the intellectual learns love takes more than brains.

**82.** *Reservoir Dogs*, 1992, directed by Quentin Tarantino, starring Harvey Keitel, Steve Buscemi, Tim Roth, Michael Madsen, Chris Penn, and Lawrence Tierney: This jewel heist film delves into the darker neuroses of men.

**83.** *El Cid*, 1961, directed by Anthony Mann, starring Charlton Heston and Sophia Loren: People have forgotten this film, but Heston plays a strong, romantic man who conquers his foes and rises to become a man of the ages.

**84.** *A River Runs Through It*, 1992, directed by Robert Redford, starring Craig Sheffer and Brad Pitt: Few movies have captured man's real connection and thus harmony with the earth as this one does. It's a lesson in brotherhood, family, and our link to nature.

**85.** *Chariots of Fire*, 1981, directed by Hugh Hudson, starring Ben Cross, Ian Charleson, Nigel Havers, and Cheryl Campbell: This is about men testing their limits and living their principles.

86. *The Shootist*, 1976, directed by Don Siegel, starring John Wayne: A gunslinger faces mortality and goes out on his terms.

87. *Patch Adams*, 1998, directed by Tom Shadyac, starring Robin Williams and Monica Potter: How a man brings redemption to others through humor and compassion.

88. *The Magnificent Seven*, 1960, directed by John Sturges, starring Yul Brynner, Eli Wallach, Steve McQueen, Charles Bronson, Robert Vaughn, and James Coburn: This variation on *The Seven Samurai* pits seven gun slingers against bandits terrorizing a village of farmers.

89. *Starship Troopers*, 1997, directed by Paul Verhoeven, starring Casper Van Dien, Denise Richards, Dina Meyer, and Jake Busey: A rich kid grows up, loses his love, and becomes a leader and hero.

90. *Wall Street*, 1987, directed by Oliver Stone, starring Charlie Sheen, Michael Douglas, and Daryl Hannah: Greed corrupts a young stockbroker, who then has to embrace honesty and take his lumps or become a villain.

91. *Cinderella Man*, 2005, directed by Ron Howard, starring Russell Crowe, Renée Zellweger, and Paul Giamatti: A man fights against overwhelming odds to keep his family together.

92. *It's a Wonderful Life*, 1946, directed by Frank Capra, starring James Stewart and Donna Reed: A good man loses faith, but then finds out what the world would be like if he had never existed.

93. *The Deer Hunter*, 1978, directed by Michael Cimino, starring Robert De Niro, Christopher Walken, and Meryl Streep: The Vietnam War forces these men to learn what manhood really is.

94. *Legends of the Fall*, 1994, directed by Edward Zwick, starring Brad Pitt, Anthony Hopkins, Aidan Quinn, Julia Ormond, and Henry Thomas: An epic about the meaning of brotherhood.

95. *Fight Club*, 1999, directed by David Fincher, starring Edward Norton and Brad Pitt: To be a man you need to prove yourself physically, though not necessarily as a fighter.

96. *Heat*, 1995, directed by Michael Mann, starring Al Pacino, Robert De Niro, Ashley Judd, and Tom Sizemore: A conflict between two men and their codes of honor.

97. *300*, 2006, directed by Zack Snyder, starring Gerard Butler and Lena Headey: Is it better to die for your country or to live as a slave? These men answer with action.

98. *Zulu*, 1964, directed by Cy Endfield, starring Stanley Baker, Jack Hawkins, Ulla Jacobsson, James Booth, and Michael Caine: Courage and honor are tested in this classic true story.

99. *Platoon*, 1986, directed by Oliver Stone, starring Charlie Sheen, Tom Berenger and Willem Dafoe: Is it right to take justice into your own hands? This movie will make you wonder.

100. *Lethal Weapon*, 1987, directed by Richard Donner, starring Mel Gibson and Danny Glover: A man finds that fighting for justice is his reason to live.

# APPENDIX II:
# 100 Books Men Should Read

1. Bible: The Bible is *the* guide for life. It covers everything including male friendship: "Greater love hath no man than this, that he lay down his life for a friend."

2. *De Officiis* (often titled "On Duties") by Marcus Tullius Cicero, 44 BC: Frederick the Great of Prussia called this the greatest book on morality and ethics ever written. It's a readable, inspiring outline of the ultimate man's philosophy.

3. *The Republic* by Plato, 380 BC: A man needs a curious mind all his life. This foundation of western philosophy will make you question everything.

4. *Meditations* (*Ta Eis Heauton*) by Marcus Aurelius, around 180 AD: This straightforward outline of Stoic philosophy will benefit every man.

5. *The Art Of War* by Sun Tzu, thought to have been written between 200 and 400 BC: This is an ancient Chinese outline for war, but its humanistic philosophy will surprise and teach things to any man.

6. *The Iliad* and the *Odyssey* by Homer, around 700 BC: Heroism, courage, cleverness, justice . . . these epics are guides to manhood.

7. *The Book of Five Rings* by Miyamota Musashi, 1645: One of the greatest Samurai who ever lived wrote this guide to manhood.

8. *Huckleberry Finn* by Mark Twain, 1884: This coming-of-age story tackles racism, propriety, and friendship.

9. *Bhagavad Gita*, written between the 5th and 2nd centuries BC: Ralph Waldo Emerson said, "I owed a magnificent debt to the Bhagavad Gita. It was the first of books; it was as if an empire spoke to us, nothing small or unworthy, but large, serene, consistent, the voice of an old intelligence which in another age and climate had pondered and thus disposed of the same questions which exercise us." The content of the *Gita* is the conversation between Krishna and Arjuna before battle. Krishna explains to Arjuna his duties as a warrior and a prince.

10. *The Old Man and the Boy* by Robert Ruark, 1957: An old man instructs a boy how to grow into a man.

11. *Captains Courageous* by Rudyard Kipling, 1897: A rich brat is forced to become a man.

12. *Fahrenheit 451* by Ray Bradbury, 1953: This haunting tale of censorship tells men to use their minds.

13. *Hamlet* by William Shakespeare, around 1600: *Hamlet* is the greatest coming-of-age story ever told.

14. *Atlas Shrugged* by Ayn Rand, 1957: This novel about individual rights and limited government has changed millions of men.

15. *The Old Man and the Sea* by Ernest Hemingway, 1952: This is the story of a man who won't give up.

16. *The Great Gatsby* by F. Scott Fitzgerald, 1925: This dramatic novel about a man maddened by love will become a part of you.

17. *Lonesome Dove* by Larry McMurtry, 1985: The character Gus is the ultimate man.

18. *Down and Out in Paris and London* by George Orwell, 1933: A gritty, yet lyrical memoir of the Great Depression.

19. *Will* by G. Gordon Liddy, 1980: An autobiography focused on honor—and the will needed to maintain it.

20. *The Brothers Karamazov* by Fyodor Dostoevsky, 1880: A drama and an argument about faith, free will, and brotherhood.

21. *A Christmas Carol* by Charles Dickens, 1843: A classic about why the just man is the generous man.

22. *Don Quixote* by Miguel de Cervantes, 1605, 1615: The lesson of this book is that men should live in reality.

23. *Glory Road* by Robert Heinlein, 1963: A man learns how to grow into a hero.

24. *Treasure Island* by Robert Louis Stevenson, 1883: A boy does things most men couldn't.

25. *U.S.A.* (the trilogy) by John Dos Passos, 1930–1936: Intertwining lives develop a picture of manhood in America.

26. *White Fang* by Jack London, 1906: A boy saves a wolf that becomes his best friend, and thereby attains a rite of passage.

27. *Big Woods* by William Faulkner, 1931: A boy goes on his first bear hunt—and finds a path to manhood.

28. *The Hobbit* by J. R. R. Tolkien, 1937: Every man should have some adventure to develop his perspective.

29. *The Lord of the Rings* (the trilogy) by J.R.R. Tolkien, 1954–1955: Though fantasy, these books are a guide to heroism.

30. *The Sun Also Rises* by Ernest Hemingway, 1926: A man navigates love and chivalry, loss and desire.

31. *The Captive Mind* by Czeslaw Milosz, 1990: This is a startling and convincing thesis on the virtues of intellectual freedom.

32. *Parliament of Whores* by P. J. O'Rourke: This is a cynical but revealing and hilarious diatribe on how the American government really functions.

33. *The Road to Serfdom* by F. A. Hayek, 1944: This book was seen as heretical for its passionate warning against the dangers of state control.

34. *The Aeneid* by Virgil, 19 BC: This Roman epic is an answer to Homer; it features a hero more in keeping with today's definition of heroism.

35. *Wuthering Heights* by Emily Brontë, 1847: Think this is a girl's book? Think again. Plenty to reflect on here about love and social status, virility and weakness.

36. *The Killer Angels* by Michael Shaara, 1974: A classic novel about the Battle of Gettysburg.

37. *Man's Search for Meaning* by Viktor Frankl, 1946: Frankl chronicles his experiences as a Nazi concentration camp inmate and describes his psychotherapeutic method for finding meaning in life.

38. *Two Years before the Mast* by Richard Henry Dana Jr., 1840: This is an American classic and one of the best coming-of-age books. It recounts a young Harvard man's decision to cut his teeth aboard a merchant sailing vessel on a two-year tour to California between 1834 and 1836.

39. *To Kill a Mockingbird* by Harper Lee, 1960: Its main character, Atticus Finch, makes a heroic stand against racism.

40. *Natural Right and History* by Leo Strauss, 1953: In this relativistic age, Strauss argues there is a distinction between right and wrong in ethics and politics.

41. *Orthodoxy* by G. K. Chesterton, 1908: The author argues Christianity is the "answer to a riddle" of mankind.

42. *Self-Reliance* by Ralph Waldo Emerson, 1841: Emerson argues that every man needs to follow his own instincts and ideas.

43. *Invisible Man* by Ralph Waldo Ellison, 1953: A novel that reminds us that men are men, no matter their color or creed.

44. *Kokoro* by Souseki Natsume, 1914: "Kokoro" literally translates to "heart," but the book is about a boy becoming a man.

45. *The Bonfire of the Vanities* by Tom Wolfe, 1987: A spoiled, wealthy man finds out the world doesn't revolve around him.

46. *The Big Sleep* by Raymond Chandler, 1939: Philip Marlowe is a private eye who uses a code of justice to stay clean as he investigates blackmail, murder, and mobsters.

47. *Shane* by Jack Schaefer, 1949: A man comes to town, with him comes justice.

48. *Casino Royale* by Ian Fleming, 1953: This is the novel that began the James Bond series and created a manly, debonair icon that still affects how men see themselves today.

49. *A River Runs Through It* by Norman Maclean, 1976: Brothers struggle to grow into men as they find a common bond through nature.

50. *Rogue Warrior* by Richard Marcinko and John Weisman, 1992: This is a first-person account of how Marcinko developed a counter-terrorism unit and battled military bureaucracy.

51. *The Wealth of Nations* by Adam Smith, 1776: This classic look at capitalism argues there are unintentional benefits stemming from men's pursuit of their desires and needs.

52. *One Day in the Life of Ivan Denisovich* by Alexandr Solzhenitsyn, 1962: Based on real accounts and experiences, this story follows a day in the life of a man in a 1950s Soviet prison.

53. *The Jungle Book* by Rudyard Kipling, 1894: These anthropomorphic tales set in India deal with the rudiments of becoming a man.

54. *Gandhi on Non-Violence* by Mohandas K. Gandhi, 1965: Gandhi said, "One has to speak out and stand up for one's convictions. Inaction at a time of conflagration is inexcusable." This book outlines his basic principles of the philosophy of non-violence (*Ahimsa*) and non-violent action (*Satyagraha*).

55. *The Last Lion* by William Manchester, 1983: This biography of Winston Churchill captivates, inspires, and teaches men to pursue their dreams boldly.

56. *Inventing Wyatt Earp: His Life and Many Legends* by Allen Barra, 2005: The legends were mostly true, and he mostly did what was right.

57. *Starship Troopers* by Robert A. Heinlein, 1959: This tale of war and adventure has a lot to say about what it means to be a man.

58. *FM 22-100 Army Leadership Manual*: From this great little book you'll learn to put people first and to achieve the mission.

59. *The Fight* by Norman Mailer, 1975: This first-person account of the "Rumble in the Jungle" is about men going for it all.

60. *For Love of the Game* by Michael Schaara, 1991: A classic about baseball and manhood.

61. *History of Christianity* by Paul Johnson, 1976: Understanding the biggest influence on Western culture in the last 2,000 years is critical to every man.

62. *Reflections on a Ravaged Century* by Robert Conquest, 2000: This book asks, "How do we account for what has been called the 'ideological frenzy' of the twentieth century?" And then answers the question.

63. *Memoirs of the Second World War* by Winston S. Churchill, 1959: Churchill begins the book by writing: "One day President Roosevelt told me that he was asking publicly for suggestions about what the war should be called. I said at once, 'The unnecessary war.' This is the great non-fiction epic of that war."

64. *The Revolt of the Masses* by José Ortega y Gasset, 1930: Gasset warns of a populist rise that will negate individual freedom in Europe; his message is as true today.

65. *On Liberty* by John Stuart Mill, 1859: This argument for freedom from tyranny is an easy, accessible read for every man.

66. *The Art Spirit* by Robert Henri, 1923: Most known for his leadership of realist painters (known as "The Eight"), Henri instructs how to find the artist in yourself.

67. *Love in the Western World* by Denis de Rougemont, 1939: Rougemont traces the "courtly love" tradition from its birth in the Middle Ages to its near collapse today in a world dominated by Eros.

68. *From Dawn to Decadence: 500 Years of Western Cultural Life: 1500 to the Present* by Jacques Barzun, 1999: A terrific and provocative overview of the modern history that every man should know.

69. *Capitalism and Freedom* by Milton Friedman, 1962: This is a fundamental book on the libertarian philosophy; it focuses on preventing the accumulation of power by any individual or group.

70. *The Death and Life of Great American Cities* by Jane Jacobs, 1961: You likely live or work in a city—here's what you should know about it.

71. *The History of the Decline and Fall of the Roman Empire* by Edward Gibbon, 1776: This classic history of Rome will teach you about empire and men—and even about America today.

72. *The Closing of the American Mind* by Allan Bloom, 1987: Education is a life-long process, and this book is proof of it.

73. *1776* by David McCullough, 2006: Every man should know the history of his country—we should know ours.

74. *Good-Bye to All That* by Robert Graves, 1958: With criticism for his class, his country, his military superiors, and the civilians who mindlessly cheered the carnage of WWI, Graves outlines the reality of man and war.

75. *How to Cook a Wolf* by M. F. K. Fisher, 1942: A well-rounded man needs to understand food; this book will make him savor the best.

76. The Declaration of Independence by Thomas Jefferson: Every man should know why America fought to be free.

77. The Constitution of the United States of America: The legal guarantor of our freedom—you need to read it.

78. *Alive* by Piers Paul Read, 1974: This is the true story of the Andes flight disaster in which people were forced to cannibalism to survive.

79. *The King Must Die* by Mary Renault, 1958: A Greek legend brought to life for modern readers.

80. *The Sea Wolf* by Jack London, 1904: An animalistic captain forces a scholar to be a man or die.

81. *Leiningen Versus the Ants* by Carl Stephenson, 1938: A plantation owner won't give up despite the man-eating ants trying to get him and everything he owns. It's a tale of man's fortitude despite nature.

82. *The Most Dangerous Game* by Richard Connell, 1924: A man hunts another for sport—and learns a mortal lesson.

83. *The Red Badge of Courage* by Stephen Crane, 1895: A young soldier in the American Civil War learns the meaning of courage.

84. *Spartacus* by Howard Fast, 1951: A novelistic depiction of the slave who rose to challenge Rome.

85. *The Caine Mutiny* by Herman Wouk, 1951: A great character study of officers aboard a World War II vessel.

86. *The Texas Rangers: A Century of Frontier Defense* by Walter Prescott Webb, 1935: Webb helps you understand Texas and its great men who held together and solidified a way of life.

87. *Style and the Man: How and Where to Buy Fine Men's Clothes*, by Alan Flusser, 1996: A man needs to know how to dress.

88. *Robinson Crusoe* by Daniel Defoe, 1719: One of the first great novels of survival.

89. *Kon-Tiki* by Thor Heyerdahl, 1950: In 1947 Heyerdahl built and sailed a raft from South America to Polynesia to make a point about who settled the islands. A great tale of true-life adventure.

90. *Henry V* by William Shakespeare, 1599: The greatest reflection on what it means to mature as a man and become a king.

91. *The Glory of Their Times: The Story of Baseball Told by the Men Who Played It* by Lawrence S. Ritter, 1992: This is the best book about the greatest game.

92. *Without Remorse* by Tom Clancy, 1993: A man of honor punishes terrible men.

93. *The Lord of the Flies* by William Golding, 1954: A group of British schoolboys are stranded on a tropical island, and then try to create order. This novel is a riveting look at human nature and boys trying to be men.

**94.** *Cold Mountain* by Charles Frazier, 1997: A novel about a Confederate army deserter searching for his love, his freedom, and ultimately himself.

**95.** *Réflexions ou Sentences et Maximes Morales* by François duc de La Rochefoucauld, late seventeenth century: Rochefoucauld's *Maximes* are never platitudes, but are a summary of living as a man should.

**96.** *The Moon and Sixpence* by William Somerset Maugham, 1919: An artist sacrifices ethics and humanity to be great—it'll leave you contemplating ambition.

**97.** *The God of Small Things* by Arundhati Roy, 1997: A novel about how it is the little things in life that shape us.

**98.** *Gulliver's Travels* by Jonathan Swift, 1726: A profound reflection on the nature of man: his ambitions, his desires, his prejudices, and his utopia.

**99.** *Glimpses of World History* by Jawaharlal Nehru, 1934: A series of essays that are meant to provide not only a glimpse at history, but a guide to life.

**100.** *The Intelligent Investor: A Book of Practical Counsel* by Benjamin Graham, 1949: Warren Buffett has described this book as "by far the best book on investing ever written."

F rank Miniter has floated the Amazon, run with the bulls of Pamplona, hunted everything from bear in Russia to elk with the Apache to kudu in the Kalahari, and has fly-fished everywhere from Alaska's Kenai to Scotland's River Spey to Japan's freestone streams. Along the way he was taught to box by Floyd Patterson, spelunked into Pompey's Cave, climbed everywhere from New York's Gunks to the Rockies, and is currently learning Kenkojuko Karate with Sensei Masakazu Takahashi. He graduated from the oldest private military academy in the U.S., a place that still teaches honor and old-school gentlemanly conduct, and believes men need this book because the U.S. has lost its code of honor as enumerated by its Founding Fathers. He is the author of *The Politically Incorrect Guide*™ *to Hunting* and has won numerous awards for outdoor and conservation writing. He was a senior editor at *Outdoor Life* magazine, and is currently the executive editor of *American Hunter* magazine.

## INTRODUCTION

**1.** Ambrose Bierce, *The Devil's Dictionary*, (Oxford University Press, 1999, originally published in 1911).

## PART I: SURVIVOR

**1.** Byron Farwell, *Burton: A Biography of Sir Francis Richard Burton* (Penguin Books, 1963).

**2.** H.G. Wells, *Mind at the End of Its Tether* (London: William Heinemann, Ltd., 1945).

**3.** U.S. Forest Service, "2005 National Survey on Recreation and the Environment," http://www.srs.fs.usda.gov/trends/Nsre/NSRE200562303.pdf.

**4.** Chuck Palahniuk, *Survivor* (W. W. Norton, 1999).

5.  Michael Ferraresi and Steve Yozwiak, "Injured hiker survives 6 days stuck in Superstitions," *The Arizona Republic*, April 20, 2007.

## PART 2: PROVIDER

1.  Jose Ortega y Gasset, *Prólogo a un Tratado de Montería* (also published as *Meditations on the Hunt*, Revista de Occidente, 1944).
2.  USDA "A History of American Agriculture," http://inventors.about.com/ library/inventors/blfarm4.htm.
3.  "2006 National Survey of Fishing, Hunting, and Wildlife-Associated Recreation," a study compiled every five years by the U.S. Fish and Wildlife Service's Division of Federal Aid.
4.  Michael S. Kimmel, *Manhood in America* (Oxford University Press, 2006), 166.
5.  Theodore Roosevelt, Seventh State of the Union Address, 1907.
6.  Lowell K. Halls, *White-Tailed Deer Ecology and Management* (PA: Stackpole Books, 1984).
7.  Mark Elbroch, *Mammal Tracks & Sign: A Guide to North American Species* (PA: Stackpole Books, 2003).
8.  Henry David Thoreau, *Walden*, (Empire Books, 2012, originally published in 1854).

## PART 3: ATHLETE

1.  William Shakespeare, *As You Like It*, 2.7, 1623.
2.  Ernest Hemingway, *Death in the Afternoon* (New York: Scribner, 1932).
3.  Larry Schwartz, "Mays brought joy to baseball," www.ESPN.GO.com.
4.  Fred Lieb, *Baseball as I Have Known It* (Lincoln, NE: Bison Books, 1996).
5.  Lenwood G. Davis, *Joe Louis: A Bibliography of Articles, Books, Pamphlets, Records, and Archival Materials* (Westport, CT: Greenwood Press, 1983).
6.  E. M. Swif, "The Golden Goal," *Sports Illustrated*, http://sportsillustrated.cnn. com/si_online/the_golden_goal/.
7.  Andy Dickes, "Tommy Lasorda," *Red, White & Green*, Commemorative Issue XIII.
8.  William Shakespeare, *Henry IV*, Part I, Act I, Scene II, 1623.

## PART 4: HERO

1.  William Shakespeare, *Julius Caesar*, 1599.

2.  Kevin Maurer, "What Makes a Hero," *The Fayettville Observer*, August 19, 2007.

3.  Raymond Douglas, "Ray Bradbury, a Biography," http://www.s9.com/Biography/Bradbury-Raymond-Douglas.

4.  *The Book of Mencius*, section 6.2.15.

5.  From a 1963 Speech in Detroit, Michigan.

6.  James Atkins Shackford, *David Crockett: The Man and the Legend* (Bison Books, 1994.)

7.  Interview to the Press in Karachi about the execution of Bhagat Singh on March 26, 1926; published in *Young India*, April 2, 1931.

8.  From a speech Theodore Roosevelt gave at the opening of the Minnesota State Fair, as it appeared in the *Minneapolis Tribune*, September 3, 1901.

9.  Mark Reisner, *Game Wars: Undercover Pursuit of Wildlife Poachers* (NY: Viking, 1991).

10. Kerri Miller, "Struggle for Survival in Tanzania," BBC, December 27, 2007.

11. See http://www.csmngt.com/churchill.htm.

12. Robert M. Utley and Wilcomb E. Washburn, *Indian Wars* (Rockville, MD: American Heritage Pub. Co., 1977).

13. Theodore Steinberg, *Slide Mountain or The Folly of Owning Nature* (CA: University of California Press, 1996).

14. Joel Diederik Beversluis, *Sourcebook of the World's Religions* (CA: New World Library, 2000), 49.

## PART 5: GENTLEMAN

1.  Ralph Waldo Emerson, "Fortune of the Republic," in *The Complete Prose Works of Ralph Waldo Emerson* (Whitefish, MT: Kessinger Publishing, 2006), 490.

2.  Jim West, *Drinking with Calvin and Luther!: A History of Alcohol in the Church* (CA: Oakdown Books, 2003).

3.  Mark Twain, "Private and Public Morals," speech, 1906.

4.  Christopher W. Bruce, *The Arthurian Name Dictionary* (NY: Routledge, 1998), 430.

5.  G. K. Chesterton, *Alarms and Discursions* (MD: Wildside Press, 2009), 53.

6.  Merle Johnson, ed., *More Maxims of Mark* (NY: privately printed, 1927).

7.  Mark Twain, "Answers to Correspondents," in Edgar Marquess Branch and Robert H. Hirst, eds, *Early Tales & Sketches, Vol. 2, 1864–1865* (CA: University of California Press, 1981).

8.  Rudyard Kipling, "The Betrothed," Departmental Ditties, 1886, http://www.readbookonline.net/readOnLine/2738/.

9.  Spanish Royal Acadamy online dictionary.

10. H. L. Mencken, *Prejudices: Fourth Series* (NY: Alfred A. Knopf, 1924).

11. Malachy Magee, *Irish Whiskey: A 1000 Year Tradition* (Dublin: The O'Brien Press, Ltd, 1998).

12. *Code of Hammurabi*, 1780 BC, http://www.wsu.edu/~dee/MESO/CODE.HTM.

13. A. H. Burgess, *Hops: Botany, Cultivation and Utilization* (London: Leonard Hill, 1964).

14. C. S. Lewis, *The Abolition of Man* (Oxford: Oxford University Press, 1943).

## PART 6: ROMANTIC

1.  H. Montgomery Hyde, *Oscar Wilde: A Biography* (Farrar Straus Giroux, 1975).

2.  Bill Zehme, *The Way You Wear Your Hat: Frank Sinatra and the Lost Art of Livin'* (Harper, 1997).

3.  Ernest Jones, *The Life and Work of Sigmund Freud* (Doubleday/Anchor, 1963).

4.  Compton Mackenzie, *Literature in My Time* (Rich & Cowan, Ltd., 1933).

5.  Katja Behling, *Martha Freud: A Biography* (Polity, 2006).

6.  Mignon McLaughlin, *The Complete Neurotic's Notebook* (Bobbs-Merrill, 1963).

7.  Allesandra Stanley, "The Dissolute Lifestyle of a Charmer and a Poet," *New York Times*, October 21, 2005, http://www.nytimes.com/2005/10/21/arts/television/21tvwk.html.

8.  Franklin Pierce Adams, *FPA Book of Quotations: A New Collection of Famous Sayings* (Funk & Wagnalls Company, 1952).

**9.** Ovid, *Ars Amatoria* ("Art of Love"), 1 BC.

**10.** Quote from Friedrich Nietzshe, TheFreeLibrary.com, http://nietzsche. thefreelibrary.com/.

**11.** Paul Janet, *Histoire de la Science Politique*, Vol. I, p. 8.

**12.** William Shakespeare, *As You Like It*, about 1600 AD.

**13.** Dave Barry, "25 Things I Have Learned in 50 Years," www.enginesofmischief. com/makers/evan/signs/barry.html.

**14.** Frank Sinatra's character "Joey" in Pal Joey.

**15.** Plutarch, *Plutarch's Morals: Ethical Essays* (B&R Samizdat Express, 2008).

**16.** C. S. Lewis, *The Four Loves* (Harvest Books, 1960).

**17.** Match.com, "10 most romantic gestures of all time," Match.com, http://www. match.com/magazine/article/3976/10-most-romantic-gestures-of-all-time.

**18.** Christina Passariello and Ray A. Smith, "Grab Your 'Murse,' Pack a 'Mankini' And Don't Forget the 'Mewelry,'" *Wall Street Journal*, September 8, 2011, http://online.wsj.com/article/SB10001424053111904900904576554380686494 012.html?mod=slideshow_overlay_mod.

**19.** Howard Hawks and Gerald Mast, *Bringing Up Baby* (Rutgers University Press, 1988).

**20.** Nancy Nelson and Cary Grant, *Evenings With Cary Grant: Recollections In His Own Words and By Those Who Loved Him Best* (Thorndike Press, 1992).

**21.** Marc Eliot, *Cary Grant: A Biography* (Harmony Books, 2004).

**22.** Betsy Drake and Robert Trachtenberg, "Cary Grant: A Class Apart," Turner Classic Movies, 2004.

# PART 7: PAL

**1.** Tara Parker-Pope, "What Are Friends For? A Longer Life," *New York Times*, April 20, 2009, http://www.nytimes.com/2009/04/21/health/21well.html.

**2.** Tom Geohagen, "What's the Ideal Number of Friends?" *BBC News Magazine*, March 3, 2009, http://news.bbc.co.uk/2/hi/7920434.stm.

**3.** "New study links number of Facebook friends to brain density," *Consumer Reports*, October 20, 2011, http://news.consumerreports.org/electronics/2011/10/ new-study-links-number-of-facebook-friends-to-brain-density.html.

**4.** "Scientists find link between number of friends and physical activity in children," *Medical Xpress*, May 7, 2012, http://medicalxpress.com/news/2012-05-scientists-link-friends-physical-children.html.

**5.** Janet Kornblum, "Study: 25% of Americans have no one to confide in," *USA Today*, June 22, 2006.

**6.** A. M. Sperber and Eric Lax Bogart, *Bogart* (William Morrow & Co. 1997), p. 504., p. 504.

**7.** "Me, me, me! America's Narcissism Epidemic," MSNBC, April 20, 2009, http://today.msnbc.msn.com/id/30312181/ns/today-books/t/me-me-me-americas-narcissism-epidemic/#.T-nPY-xn2uI. And Christopher Lasch, *The Culture of Narcissism: American Life in an Age of Diminishing Expectations* (W. W. Norton & Co., 1979).

**8.** The Bible (King James version), Ecclesiastes 4:9–10.

**9.** "U.S. Census Bureau Reports Residents Move at Higher Rate in 2009 After Record Low in 2008," U.S. Census Bureau, May 10, 2010, http://www.census.gov/newsroom/releases/archives/mobility_of_the_population/cb10-67.html.

**10.** Christopher J. Carpenter, "Narcissism on Facebook: Self-promotional and anti-social behavior," *Personality and Individual Differences*, Vol. 52, No. 4, March 2012, http://www.sciencedirect.com/science/article/pii/S0191886911005332.

**11.** Samuel Johnson, reported in James Boswell's, *Life of Johnson* (Indy Publish, 2002, originally published in 1755).

**12.** The Bible (King James Version) John 15:13.

**13.** Aristotle, *Rhetoric*, http://rhetoric.eserver.org/aristotle/rhet2-4.html#1381b.

**14.** George Washington, *The Maxims of Washington* (Kessinger Publishing, LLC, 2010).

**15.** Larry Bird and Earvin Magic Johnson, *When the Game was Ours* (Mariner Books, 2010).

**16.** Marc Serota, "Magic and Bird: A Rivalry Gives Way To Friendship," NPR, November 3, 2009, http://www.npr.org/templates/story/story.php?storyId=120053152.

**17.** Ibid.

**18.** Joseph Ellis, *Founding Brothers: The Revolutionary Generation* (Alfred A. Knopf, 2000).

19. John Adams, letter to Thomas Jefferson, July 13, 1813.

20. Lewis A. Armistead biography, http://www.encyclopediavirginia.org/Armistead_
Lewis_A_1817-1863.

21. Derek Smith, *The Gallant Dead: Union & Confederate Generals Killed in the
Civil War* (Mechanicsburg, PA: Stackpole Books, 2005).

22. Stephen McFarland, "Dean Martin is Dead at 78 Star Lived it Up On and Off
the Stage," *Daily News*, December 26, 1995.

23. George Patton, *Cavalry Journal*, September 1933.

24. LTG William B. Caldwell, "Honoring CPL Jason Dunham," April 16, 2008,
http://www.soldiersperspective.us/2008/04/16/honoring-cpl-jason-dunham-2/.

25. The Bible (King James Version) 2 Samuel, 1:26.

26. The Bible (King James Version) 1 Samuel, 18:1–4.

27. The Bible (King James Version) 1 Samuel, 20:30.

28. Avot 5:16, http://www.uscj.org.il/haftarah/Toldot5765.html.

## PART 8: PHILOSOPHER

1. Mencius, quoted in Wing-Tsit Chan, *A Source Book in Chinese Philosophy* (NJ:
Princeton University Press, 1963), 59.

2. Marcus Tullius Cicero, *Second Philippic Against Antony*, 44 BC.

3. Plato, *The Apology*, around 400 BC.

4. Mencius, "The Mencius," 2A:6, quoted in Wing-Tsit Chan, *A Source Book in
Chinese Philosophy* (NJ: Princeton University Press, 1963), 65.

5. The Bible (King James Version), Matthew 7:12.

6. *Babylonian Talmud*, tracate Shabbat 31a.

7. *Seneca the Elder*, Suasoriae, VI.

8. Thomas Paine, *The American Crisis*, collection of articles, 1776–1783.

9. Ayn Rand, *Philosophy: Who Needs It*, ed. Leonard Peikoff (Indianapolis, IN:
Bobbs-Merrill, 1982).

10. Robert Bolt, *A Man for All Seasons* (New York, NY: Vintage Publishers, 1990).

11. Bhante Gunaratana, "Taking the Eight Lifetime Precepts," Bhavana Society
http://www.bhavanasociety.org/resource/taking_the_eight_lifetme_precepts/.

12. Livia Kohn, *Cosmos & Community: The Ethical Dimension of Daoism* (Magda-
lena, NM: Three Pines Press, 2004).

13. Jay B. Hubbell, *The South in American Literature: 1607-1900*, (Duke University Press, 1954).

14. Ron Tinkle, *3 Days to Glory: The Siege of the Alamo* (McGraw-Hill, 1958).

15. Plutarch, *Parallel Lives* (Life of Crassus), around 100 AD.

16. Herodotus, *The Histories*, trans. George Rawlinson (J. M. Dent & Sons, 1992).